For Eleanor and Anna

Other football books by Steve Leach

Conference Season

Tangerines and Pies

TWENTY
FOOTBALL
TOWNS

STEVE LEACH

Published by Saraband
Digital World Centre, 1 Lowry Plaza,
The Quays, Salford, M50 3UB

www.saraband.net

ISBN: 9781912235919
ebook: 9781912235926

Printed and bound in Great Britain by Clays Ltd, Elcograf S.p.A.

1 2 3 4 5 6 7 8 9 10

CONTENTS

PART II: HOPES AND DREAMS

FOREWORD

*The sense of place is one of those things that is supposed to
have died in football, its power dissipated by remote fandom.*

Barney Ronay, *The Guardian*, February 14th, 2020

In 1997, the photographer Stuart Roy Clarke opened 'The Homes
of Football', a gallery dedicated to exhibiting his images of football grounds and fan culture in the UK. Surprisingly, Clarke did
not choose to locate his gallery in London or Manchester or
Liverpool or Birmingham; instead, he opted for Ambleside, right
in the middle of the Lake District National Park. The doors of
'The Homes of Football' remained open in Ambleside for fourteen years and, throughout that time, visits to the gallery were
characterised by a sense of cognitive dissonance – to step out of
the rain and into 'The Homes of Football' was to be transported
to an imaginative elsewhere. Visitors were invited to momentar-
ily block out the Cumbrian landscape of rocks and screes, tarns
and becks, and to focus instead on photographic reminders of the
places from which they'd travelled and the football grounds that,
every other Saturday, they called home.

Looking back, Clarke's photographs from the 1990s docu-
mented a game in flux. His images of top-tier football examined
the idiosyncrasies of match-going: burger vans were elevated to
the status of street-corner altars, and fans were captured leaving
grounds early in order to beat the traffic. In one sense, then, his
photographs were concerned with the comforting familiarity of
ritual and routine. At the same time, though, Clarke's wide-angle
images of major stadia offered a visual record of elite football's
evolution in the years following the Hillsborough tragedy – a
period that also witnessed the Murdoch-fuelled formation of the
FA Premier League in England.

Although Clarke recorded the top levels of British football, however, some of his most memorable photographs were warmly attentive to the lower league game: unvarnished worlds in which sheds served as ticket offices in car parks and Portakabins doubled up as licensed bars. In looking away from the increasing sheen of the elite game, Clarke captured the messy materiality of watching football – and especially football in the north of England – on a habitual basis.

In this book, Steve Leach explores similar imaginative – and often geographical – territory to Clarke's photographs. He presents a world of meat-and-potato pies and difficult-to-describe club mascots, standing room paddocks and hyper-local sponsors. The book opens with a Contents page that reads like Johnny Cash's *I've Been Everywhere* reimagined by Victoria Wood: for Reno, Chicago and Fargo, read Manchester, Barrow and Morecambe. Steve then compiles a personal footballing map that weaves together autobiographical reflection, topographical description, local history and socio-political commentary. And, in doing so, he opens up thinking about the rich relationships between clubs and the landscapes and communities in which they are rooted.

Along the way, Steve reflects on our sense of place in a number of original and revealing ways. First, he captures the sense of embodied physicality – of both fans and players – that is present in so many of Stuart Roy Clarke's photographs. Food and drink invariably figure prominently in the match-day experience and journeymen players are watched from close proximity.

Second, he draws upon his professional expertise to look at how local politics – and, more specifically, local authority boundary changes – can intersect with the lives of football clubs in the construction of a sense of place. When visiting the Globe Arena, to give one example, he reflects on the loss of civic identity suffered when, in 1974, the town of Morecambe ceased to be a local authority in its own right and was absorbed into Lancaster City Council.

Third, he considers how football clubs and communities are affected by events and changes in the wider world. The focus on the near-at-hand does not preclude discussion of national politics and, saliently, the spectre of Thatcher haunts much of this book. Steve is similarly alert to the fact that, in the twenty-first century, the local and the national are invariably and inextricably intertwined with the global. Reflecting on the severing of his lifelong relationship with Manchester City, he asserts that he 'didn't want to be part of a world of football dominated by global capitalist institutions'; but, later on in the book, he registers that, just down the road, even Macclesfield Town is now owned by the Iraqi-based Alkadhi brothers.

By moving from club to club, and town to town, Steve offers an intriguing new style of writing about the concepts of self, football and place. Many books about life as a football supporter – some of which have emerged out of the culture of fanzine writing that Steve himself enjoys – understandably concentrate on the articulation of a deep-rooted affinity with the one club. Perhaps the most celebrated example is Nick Hornby's *Fever Pitch* (1993), in which the protagonist uses his love of Arsenal as a means of coping with the complexities of life. Another is *A Season with Verona* (2002), a non-fictional text in which Tim Parks documents a year spent following Hellas Verona all over Italy. Both these books interrogate what it means to steadfastly support *a* team that is rooted in *a* particular place. In different ways, therefore, both books are concerned with the assertion of what might be described as authentic insiderness. But in *Twenty Football Towns*, Steve reflects on a life of relative footballing promiscuity. Instead of digging deep into a monogamous relationship with just one club, he considers what it means to have had affairs – of differing lengths and intensities – with twenty different teams.

As a result, this book makes a strikingly original contribution to the library of football fan literature. At the same time, and perhaps more surprisingly, the book offers an intervention in the ever-expanding field of contemporary place writing. As the shelves of our bookshops testify, there has been, over the past two decades, a proliferation of creative non-fiction books that take place as their principal preoccupation: from the psychogeographic wanderings of Iain Sinclair to the 'new nature writing' of Kathleen Jamie; from the memoirs of Amy Liptrot to the deep mappings of Rachel Lichtenstein. Through the artful braiding of a range of literary genres, many of these books defy conventional categorisation. As a result, the label 'place writing' has emerged as a helpfully malleable term to describe a wide range of books for which no existing label readily exists. *Twenty Football Towns*, then, can be framed, I would argue, as a work of place writing. It is a reading that is supported by the blunt directness of the book's opening two-word sentence: 'Place matters.'

Steve contends 'that there is much more about "going to the match" than the match itself'. In a similar way, then, *Twenty Football Towns* is much more than 'about' football grounds. Read as an act of place writing, the book opens up thinking about the role that football can play in the shaping of geographical experience. Much place writing is vulnerable to the critique that it makes a virtue of solitariness. The routine of 'going to the match', though, is predicated on the sharedness of space, and this sense of communality is most evident on the terraces and in the stands. But it actually begins way outside the ground: as Steve makes clear, the practice of getting to the match – by public transport and/or on foot – involves the individual forming part of the collective. As with much contemporary place writing, walking does feature in *Twenty Football Towns*; but, even when Steve recounts walking alone, he inevitably finds himself being swept along, with hundreds of others, by the gravitational pull of the ground. The process of journeying to the match, there-fore, can lead to a momentary transformation of our cities, towns and even edgelands into sites of communality. It is probably only football, for instance, that could entice busloads of people out to the 'industrial wastelands' of Stoke-on-Trent on a predictably wet November evening.

It would be disingenuous, of course, to ignore the fact that football culture is also founded upon crude binary oppositions and even raw tribalism. Steve reminds us, however, that the ritu-alistic practice of match-going also allows the supporter to break out of bubbles of isolation, if only for the afternoon or evening, and to experience place as part of a collective.

In presenting place in this way, Steve shares some common ground with a fellow Mancunian: the geographer Doreen Massey, who, in spite of spending much of her childhood in Wythenshawe, was a passionate Liverpool supporter up until her death in 2016. In an influential book chapter published in the 1990s, Massey argued that 'what gives a place its specificity is not some long internalised history but the fact that it is constructed out of a particular constellation of social relations, meeting and weav-ing together at a particular locus'. Steve Leach – in writing about Accrington and Kidderminster, Gateshead and Fylde – offers the reader an analogous understanding of place and its meanings. As a result, the autobiographical reflections of *Twenty Football Towns* go some way to explaining why, in the Lake District – a landscape that, for many, is seemingly 'remote from every taint / Of sordid industry' – tourists found themselves being drawn into a gallery to look at photographs of the shared, intimate spaces of their foot-balling homes.

Dr David Cooper

Co-Director, Centre for Place Writing, Manchester
Metropolitan University, March 2020

PREFACE

This is a book that explores the ways in which football is, for many of us, an expression of our attachment to the towns and cities we've called home at different stages in our lives – and how local football teams operate as symbols of community identity. It illustrates these ideas from a personal perspective, in the light of visits I made to twenty towns that have been of significance in my own life. In all but two of these chapters I describe a football match that I attended in the town concerned. I have also included chapters on Manchester and Liverpool, both of which have played an important part in my personal life. However, because my interest as a football spectator is now focused on the lower tiers (Leagues One and Two and the National League, with occasional forays into the Championship), I decided not to attend a Premier League match at any of the clubs concerned, not least because of the slim chance of obtaining a ticket!

The book is a celebration of the distinctiveness of place – the fascinating differences between Lincoln and Leyton, Barrow and Birmingham, Macclesfield and Morecambe, and all the other towns I visited with non-matching capitals to their names. It is an evocation, using football as the focus, of what these places have meant to me on my journey through life. As a result, there are strong elements of memoir and autobiography in what follows. I make no apologies for this. Everyone's life story is interesting; more people should write one. In my case, 'The life of a middle-ranking academic specialising in local government' is not, I suspect, a title that would evoke much interest, either from the public or a publisher. But by bringing in an extra ingredient, the joys of watching football – not just the games themselves, but the unique qualities of the grounds and the crowds, the histories of the clubs concerned and the characteristics of the towns they represent – the appeal of the book will hopefully be greatly enhanced. The relationship between time, place, life and football, as experienced by one individual (me), is something about which I have long wanted to write. This personal approach also provides an opportunity to include details of other enthusiasms of mine – politics, rock music and my own experiences in schoolboy and local amateur football – where they played a big part in my experience of that place at that time.

The book chapters follow the sequence of the places I visited, starting with Barrow-in-Furness in late December 2017 and finishing with Walsall in late December 2018. Naturally, this is not the order in which the places featured in my life, so readers trying to make sense of my personal history will just have to cope with some backward and forward time-travelling! Ten of my visits took place in the second half of the 2017–18 season; the other eight during the first half of the 2018–19 season. A chapter dealing with how each of these teams subsequently prospered (or otherwise), in the period up to the end of the 2018–19 season, is also included. The first chapter discusses in some detail the appeal of football and its relationship with place and community identity. The final chapter adds further reflections on these issues, in the light of my wanderings across northern and middle England. I hope you enjoy sharing my journey.

Post scriptum

In the spring of 2020, when this book was undergoing its final edit, the impact of the coronavirus pandemic in Britain reached crisis point. All Football League fixtures were suspended from March 14th, and National League fixtures ten days later. Within weeks, Leagues One and Two of the Football League and the National

League (including North and South divisions) had decided not to attempt to complete the remaining fixtures, but to regard the league tables as they stood when football was suspended as final, subject to a 'points per game' adjustment. On this basis (which had its critics), champions were identified, automatic promotion and relegation issues were decided and play-off matches scheduled for later in the summer.

On the other hand, the Premier League and the Championship authorities eventually decided to fulfil the season's scheduled fixtures, all to take place behind closed doors, from mid-June onwards. At the time of writing (early July), Liverpool have amassed enough further points to emerge as champions (no surprise there!), and Barrow have returned to the Football League after forty-eight years in the wilderness as National League champions. Championship play-offs are due to take place early in August.

The consequences of the pandemic and the loss of income involved for the future of football clubs are potentially disastrous, particularly for those in the lower divisions and the National League. In an interview with David Conn (*Guardian*, June 15th), Simon Sadler, owner of Blackpool FC, predicted that 'clubs will go down like dominoes' (although not Blackpool, apparently). In fact, the first casualty was unexpected. On July 1st, Wigan Athletic went into administration, not directly as a result of the impact of the Covid pandemic, but because of a recurring syndrome that many football fans are familiar with: 'issues with the owner'. A Hong Kong-based owner who had purchased the club in June from the existing owners (another Far Eastern consortium) suddenly opted out, amidst rumours of a large bet being placed in the Philippines on Wigan's likelihood of relegation at the end of the 2019–20 season. All very mysterious, but devastating for Wigan, who had during the previous few weeks pulled themselves up from a relegation slot to a mid-table position.

The future of several of the football clubs covered in this book looks extremely shaky. Can Macclesfield Town, already in deep financial trouble, survive (even if they manage to avoid relegation to the National League, which remains uncertain)? And what of other clubs running on shoestring budgets, such as Morecambe, Accrington Stanley and Chester? It would be a tragedy for such clubs, their supporters and the towns in which they are located if they were to experience a fate similar to that of Bury FC, expelled from the Football League in August 2019. If, as seems likely, the government is not prepared to step in with a rescue package, wouldn't it be wonderful if a modest portion of the finance channelled to the big-time clubs of the Premier League by Sky and BT could be diverted to prevent this outcome?

Steve Leach
July 2020

PLACE, COMMUNITY AND FOOTBALL

Place matters. The town where we grew up, the city we chose to move to – indeed, all the places where we've ever lived – form reference points in our lives, bringing with them a potent mix of associations: first girlfriends or boyfriends, where our kids were born, moves to new jobs, our achievements and failures ... and (for many of us) the football teams we supported. Writing in *The Municipal Journal* in November 2017, local government expert Barry Quirk puts it like this:

> *Localities are woven into our personal lives: of where we're from, where we've been, where we are now, and where we imagine we're going. Specific localities give colour to our origins, our journeys and our imagined destinations.*

I was born and brought up in Manchester, experienced my adolescence in Stockport and spent three years at the university in Birmingham, before moving back to Manchester for my first job. My next work move was to Chester, followed by Liverpool, back to Birmingham, and finally Leicester. Domestically, I've also been based in Silverdale in north Lancashire, Gateshead (where my first son, Callum, was born) and Kendal, on the edge of the Lake District (where Fergus was born, seven years later).

In all these places, as a long-term football enthusiast (spectator and amateur player), I have sought out and watched local football clubs, ranging from the Premier League to the National League North. From the age of eleven, I was a dedicated Manchester City supporter, but also attached myself to Stockport County, when we moved to Stockport in 1956. Since then, I have watched a good deal of football at Chester, Morecambe, Carlisle, Blackpool, Wigan and Barrow, with more sporadic visits to various other venues. In each of these towns, memories of football are inextricably intertwined with memories of key events in my personal life. To quote Barry Quirk again:

> *The fabric of locality gives texture to our lives. We may remember with fondness and tenderness the conflicting rhythms of life we experienced in specific places during specific times in our lives. These memories tether us to places in our past.*

If the link between place and football has been important to me in my meanderings around north and middle England, how much more must this be true of those who remain rooted in the area in which they were born and raised? Martin Tarbuck, editor of the Wigan Athletic fanzine, *Mudhutter,* was born in Wigan and has never left the town of his birth. He started watching Wigan Athletic in 1988 and is an example of the true football fan – one town, one club, a lifetime's experience focused on a single place. The pattern of my career and domestic life has made such consistency impossible, but the link between place and football over time has, in its own way, been just as significant for me.

Once we have developed an affection for a particular place – because we were brought up there, raised a family there, or have chosen to live there – it becomes important symbolically as well as functionally. We want the qualities of the place that attracted us to it, or motivated our continued attachment to it, to be recognised and celebrated. And what better opportunity for recognition and celebration than the exploits of the football team that bears the town or city's name? When a football team reaches a Wembley final (even if it's only the EFL Trophy!), it is invariably the case that large numbers of the town's population make their way there, many of whom may not have attended more than the odd match during the season. This is the day when the achievements of Walsall or Forest Green Rovers or Brackley Town have brought the existence of these places to wider public attention, and their residents want to be there in profusion to celebrate this outcome.

But there are recent social trends that have weakened the strength of the link between local community and the support of a football (or rugby league) team. In *A Yorkshire Tragedy*, a powerful and passionate review of the decline in fortunes of the football, rugby league and cricket clubs of Yorkshire since the 1980s, Anthony Clavane argues that the legacy of the Thatcher years – the decimation of the Yorkshire mining industry, the disappearance of the fishing industry and the major decline of other manufacturing concerns such as steel – has had a major impact on the community cohesion of towns and cities such as Barnsley, Hull and Sheffield, and the strength of the link between place, community and football team:

Old Yorkshire as an idea can be sentimentalised, romanticised even, its insular and bigoted tendencies ignored by nostalgia-ridden advocates. But the loss of a belligerent, solidaristic communal culture is more than a Yorkshire tragedy. It is a national one. Many of the county's clubs are no longer the heartbeat of their communities; their players, an ever-decreasing number of whom are recruited locally, exist in a completely different financial orbit. The communal to-and-fro of the old, standing terraces belong to a different world of well-paid skilled jobs, crowded pubs and terraced streets. The evisceration in the eighties of that world sounded the death-knell for a simpler, purer, harder, edgier version of sport.

This is a convincing argument, which undoubtably has resonance beyond Yorkshire. The decline of the cotton industry in Lancashire from the 1950s onwards has had similar adverse consequences for community cohesiveness in towns such as Bolton, Bury, Accrington and Burnley. And in the big cities, the slum clearance schemes of the 1950s and 1960s dispersed close-knit inner-city communities to council estates on their fringes, where community identity has been slow to develop. The Northeast has experienced a similar industrial upheaval, with coalmining now a thing of the past and shipbuilding in terminal decline. So, if Clavane is right, the decline of community cohesion and identity would be equally apparent right across the North, from Lancashire to Sunderland, and even in big cities such as Manchester and Leeds, which have prospered recently as retail and commercial centres.

It is hard to disagree with Clavane's conclusion that traditional working-class communities, focused on locations where peoples' work patterns, domestic lives and leisure-time activities are closely interwoven, have become much less common over the past forty years. He talks about Featherstone in West Yorkshire as a potent example of how things used to be, and what has been lost. Featherstone is, or rather was, a small mining town where social life revolved around the pit, the Miners' Institute and other community organisations, and the rugby league club, Featherstone Rovers, many of whose players worked at the pit, where the first topic of conversation on the Monday shift was always 'how did the Rovers get on?' But in the 1980s the mine was closed, and the life force of the town ebbed away. Rovers are still punching above their weight, but their role as a binding social force in a town with a high unemployment rate has clearly declined.

There remain a few exceptions to the dominant pattern of industrial decline, and here, support for local teams remains strong. Barrow-in-Furness, where the building and re-fitting of nuclear submarines is still the dominant industry, is one town where a traditional working-class community has largely survived; the shipyard's seven thousand employees are drawn mainly from the town itself, and Barrow AFC, unsuccessful though they have been in recent years, remains a source of local pride. The large steelworks at Scunthorpe still dominates the town's economy, and Scunthorpe United fans still chant 'Come on the Iron'. But these are the exceptions. For every Barrow or Scunthorpe there are plenty of towns that have lost their basic industry – or it has become much reduced in scope – and the traditional bonds between home, workplace and leisure have been greatly weakened. Barnsley, Oldham, Accrington, Crewe, Wigan and Middlesbrough are among the Northern places which have experienced this kind of decline, along with many others in the Midlands – Walsall, Stoke-on-Trent and Mansfield, for example.

And yet, despite industrial decline, the loyalty to football clubs remains. It may, in most cases, be less of an expression of community identity than it was, and more a symbolic attachment to a town that has lost its economic identity; but it nevertheless remains. Indeed, attendance numbers at grounds have risen since the early 1980s, when the Thatcher-inspired hollowing-out of our industrial base was just beginning. Amongst many Premier League clubs, there has, I suspect, been a major shift in the social background of their clientele – if you're on the dole or in a part-time or zero-hours contract job, you're not going to be able to afford a season ticket at Manchester United, Manchester City, Chelsea, Arsenal or any of the other corporate big-time clubs. But moving down a level or two, things are different. When Barnsley came to Wigan on the last day of the 2015–16 season, they needed a win to make it to the play-offs. Five thousand Barnsley supporters, bedecked in red, made the journey across the Pennines to cheer their team on, filling the whole of the North Stand of the DW stadium. Their journey and the passion of their support was rewarded with a 4-1 victory that secured a play-off place and later promotion to the Championship. My conclusion was that, whilst traditional working-class communities may well have declined, the importance of 'supporting your local club' has continued. Indeed, it can be argued that it has helped supporters cope with the economic insecurity into which so many have been plunged, since the 1980s.

* * *

The significance of football clubs as expressions of the strength of community identity with a town can, however, be much more than a symbolic feature. It can operate for many as a major influence on the quality of their lives. Nowhere is this better illustrated than in situations where the very existence of a club is threatened. In August 2019, three months after gaining promotion from League Two in some style, Bury were expelled from League One due to insurmountable financial problems. A BBC documentary powerfully illustrated the impact of this expulsion. 'When I heard the devastating news, I cried in my dad's arms for an hour,' admitted one woman. Her dad had bought her first season ticket when she was six, over twenty years ago. Every other Saturday, Kenny Hindle, seventy-eight years old, would leave his sheltered housing, take the bus into town, go for a pint and then watch the team he has supported for more than seventy years. 'What do you do without bloody football!' bemoaned Kenny. Joy Hart, a former director of the club, chained herself to a drainpipe outside the stadium. Zoe Hitchin, a former club photographer, has since put together an exhibition covering the 134 years of Bury's history because 'the true value of Bury FC – which is people and community – has been forgotten. I care, because that football club was my extended family.' Many supporters claimed that they have found it too painful to watch any football since the club went out of business. Such is the power of the link between football teams and local communities to stir deep emotions.

Such traumatic developments have a resonance that extends way beyond the town in which they occur. I, too, was greatly saddened by the news of Bury's demise (which hopefully doesn't preclude a resurrection). When I lived in south Manchester in the 1960s, I made regular visits to Gigg Lane, Bury's friendly stadium, surrounded on two sides by mature trees. They were in what was then the Second Division, punching above their weight; although, going further back in time, they twice won the FA Cup in the early 1900s and often graced the old First Division with their presence until as late as 1929. As recently as 2016, I was at Gigg Lane to watch Bury beat Blackpool 4-2. Many other occasional visitors and supporters of teams visiting Bury are likely to have experienced reactions of dismay similar to my own. There is a camaraderie amongst football fans, particularly down in the lower leagues. There but for fortune!

At the time when Bury's future was in the balance, I hoped that one of Manchester's elite Premiership clubs might come to their aid, financially or otherwise. After all, Manchester City, for example, owe a large debt of gratitude to Bury, from whom they signed Colin Bell, one of their iconic players of the 1960s and '70s. Sadly, no such help was forthcoming.

The strength of the relationship between local community and local football club is further illustrated by the way in which local political action has been stimulated by concerns about the future of a football team. The demonstrations outside Gigg Lane provide one notable example. Other triggers include inertia on the part of the local council, or opposition to the behaviour of the club's owners. Charlton Athletic's long exile from its traditional home, The Valley, in the 1980s led to an organised and ultimately successful campaign for a return. When the local council – the London Borough of Greenwich – was perceived to be dragging its feet, the pressure group involved nominated several of its members to stand in local elections on a specific 'back to The Valley' programme. They didn't win any council seats, but it certainly spurred the council into taking action.

When Wimbledon's owners moved the club to Milton Keynes in 2005 (where it became MK Dons), the club's outraged supporters started a new Wimbledon-based club, which in 2012 was promoted to the Football League, having worked its way up the non-league pyramid. They have since joined their 'parent' club in League One.

A breakaway group of Manchester United fans, angry at the takeover of the club by American businessman Malcolm Glazer, founded a new club, FC United of Manchester, which currently plays in the National League North in Newton Heath (the original home of Manchester United) before crowds regularly topping two thousand.

In 2015–16, when I was writing *Tangerines and Pies*, a book about Blackpool and Wigan Athletic, there were regular demonstrations outside Blackpool's Bloomfield Road on match days, protesting about the way Oyston family ran the club. At the last home game of the season, there was a march from the town centre to the football ground, in which I took part. It attracted over two thousand fans. At a similar event the following season, supporters from other clubs who were experiencing problems with owners were invited to attend. There was a large contingent from Leyton Orient, then in the hands of Italian businessman Francesco Becchetti and already doomed to relegation. Groups of supporters from Blackburn Rovers and Coventry City also took part. The camaraderie amongst the different groups, united in their opposition to the attitude of their owners and in their determination to do something about it, was both encouraging and moving. There have also been several instances of clubs being bought out by supporters' associations: Portsmouth, Exeter City and Wycombe Wanderers provide successful examples of such takeovers.

All these different examples of community action (to which more could be added) can be seen as expressions of the importance of their local town to those who have taken such action, and of the way the local football club symbolises this attachment. Despite the fragmentation of traditional working-class communities, a sense of place clearly does continue to matter, not least to the vast number of football fans who support their team week in, week out.

And, of course, there is the social dimension of 'following your team'. Because I tend to travel to a range of different venues, rather than attend regularly at one particular club, I often go to games on my own. In this, I know I am not typical. Although I am usually aware of a handful of other solitaries in the vicinity, it is clear that the majority of those present have come as groups: sometimes fathers and sons, sometimes whole families (mums and daughters included), but particularly groups of mates, some school-aged, some in their twenties or thirties, and some senior citizens, who've probably been coming since they were lads. Many will have enjoyed a few pints in a local pub, on the way to the match. The social ritual involved is a crucial element of being a supporter.

Martin Tarbuck described to me his experience of away-days in the following terms: 'I love the day out, the beers, the planning, the train or coach journey, meeting up with friends, the rivalry, the anger, the smell of the pitch, and yes, the pies; everything about the day is a great occasion.' He quotes a comment from a friend of his: 'Anyone who knows anything about football knows that football has got nothing to do with football.' That sounds nonsensical, but I know what he means! Attending football matches is for most of us a collective, social activity and as such should be treasured, as an antidote to the increasing domination of individual pursuits, typically IT-based.

Daniel Gray's evocative book, *Saturday, 3pm: 50 Eternal Delights of Modern Football*, includes a chapter entitled 'Knowing where you were', in which he explains the strength for him of the association between major events in one's life and football matches: 'I don't know why it matters,' he writes. 'Life events should be significant enough in isolation without football fixtures clamping onto them like limpets.' But there is a sense in which individual football matches do, for many of us, act as landmarks in our progression through life. For others, such life associations operate through popular songs. For football fans, though, it's 'the game we'd been to on the day we got engaged', or some such soccer-linked memory that survives over time. In this respect, time, place, life and football become inextricably intertwined.

MANCHESTER

Old Moat Juniors, Parrswood Athletic and the Sky Blues

I still get asked to do the occasional training sessions for councillors of Manchester City Council. In introducing myself, I always make a point of establishing my credentials as a Mancunian. I've found that it's helpful to my credibility at such events to be able to demonstrate some kind of affinity with the local authority for whom I'm working, even if it's only 'we used to come on holiday here...'

I was born in Rusholme (a couple of miles south of the city centre), I tell them. I lived for the first fifteen years of my life in a semi-detached house in West Didsbury and attended Old Moat Primary School (of which more shortly), situated in the middle of a large council estate. I went on to gain a place at Manchester Grammar School, which I can't say I much enjoyed, particularly in my third and fourth years when our form master was the notorious and tyrannical Billy Hulme. After attending university in Birmingham, I moved back to Manchester, and worked as a junior town planning officer for the city council for five years, before moving on to Chester. So, I conclude in my self-introduction, we share the same heritage. We are all Mancunians.

This claim is perfectly genuine. I do still feel deeply rooted in Manchester, even if I have not lived there since 1969, although whenever I revisit the city nowadays, I am struck by how fast the landscape of the centre is changing – it is currently the dominant provincial rival to London in terms of the pace and scope of new developments, and cranes are always in abundance.

My love of football – both as a spectator and an enthusiastic, but run-of-the-mill amateur player – developed during my time there. I was a member of the talented (though I say so myself)

11

Old Moat Primary School football team. We played in yellow and brown shirts, a combination I've never come across anywhere else, and I can't say I'm surprised; why would anyone in their right mind choose such a bizarre combination? We ended up as area league champions, playing twelve and winning twelve, including two victories over our traditional rivals, Ladybarn Primary. And we made it to the quarter-final of the all-Manchester primary school cup, which was no mean feat, with over eighty schools competing. But there we met our match: we were drawn away to Ravensbury Street, a school in Clayton. It was a big occasion for Old Moat. A coach was hired to transport us to the unknown territory of industrial east Manchester. We changed in the school and then trooped in the pouring rain to the school's pitch, which was situated on a plateau above the murky River Medlock. The pitch, when we reached it, elicited gasps of astonishment from the Old Moat team. There wasn't a single blade of grass on it. It was grey in colour and the consistency of glutinous powdered cinders, which became increasingly saturated as the rain continued to fall. How were we expected to play on that morass?

Well, if we couldn't, Ravensbury Street certainly could. They beat us 4-0 and it could easily have been more. At the final whistle, we were escorted to the local swimming baths, where we immersed ourselves in steaming hot tubs (three to a tub), managing to remove all traces of the muddy playing surface glued to our bodies, before emerging pink and relaxed, but still chastened by the comprehensiveness of our defeat.

The reality was that Ravensbury Street were a very good side indeed – they went on to win the cup and would have beaten us equally decisively on sea-washed turf. But that was not the way our form master and football coach, Mr McVeigh, saw it. He was convinced that, on our own uneven but partly grassed playing surface at Old Moat, we would prove their equal. Accordingly, he invited them for a return friendly match a couple of weeks later. A major error of judgement, as it turned out! They were four goals up by halftime, and eventually cruised to a 5-0 win. Mr McVeigh and the entire Old Moat squad were forced to conclude that Ravensbury Street were in a different class to us.

By 1954, when these matches took place, I was already an occasional spectator at Maine Road or Old Trafford, where I would be taken whenever my dad and Uncle Arthur could be spared from Saturday domestic duties. They didn't seem bothered whether it was City or United we went to see; so much for the expectation that everyone in Manchester would attach themselves to one or other of these traditional rivals and would not dream of attending any of the other team's matches! But by some mysterious process that I can't recall, my friend John Davies and I had, by this time, decided we were Manchester City supporters. Perhaps there was an element of supporting the underdog, because that was certainly City's status at that time.

We watched Manchester City as often as pocket money and other commitments would permit over the period 1957 to 1969, when we both moved away from Manchester. There were bad times and there were good times. In the memorable 1958–59 season, City both scored and conceded over a hundred goals in their forty-two League games; that's an average of five goals per game. One of the outstanding City players of the time was George Hannah, an inside-forward previously with Newcastle United. His speciality was defence-splitting passes, and I can still see him making them, in my mind's eye, sixty years later. City also had a speedy right-winger called Colin Barlow, not particularly tricky with the ball, but he could run very fast. Hannah would receive the ball in midfield, look up and dispatch a forty-yard pass inside the full-back to the feet of the on-rushing Barlow, who would either make straight for goal, or take the ball to the bye-line and cross it at head height for

Billy McAdams to nod in. Hannah's pass, and indeed this whole sequence, could aptly be described as a thing of beauty.

In 1962, City were relegated to the Second Division, much to our indignation. After a particularly galling 5-1 defeat at home to West Bromwich Albion, John and I joined an impromptu demonstration outside the Maine Road main stand, hurling pennies at the reinforced glass windows of the club offices. When one of our missiles actually cracked the glass, we quickly scarpered. John was present in the lowest home crowd in living memory – something over eight thousand – that witnessed a 2-1 defeat by Swindon Town. This was the time when the genial, pipe-smoking (and totally useless) George Poyser was manager. He features in one of my all-time favourite football jokes. One Friday, during a dismal run, with attendances slumping, he bumps into a City fan. 'Hello, George,' says the fan, 'I'm thinking of coming to the game tomorrow. What time's kick- off?' George's face lights up, and he replies: 'What time can you come?'

After three years in the Second Division, City finally got their act together under the formidable management team of Joe Mercer and Malcolm Allison. John and I were at Millmoor to witness the 1-0 win against Rotherham United in the spring of 1966 that guaranteed promotion. That was the start of a golden period in City's history, which lasted until the mid-1970s. We were present at St James's Park on the final day of the 1967–68 season to see them clinch the First Division title with a 4-3 win against Newcastle United. The following season we were at Wembley to see City lift the FA Cup with a 1-0 victory over Leicester City. In May 1970, we flew to Vienna to watch City win the European Cup Winners' Cup, with a 2-1 win over Górnik Zabrze. The stadium didn't have an iota of cover, and the rain hammered down for the whole of the match, so it wasn't the most pleasant experience. But at least we were there!

All these achievements were down to a group of players recruited largely from the Greater Manchester area. Francis Lee came from Bolton, Colin Bell from Bury and most of their teammates from Manchester itself. The one outsider was Mike Summerbee, who hailed from Swindon. There was not an overseas signing in sight, which was normal then. At that time, the link between football club and local community was stronger than it is now – we were watching players who we might have unknowingly faced in a school fixture.

* * *

It was in Manchester that I played a major role in setting up a proper football club in a proper league, namely Parrswood Athletic in the Manchester Amateur Football League. The way it came about was this. When I returned to Manchester in 1964, after three years at Birmingham University, a small group of friends and I started meeting every Sunday morning at the football pitches at Parrswood, East Didsbury, for a kick-around session: attack-against-defence and that kind of thing. As the numbers grew, we realised that if we could interest a few more players, we would have enough for a full football team. Friends of friends were roped in, and towards the end of 1965 we had a dozen reasonably competent young footballers in tow. We began to organise friendly matches, including one against the local tennis club, West Heaton, a middle-class establishment who'd taken to running a football team in the winter months, when tennis was off the agenda. By the time we met them, they'd already had a few matches under their belts, and clearly fancied themselves. We beat them 6-4 (an appropriate score for a game against a tennis club!), a result which encouraged us to apply to join the Manchester Amateur Sunday Football League (Division Six) for the 1966–67 season. All you needed was a club secretary and the guarantee of a pitch, typically in a public park. If you had nets to attach to the goals, which we did, that was a bonus, but not a requirement.

To our delight and amazement, our application was accepted. We later realised that it perhaps wasn't so amazing; there was always a high drop-out rate, not just from Division Six, but also from the higher divisions. There was a track record in this league of new clubs surviving for two or three seasons, and then expiring, as indeed Parrswood Athletic did in 1969.

I'd watched Manchester Amateur Sunday Football League Division One games at Hough End Fields in the mid-1950s, some of which attracted impressive attendances: rows of spectators were often two deep on all sides of the pitch. Indeed, it was not just Sunday League football that attracted this size of crowd. In the Lancashire and Cheshire Amateur League, leading clubs like East Chorlton, who played at Hough End Fields on one of the thirty or so pitches there, and Rusholme, who played at nearby Christie Fields (now a business park) often played in front of capacity crowds, 'capacity' being how many you get standing on all four sides of the pitch, able to see enough of the play to make it worthwhile. In the 1950s, there was still an appetite for watching football at all levels, following the years of deprivation during World War Two.

My favourite local team was East Chorlton, who managed to win the Lancashire Amateur Cup in the late 1950s. Their star attraction was Eddie Joyce, a stocky centre-forward, probably approaching his mid-thirties. Eddie was a prolific goalscorer with a venomous shot and a capacity for bullet-like headers – always a joy to watch. Just before their cup final, there was a radio programme in which Eddie was interviewed together with the much more famous Stanley Matthews, who stressed the importance of abstinence from alcohol and tobacco in maintaining your football career in your thirties. Eddie's response was that smoking and drinking were two pastimes he very much enjoyed, which he had no intention of giving up!

In the Manchester Amateur Sunday Football League in the 1950s, many of the leading teams were pub-based, Elsdon being a dominant force at that time. But there was also a club called 'The Wanderers' who were still in the league in 1966, when we joined. By this time, clubs based on Catholic churches had moved into prominence, notably St Bernadettes and St Kentigerns, both to be found in south Manchester.

'Where did it all begin?', an evocative article by Fred Brocklehurst on the Manchester Amateur Sunday Football League website, brings back a lot of memories for me. He confirms the popular appeal of the top league matches: 'It was not unusual for crowds of hundreds to watch famous local teams like Elsdon, Clynes, Little Alex and Brookes Bakers,' all of whom I recall seeing. In 1948, Fred became player-manager of a relatively undistinguished team called City Rangers and he recalls that the highlight of his managerial career was 'to hold the mighty Little Alex 0-0 in a cup-tie for 80 minutes before we eventually collapsed to a 4-1 defeat'. He notes that many of the players of these top clubs also turned out professionally for teams in the Lancashire Combination and Cheshire County League, a practice that was also in operation when we were playing in the 1960s.

None of the 'big clubs' mentioned above exist now. The most likely reason for their collective demise is that most of them were pub-based teams from working-class areas in the inner city, to the south of the city centre. From the mid-1950s onwards, the city council's relentless slum clearance programme gradually obliterated the streets of terraced housing in these areas, and with them, the vibrant working-class communities that had grown up there. No doubt clubs like Elsdon, Clynes and Little Alex became unviable as a result.

Our first fixture in 1966 was at home at Cringle Fields against FC Zurich, not a visiting team from Switzerland, but rather one representing a Manchester-based insurance company. At halftime we were 4-1 up, and feeling pretty pleased with ourselves – promotion, here we come! Our opponents dominated the second half and pulled it back to 4-4, but nonetheless, it was an encouraging start; we could surely at least survive at this level.

The next Sunday we were away to Camberwell, a young pub-based team from Wythenshawe. We were quietly confident. Less so after thirty seconds, when they carved through our defence straight from the kick-off and scored. Six minutes later, they scored again, and yet again after fifteen. When the final whistle was mercifully blown, they had found the net fifteen times; we had managed nothing in response. A rude awakening indeed! The results of the league were published in the Monday edition of the *Manchester Evening News*, so we knew the world would learn of our ignominious defeat. In fact, the published score was 13-0: either a misprint, or the referee had lost count. But we knew the reality.

It was with some trepidation that we faced Inter-Gorton at Debdale Park the following Sunday. Inter-Gorton clearly had illusions of grandeur, naming themselves after the famous Milan club. Perhaps we should have styled ourselves Real Parrswood. The pitch we played on at Debdale Park was unusual in that, at the edge of the penalty area at one end, there was a sudden dip, so that in that location, the crossbar was at ball height. No doubt Inter-Gorton were accustomed to this bizarre feature, but as we escaped with a 2-0 defeat, we weren't complaining. At least that was a real score!

As the season progressed, things gradually improved, and we finished in a lower-middle position. It was a wet winter with many postponements, and no team fulfilled all their fixtures. As it turned out, we didn't have to face Camberwell (who finished as champions) again, which was a relief; I'm not sure 'home advantage' would have made a lot of difference to the outcome.

Was there an improvement in the following season, you will no doubt want to know? The best way of satisfying your curiosity is to quote from the 'Parrswood Athletic Annual Report and Balance Sheet for the Season 1967–68', penned by club secretary Steve Leach and which my friend and fellow team-member John Davies kindly unearthed for me recently:

The playing record of the club in its second season showed a distinct improvement on the first. Although inconsistency was still apparent, Parrswood managed to avoid the heavy defeats experienced in the first season (epitomised by the Camberwell disaster), and on occasions turned out some really good performances. The highlight of the season was undoubtably the cup game against St Bernadettes, who had won the Triple Crown of the Division One Championship, League Cup and Manchester Sunday Cup the previous season. After taking an early lead, Parrswood played well above themselves and were perhaps unlucky to go down 5-3 to one of the elite of Manchester Sunday Football. The best league performance was probably the fine 5-0 win against a strong Mermaid side in the Cringle Fields mud, and the club finished the season in fine style, by scoring ten goals in the second half of the game against British Road Services Contracts, to end up 12-2 winners.

It is only fair to add that St Bernadettes played the game with ten men. Scorer of two of St Bernadettes' goals was the legendary (in the world of Manchester Sunday football) Ricky Green, who played for a semi-professional club at the time. It should also be noted that BRS Contracts were by far the most useless team we had encountered in our three seasons in the league, and to be held to a 2-2 draw at half-time by that shower was a disgrace. Still the eventual 12-2 outcome did help to dull the pain of the Camberwell experience.

Encouraged by our improvement, we decided to apply for promotion to Division Five. With a playing record of played twenty, won seven, drawn four and lost nine, you might think this a long shot, not to say presumptuous. But just as entry to the league benefitted from the drop-out rate, so did the prospects of promotion. Perhaps also impressed by my letter of application, in which I drew attention to our excellent record of sportsmanship, our application was successful, and in 1968–69, we played in Division Five.

I can't remember the details of our playing record, but I do recall that it was our most successful season, culminating in a 1-0 win over division champions Didsbury United at Hough End Fields. Another cringeworthy application ensued, which was again successful. But sadly, our plan to take Division Four by storm never materialised. Several of our founding members had already moved elsewhere, and when I accepted a job offer in Chester in the spring of 1969, there was no one able or willing to take over the task of running the club. So, like many before us (and no doubt since) we folded, and I went on to sign up with St Theresa's FC in the Chester suburb of Blacon.

Although I doubt if anyone now remembers Parrswood Athletic, apart from its ex-players, I am pleased to have been part of their brief history. As someone who has always enjoyed watching football, at a variety of levels, I have also derived great satisfaction from actually playing the game, albeit at the most grass-roots of levels, and to have been involved in the fascinating and ever-changing world of the Manchester Amateur Sunday Football League, which still exists. Long may it continue!

* * *

I had returned to Manchester in 1964, with my social science degree in my pocket, and started looking for a job. The problem was that a university degree in sociology, interesting though that subject is, did not lead to any obvious career pattern, in the way that a qualification in civil engineering or law would have done. So, what was I to do?

The way I obtained my first proper job seems hardly believable, fifty years later. My dissertation at Birmingham had addressed the topic of green belts in metropolitan areas, an issue that I knew town planners had to deal with. I wrote a brief letter to Manchester City Council and Stockport Borough Council explaining that I had just obtained a university degree in sociology, and that I was interested in town planning, and would they consider employing me? Stockport never replied, but Manchester wrote back within a couple of weeks, inviting me for an interview. Whatever I said at the interview must have made a favourable impression, as I was offered a job in the city's planning department, at the princely salary of £850 per annum, which seemed generous enough, compared with my wages in previous jobs (summer holiday work in a Cheadle battery-making factory and a Stockport bakery, and two stints on Christmas post).

I had five enjoyable years in the planning department, but there was one aspect of the work I did there that I felt uneasy about. By 1964, when I joined the department, the Manchester slum clearance programme had developed an unstoppable momentum. One of my tasks was to analyse the household structure in the areas to be demolished, so that an assessment could be made of the overall rehousing requirements. The problem I had, as a recently qualified sociologist, was that I'd read Michael Young and Peter Wilmott's classic 1950s study of Bethnal Green, which revealed the close-knit networks of extended families and friends in such communities and warned against the social costs of disrupting them.

One of the first areas I had to deal with was Lodge Street in Collyhurst. I carried out a survey of the family structure there and argued that rehousing the residents in the same area would help maintain the social fabric. But such responsiveness was not a priority for the council; indeed, there was no awareness that social networks needed to be taken into account: 'They're all getting a council house, aren't they? What more do they want?' I did express my concerns to anyone who would listen, but my words fell on deaf ears. In the 1970s, following increasing pressure from residents, there was a switch from redevelopment to area improvement – and not before time.

A condition of my appointment at Manchester City Council was that I should enrol on a part-time town planning diploma course at Manchester University, which would, after three years, lead to my becoming a professionally qualified planner. This I duly did, little realising what a restrictive effect it would have on my social life over that period. The worst part of it was the evening sessions, after a full day's work in the office. In the first year, there was an hour and a half of 'Engineering Construction' followed by an hour and a half of 'Sewerage', both delivered by the same lecturer in a droning monotone. It was difficult to concentrate, or indeed, at times, to stay awake.

During 1968, I went out for a while with a colleague in the planning department called Pamela (widely known amongst the male fraternity as 'Little Pamela' in that notoriously non-PC era). One evening we went into the Sawyers Arms on Deansgate. Who should be there but the legendary Georgie Best, then still at the peak of his career (or perhaps slightly past it). He was obviously taken with Little Pamela and repeatedly tried to catch her eye during the half-hour we were there. Now there's a claim to fame for you – 'Georgie Best eyed up my girlfriend' – but I guess more so for her than me.

The 1964–69 period was one in which the world of popular music was transformed and a key figure in this sea change was Bob Dylan, who appeared twice at the Manchester Free Hall when

I was working in the city. His first performance was in1965, when he was still singing protest songs. There was just him, a harmonica and an acoustic guitar on stage, and a spellbound capacity audience who cheered every song.

He was back in 1966, with a very different persona and musical output. The first half of the concert was not unfamiliar; Dylan on his own, singing a new set of songs, more poetic and introspective than the protest material, but a close enough approximation to what the audience were hoping for, to earn him a reasonably enthusiastic reception at the interval.

In the second half, that mood was blown away. Dylan came back on stage with a group of musicians (in fact, the Band, although we didn't know that at the time). They all, including Dylan, plugged their instruments into a formidable bank of amplifiers, before blasting into a very loud rock number called 'Tell Me, Momma', in which the words were a mixture of the inaudible and incomprehensible. Applause was lukewarm, and the hostility of the audience grew as Dylan and the Band worked their way through strident versions of several as-yet unrecorded songs, including 'Ballad of a Thin Man'. 'Leopard-Skin Pill-Box Hat' came in for particular derision – could this really be the work of a man who less than a year ago was delighting his audience with 'The Times They Are A-Changin'' (which they clearly still were)?

Towards the end of the set came the infamous shout of 'Judas' from one of the remaining members of the audience who hadn't already walked out. 'I don't believe you; you're a liar' was Dylan's response before storming into a very loud and angry version of 'Like a Rolling Stone'. I was still there at the end, applauding the musicians as they hurriedly left the stage. It seemed to me to be healthy that Dylan was moving in a new direction and wasn't intending to go on performing 'Blowin' in the Wind' for the rest of his life. Despite the dire quality of the sound, I thought the new songs sounded good, as indeed they were later acknowledged to be. I've long dined out on the fact that I was present at one of the most turbulent and celebrated gigs of the twentieth century.

* * *

A couple of months before watching Manchester City beat Leicester 1-0 in the FA Cup Final of 1969, I had moved to Chester to work for Cheshire County planning department. I never again lived in Manchester, and when my parents retired to Alderley Edge (which regards itself as a different world entirely, despite being linked to the city centre by a twenty-five-minute train journey), the family link with my place of birth and upbringing was finally broken.

And what became of my allegiance to Manchester City, the club I had supported since the age of nine? In the early 1970s, I travelled back to Maine Road to watch them from time to time. This was the era of Mick Channon, Wyn Davies and Brian Kidd, and City played to the strengths of this formidable strike force. They were always entertaining to watch, and regularly finished in the top six of Division One but proved too inconsistent to ever emerge as champions. I was at Villa Park in 1981 to watch City defeat Ipswich Town in the FA Cup semi-final, with a late goal from Paul Power (they went on to lose to Spurs in a replayed final, undone by the magic of Ossie Ardilles and Ricky Villa). When living in Silverdale, Lancashire, in the early 1990s, I was again drawn back to Maine Road, this time by the quality of football played by a team dominated by locally born and nurtured young-sters, amongst them David White, Ian Brightwell, Neil Pointon, Steve Redmond and, before an injury prematurely ended his career, the talented Paul Lake. City finished fifth in two successive seasons. One abiding memory is a game against Derby County, when early in the second half, keeper Tony Coton was sent off for fouling Dean Saunders. Niall Quinn, who had already scored, replaced him in goal, saved Saunders's penalty and went on to display an aptitude as a keeper that no one (including, I suspect, himself) would ever have guessed he possessed. He remained unbeaten, despite much Derby pressure, and ten-man City went on to win 2-1, an outcome that owed much to the team spirit of a side which always looked like they enjoyed playing together.

After that, my active involvement with City declined, but not, for a while, my nominal support. From 1993 onwards, I had a young family that took up most of my spare time; trips from Kendal, where I now lived, to Manchester would have seemed like a self-indulgence. On my sixtieth birthday (November 2002), my wife, Karen, planned a surprise day out in Keswick – I thought it was going to be a family excursion, but when we arrived in the town, I was ushered into a pub, where old friends John and Bill had been primed to meet me. It was the day of the Manchester derby – City versus United – which we watched on a big screen, whilst Karen and the boys went off for a walk. City won 3-1, their first win against United in a long time, and included a stunning goal from Shaun Wright-Phillips (a shame his career stalled and then declined at Chelsea). In 2005, for a celebration of John's sixtieth, I treated him to a visit to the Etihad Stadium – the first and only time I've been there. It was a less inspired choice for a birthday surprise, as it turned out; it was the time when Stuart Pearce was manager, and the emphasis was on defence. The opponents were Blackburn Rovers, it was a goalless draw, and, as I recall, there wasn't a single shot on target from either team. There was, however, a spectacular sunset, which mercifully distracted us from the aridness of what was taking place on the pitch.

Then, in 2007, came the arrival of the former Thai Prime Minister, Thaksin Shinawatra, armed with a previously undreamed-of level of riches to invest in the club. His dodgy political background would, in itself, have caused me to distance myself from City, but equally unacceptable, at least to me, was the way in which these newfound millions were used to entice players from other clubs by offering them much bigger salaries than their existing clubs could afford. A year later, an immensely wealthy private equity company called the Abu Dhabi United Group took over City from Shinawatra. Expensive superstars from all over the globe came and went; high-profile overseas managers likewise. The chances of a local-born (or even locally developed) young player making it to the first team became increasingly remote. Admittedly, these star-studded line-ups delivered: Premier League titles in 2012, 2014 and 2018, and in the process, there was much scintillating football played, particularly in 2018, when City were virtually unbeatable.

But, by then, I'd severed my fifty-five-year connection with the club. I didn't want to be part of a world of football dominated by global capitalist institutions. I wondered, too, how many of the local population could now afford the price of a season ticket. East Manchester has always been a working-class area. Its population fell by as much as 60%, as a result of the slum clearance programme of the 1960s and 70s, and the area became further impoverished by the disappearance of what remained of the industrial jobs in the area during the Thatcher years (and more recently by the post-2009 onset of austerity). My guess is that the slack will have been taken up by the young professionals who have poured into the plethora of apartment blocks constructed in the city centre over the past ten years. As for me, I am happy to be left with my memories of the packed terraces of Maine Road, and the delight of watching the likes of Ivor Broadis, Bobby Johnstone, George Hannah, the local lads who made up the bulk of the 1992 team and, of course, the class of 1968, who fifty years ago clinched the First Division title with a thrilling 4-3 win at St James's Park, watched by a crowd of 55,000, my friend John Davies and I amongst them.

PART I

DAYS OF RECKONING

BARROW-IN-FURNESS

You are awful (but I like you)

Barrow has been described over the years in various ways, most of them uncomplimentary. Before the advent of rail links, access from Lancaster and anywhere to the south of it was by stagecoach, horseback or foot, across the sands of Morecambe Bay, a perilous journey at the best of times. The graveyard adjacent to Cartmel Priory is full of the gravestones of those who failed to complete the crossing alive. *Crap Towns* (2003 edition) is particularly dismissive:

> *'Grey pebble-dash galore, Barrow is never without rain for more than a few minutes, and most people will only have heard of it thanks to a well-publicised outbreak of Legionnaires' disease.'*

It's arguably the best remaining example of a 'company town' in Britain – in most of its rivals, 'the company' closed during the Thatcher era, if not before. Shipbuilding is its economic raison d'être, carried out in the vast complex of yards that used to be run by Vickers, and now operated by BAE Systems. But we're not talking about any old kind of ship. Nuclear submarines are the yard's speciality, indeed currently its sole product. As *Crap Towns* puts it: 'Barrow is a shipbuilding town where hardly any ships are built, a shadow of its former self, dependent on the manufacture of a few murderous nuclear submarines for its survival.'

That's perhaps an overstatement (an attribute to which *Crap Towns* is prone), or at least the bit about the town being a 'shadow of its former self' is. The yard employs around 7,500, working on the next generation of submarines, which may be a lot less than the workforce of 16,000 in the 1990s, but it is still by far the biggest employer in the town. However, in the longer term, its future is uncertain. If the shipyard were to close, the biggest employer in the town would be Kimberly-Clark, which manufactures toilet rolls, amongst other paper goods. What an indignity that would be! A switch from a shipbuilding town to a toilet roll town. It would be reminiscent of what happened to Consett in County Durham in the 1980s: the steelworks closed, and a manufacturer of potato crisps moved in. Steel to potato crisps; ships to toilet rolls – it says a lot about the change in the country's economic base over the past fifty years.

The BBC Cumbria website emphasises the town's isolation, noting that 'one of the most significant things about Barrow is that only the most hapless dazed orienteer could possibly visit by accident – you have to have a purpose to get there'. In the late 1960s, the manager of the 99 Club, the only nightclub in town, booked The Who, then at an early stage in their career. Pete Townsend later described Barrow as 'the armpit of the universe'.

But there are those with a less jaundiced view of the qualities if the town. In his book *You Are Awful (But I Like You)*, a hilarious journey round 'unloved Britain', Tim Moore was pleasantly surprised by the town. He found Barrow to be 'a town clinging tenaciously to its roots ... as a British industrial town, Barrow must have endured its fair share of economic kickings, but somehow the bottom has never fallen out of the place'. It is one of the few locations in his book that he does end up 'quite liking'.

I agree with him. Ever since first visiting it, I've admired its gritty, unashamedly working-class ambience. It must have one of the highest proportions of working-class people in its population in the country, simply because there are still over seven thousand traditional manual jobs to be had in the town, and due to the fact that few of the executive/managerial employees of BAE Systems actually live there. The Barrow tourist literature portrays the town as being 'where the Lakes meets the sea', but this is something of an exaggeration – the boundary of the Lake District National Park is some twelve miles away. But there are plenty of pleasant small towns and villages within easy reach of Barrow, in the direction of the Lake District, and that is where the BAE managers choose to live.

I like Barrow's areas of criss-crossing streets of terraced houses, such as Hindpool, adjacent to the football ground, which are a physical embodiment of its working-class persona. They have survived more or less intact, partly as a result of the Luftwaffe's inability to target their bombs on Vickers' shipyards and adjacent areas – one load landed in the middle of the limestone plateau of Birkrigg, near Ulverston, eight miles away – and partly due to Barrow Council's commendable decision not to replace them with high-rise flats in the 1960s, when many urban councils bought into the architects' hype and did just that. And the Dock Museum is an imaginative tribute to the development of the town's basic industry. But, most of all, I warm to the town's strong sense of community, well illustrated in Nella Last's published diaries, which she wrote from 1940 until 1955, as part of the Mass Observation project. That communal spirit appears to have survived to the present day. Barrow a crap town? I don't think so.

My first experience of Barrow was in the early 1980s. I had recently moved from Birmingham to north Lancashire, with my first wife and two stepdaughters. We were all active members of the Campaign for Nuclear Disarmament and took part in a mass CND-organised protest in Barrow against the construction of Trident nuclear submarines. The highlight of the demonstration was a simulated die-in: at the appointed time we all collapsed to the ground and lay there prone for five minutes, to illustrate the impact of a nuclear attack. A great idea, but I don't suppose anyone took much notice, either in Barrow itself, or in the world beyond.

Amongst the demonstrators was my future (second) wife, Karen, although a dozen years would elapse before I met her. In the 1960s and 1970s, her dad had worked at Vickers. Karen remembers that, when a little girl and shopping with her mother in Barrow, she'd sometimes be in the vicinity of the factory when the hooter sounded for the lunch break. She recalls being awe-struck at the deluge of workers – some on foot, some on bicycles – pouring out of the factory gates.

The football history of Barrow AFC is typical of the many clubs based in medium-sized towns that joined the League in 1921, when it was expanded from two to four divisions (Third Divisions North and South). Barrow were usually to be found in the lower to middle ranges of Third Division North, rarely being amongst the promotion challengers (of whom, until 1958, only the champions made it to the Second Division). They fared no better in the Fourth Division, until 1967, when they were promoted to the Third Division, where they survived for three seasons, before dropping down to more familiar habitat.

But worse was to come. Having finished twenty-second in the division, they suffered the rare (at the time) indignity of failing to secure re-election, losing out to Hereford United, fresh from their giant-killing FA Cup run (including Ronnie Radford's wonder goal against Newcastle United). So much for the familiar Old Pals' Act, which secured numerous survivals for Hartlepool United in the 1970s and 80s! It all seemed so unfair; both Crewe Alexandra and Stockport County finished below Barrow. So why not them? Apparently, Barrow didn't have enough pals, old or new, which maybe isn't surprising. It's a long trek to Barrow from anywhere outside the Northwest, and Holker Street is an inhospitable, windswept venue.

Since their abrupt ejection from the Football League, Barrow have zigzagged between the first and second tiers of non-league football. They struggled for seven years in the Northern Premier League, having been admitted in 1972 only on condition that they removed the speedway track that had been installed a few years earlier to generate extra income for the club. Then they were invited to join the newly formed Alliance Premier League (which later became the Conference, and more recently the National League). Until recently, it has not been an easy time for the club. There have been unreliable owners, notably Stephen Vaughan, who, having put money into the club, suddenly withdrew his investment in 1998, which resulted in Barrow being forced into liquidation (he later went through a similar sequence with Chester). Barrow's financial crisis lasted for three years, a period when there was a dispute as to who owned Holker Street.

But there have been compensatory highlights, despite all the turbulence. Barrow won the FA Trophy in 1990, beating Leek Town 2-1 at Wembley. They prospered in the late 1980s and early 1990s under a much-loved manager, Ray Wilkie, who was so greatly revered that they re-named the road adjacent to the ground in his honour, when he died in 2002. And there was the epic contribution of Colin Cowperthwaite (now there's a good local Barrovian name for you) who played 704 games for the club and scored 282 goals. We need more like him in the modern game.

Then, in 2014, came the boost that all non-league clubs aspire to, but relatively few achieve: the arrival of a wealthy benefactor. In 2013–14, Barrow finished the season becalmed in mid-table in the Conference North (as it then was). Their return to the big time (relatively speaking) of the National League owes much to the subsequent arrival of a new chairman and benefactor, Paul Casson, a self-made multi-millionaire businessman who was born and brought up in Barrow but made his money in the USA. In 2014, he decided he wanted to revive his home-town club. In his first full season as chairman, Barrow won the National League North title. The following season they finished mid-table, and in 2016–17, came within striking distance of promotion to the Football League. Now that would have been an inspiring achievement – Barrow returning to the League after a forty-four-year absence. It would come close to matching Accrington Stanley's return from the dead after their expulsion from the League in 1962.

Millionaire owners do make a difference in the National League, as they do at higher levels. If you see a hitherto little-known club emerging from obscurity (examples include Salford City, AFC Fylde, Eastleigh and Forest Green Rovers), such benefactors are typically behind this move into the spotlight, although it is worth remembering that Boreham Wood and Braintree Town have both prospered recently in the National League without such financial backing.

Paul flies over for many of Barrow's home games and writes a lively column in each home match programme. Halfway through the 2015–16 season, he replaced manager Darren Edmondson with Paul Cox, whose track record evoked hopes of a return to the Football League after a long absence. After a not particularly distinguished playing career, he achieved miracles with a small-time Derbyshire club, Eastwood Town, master-minding a rapid climb from obscurity to the Conference North play-offs in 2010, in which they were unfortunately not permitted to compete, owing to the limited capacity of their ground. His success there inspired Mansfield Town's millionaire owner John Radford to appoint him as manager, and in 2013, he steered Mansfield back into the League after a six-year absence. He kept them up the following season but left the club by mutual consent in November 2014. After a brief spell with Torquay United, which he left after ten games, having not been paid, he was appointed by Barrow in November 2015.

The soundness of the chairman's judgement in appointing him was confirmed the following season (2016–17). In the close season, Cox brought in a raft of new signings, as new (and established) managers invariably do at this level – perhaps as a result of the short-term contract culture. His acquisitions quickly gelled into a coherent unit and were up with the front-runners from early on. Indeed, had it not been for an impressive run in the FA Cup, where they reached the third round with a 2-1 win away to League One's Bristol Rovers, they could well have ended up in a play-off place. But the decline in League form which followed the cup exit put paid to that. Nevertheless, Barrow finished a respectable seventh.

During that 2016–17 season, I paid several visits to Holker Street, now retitled the Furness Building Society Stadium, but still, in reality, the endearing un-reconstituted Holker Street of old. I did so in the company of a family friend, John Pearce, who had recently moved back to Cumbria, after long stints teaching in Brunei and Luxembourg, and who shared with me some of his memories of growing up as a Barrow supporter. John was born and brought up in Barrow and was first taken to a match by his dad in 1959 to see a cup-tie against the then-mighty Wolves. Barrow lost 2-4 but gave a good account of themselves. That was the one and only time he was taken by his dad, who wasn't particularly interested in football. But John had 'caught the bug', started going on his own from time to time and then, later, when he went to secondary school, with a group of school friends. As with so many school-age supporters, 'going to the match' was enjoyed as much as a social occasion as for the game itself.

There are particular games that stand out in his memory: Barrow's first game under floodlights, when they were thrashed by Greenock Morton (who must have been a more impressive outfit in the early-1960s than they are now!), and a cup-tie against Leicester City, marred by 'crowd trouble' (which has been a recurrent theme at Barrow over the years). The trouble did not involve a clash between the respective fans; rather it resulted when a group of Leicester fans began to dismantle the roof above the Gents urinal, which consisted of a shallow trough in the ground next to a wall – their action was possibly a comment on the primitive nature of the facilities. The urinal and trough are still there, however.

In 1967, he saw them achieve their one and only promotion to the Third Division. 1967 was a good year for sport in Barrow, as the rugby league team also made it to the Challenge Cup final at Wembley. A game the following season is forever etched in John's memory. On December 30th, 1968, he saw Barrow beat Oldham Athletic at Holker Street; later that evening, he was dumped by his girlfriend of the time. It is not unusual for personal crises and football matches to be linked in the memory in this way. A few days after my dad died in a car accident, I went to watch Stockport County play Peterborough, and in a strange way found the visit a source of solace.

Barrow lasted three seasons in the Third Division before relegation, and two years later, the failure to secure re-election and the descent into the murky depths of non-league football. By this time, John was away at university, and destined to suffer from afar. But he did travel all the way from Luxembourg to Wembley in 1990, with his son Joe, to witness Barrow defeat Leek Town in the FA Trophy final; a rare highlight in Barrow's otherwise undistinguished history.

On our joint visits during the 2016–17 season, I'd warmed to the friendly atmosphere of the club, and the passion of the home supporters, which unfortunately at times borders on the vitriolic, particularly when it comes to referees they regard as incompetent – a frequent though not always justified judgement.

But, in the 2017–18 season, there was to be no repeat of the achievements of 2016–17. First, several of Barrow's outstanding players were signed by League clubs: Jordan Williams went to Rochdale, Nick Anderton to Blackpool, and Richie Bennett to Carlisle United. Their replacements were less impressive. Then Paul Casson and Paul Cox fell out. The manager wanted funds to be made available to strengthen the squad, after a mediocre start; the chairman wasn't prepared to release them. Paul Cox then resigned and moved to Guiseley (which didn't sound like a good career move to me) and was temporarily replaced by his assistant, Mick Moore, under whose stewardship things went from bad to worse. By October, Barrow were in the bottom four, and went out of the FA Cup at the first time of asking to Shaw Lane (no, I don't know where it is either). Moore was sacked and replaced by Adrian Pinnock, whose track record can best be described as variable, although he did manage to save Gillingham from relegation in the previous season. Results then improved, at least away from home, with Barrow managing four away wins in succession towards the end of 2017. At Holker Street, however, Barrow couldn't seem to beat anyone.

BARROW v SOLIHULL MOORS
National League, Saturday December 30th, 2017

In these circumstances, it was with no great optimism that John and I made our way to Holker Street for the last fixture of 2017. Barrow were one place clear of the bottom four, but eight points better off than Chester, the team immediately below them. Solihull had struggled all season and were currently entrenched at the very bottom of the table. On the face of it, it should have proved a straightforward home win, lifting Barrow further from the danger zone, and even raising the – admittedly remote – possibility of a play-off place. There was no breakaway leadership group this season, and six rather than the customary four play-off places were available. There were only twelve points separating seventh placed Boreham Wood and Barrow. Stranger things have happened. Such is the stuff of pipedreams!

Solihull Moors is a perplexing name for those familiar with the Birmingham area, who will know that there is no moorland in or near Solihull. But those nerdish individuals who follow the fortunes of non-league clubs over the years would not be perplexed. They would know that the name is an amalgamation of those of two different clubs: Solihull Borough and Moor Green, which is a south Birmingham suburb (maybe they should have called themselves Moor Green Rovers, and modelled themselves on the other 'Green Rovers' now gracing the Football League with their presence). With both clubs struggling to attract sustainable crowds, they decided, in 2007, to merge, and Solihull Moors, one of the youngest clubs in senior non-league football, was formed. This proved to be a shrewd move; although attendances continued to disappoint (it's hard to imagine Solihull as a 'football town'), the quality of the football improved, and May 2016 brought promotion (as champions) from the Conference North to the National League. In their first season at this level they finished a respectable sixteenth, but the 2017–18 season had been a struggle from the start. Solihull Moors recently appointed their third manager of the season; Mark Yates, who had previous managerial experience in the Football League with Cheltenham Town and Crawley Town.

John likes to get to the ground early, possibly to soak up the pre-match atmosphere, although in reality there's precious little of that until ten minutes before kick-off. That's fine by me on a pleasant afternoon in September, but not on a bitterly cold and windy day in late December. Having arrived at Holker Street at two o'clock, I managed to persuade him to savour the pre-match atmosphere in the bar overlooking the pitch, rather than on the deserted terraces. I always enjoy the pre-match buzz in such places: the analysis of what went wrong last week, and the critical examination of the Barrow team selection. We were also able to enjoy the last twenty minutes of the Aldershot/Maidstone game, a 12.30 kick-off being shown on Sky Sports, and which suggested to me that, if Aldershot were one of the front-runners, then Barrow's survival looked assured. An injury-time equaliser earned the home side an undeserved point.

Soon after we'd moved out on to the terraces (still able to secure our favourite spot at 2.45), the Solihull starting line-up was announced. It became apparent that one of their new manager's early decisions had been to bring in a lot of new players. Of the first seventeen names listed in the programme, only three were playing today. The majority of today's team were clearly recent signings, with shirt numbers in the 20s or, in three cases, the 30s. This is of course what new managers tend to do, drawing on their network of links with players they've encountered in previous jobs. Whether it's a good idea is a moot point.

When the two teams emerged from the dressing rooms, it was clear that someone associated with Solihull Moors had made a thoroughly bad decision. Whoever chose their bizarre away strip needed to be dispatched to the nearest job centre. The shirts were striped grey and a pallid shade of red. The shorts were grey, and the socks likewise, with a splash of red. The whole ensemble looked like it had been put through the washing machine at far too high a temperature. It's not surprising Solihull were propping up the table, requiring their players to turn out in a strip like that had surely undermined their self-respect, and contributed to their unimpressive away record.

The first half was dismal. Solihull posed no threat at all, but Barrow were little better. They played three up-front: Donald White (ponderous), Grant Holt (useless) and Byron Harrison (a class act, but not at his best today). But neither they nor anyone else in the Barrow team could cope with the wind. Long balls from defence or midfield invariably scudded well beyond their intended recipients and rattled harmlessly into the hoardings. You would think, wouldn't you, that there would be a game plan for such conditions? After all, a west wind blowing straight down the pitch is a common enough occurrence at Holker Street. But today's evidence suggested no such plan existed. John's view was that Barrow needed to be at least one goal up by halftime, given that they'd be playing against the wind in the second half. I wasn't so sure – it's sometimes easier knowing that the wind will hold the ball up; adept forwards can exploit such opportunities. But not, I suspect, White or Holt, on today's showing. Several of the players on both sides looked like they would rather be somewhere else. I sympathised with them. Halftime came, with the game still goalless.

Would things improve in the second half? Barrow certainly generated more goalmouth action, often resulting from long throws by Dan Jones, a specialist in this device. But the Solihull defence rarely looked troubled by them. 'These long throws are a total waste of time,' I said to John. But I spoke too soon. A couple of minutes later yet another of Jones's trademark throws found the head of Asa Hall, who dispatched it coolly past the Solihull keeper.

For a short time, it looked like a routine win against the bottom club was on the cards. But it was not to be. First, Solihull's pony-tailed captain Darren Carter latched on to a loose ball on the edge of Barrow's penalty area and scored emphatically with a well-placed shot. Solihull then proceeded to demonstrate an ability to take advantage of the wind in a way that had proved beyond their opponents; no long balls sailing over the heads of forwards and into touch, but rather measured passes out to someone out on the wing, who then headed for the goal-line and put in danger-ous crosses. It was no surprise when, ten minutes from the end, following just such a move, a Solihull player was unceremoni-ously upended in the penalty area by Moussa Diarra, and Jamie Reckford scored from the spot. What was more surprising was the allocation of the Man of the Match award to Diarra, a couple of minutes later. Maybe the award sponsor (everything connected with Barrow AFC has a sponsor) had left before the penalty inci-dent. I wouldn't have blamed him (or her) – the temperature was dropping, and there are no executive boxes at Barrow.

Barrow brought on substitutes for White, Harrison and Jones, but not for Grant Holt, who had contributed nothing, apart from a tendency to fall over at regular intervals, even when unchal-lenged. I began to wonder whether his status as coach gave him immunity from being substituted. The substitutions were in vain; the visitors held on to their lead. At the final whistle, Barrow were booed off the field, but the Solihull players ran to celebrate a rare away victory (the first since September) with their twenty-seven travelling fans. Now that's what I call loyalty – travelling to Barrow on a perishing cold December day, when your team's bottom of the table. As John and I made our way to the car park, I felt pleased for them.

MORECAMBE

Never do business with Mr Blobby

Morecambe was once a flourishing holiday resort, full of big attractions such as piers, autumn illuminations and the Winter Gardens. It hosted political party conferences until the mid-1950s, and, until the 1970s, the annual event to discover 'Miss Great Britain'. All this has long gone. At least Morecambe Bay is home, or staging post, to an impressive variety of seabirds – you can see them congregating on the edge of the sands, waiting for the tide to recede – and the ornithological theme is highlighted in the plethora of impressive statues of birds on the promenade and pier. But twitchers do not come to Morecambe in the kind of numbers that used to pile in from West Yorkshire, until cheap holidays in the Costa del Sol became the norm in the 1960s. Nor are they likely to stop overnight in the town; there are many much pleasanter locations dotted around the bay.

Morecambe has become a place to retire to, as movingly depicted in Alan Bennett's 1975 TV play 'Sunset Across the Bay', which deals with the experience of an elderly couple, who find that retirement in Morecambe, a favoured holiday destination of their younger days, does not fulfil their hopes and dreams. The couple had moved from Leeds, which (together with Bradford) is where many of Morecambe's holidaymakers hailed from. Like so many resorts, its clientele was influenced in their choice of destination by the railway system; there is a direct link from West Yorkshire to Morecambe. Nowadays it is hard to imagine the town fulfilling anyone's hopes and dreams. Although it remains a place for retirement, it has increasingly become a location for those needing cheap accommodation, of which there is an abundance in the town. The B&Bs and guesthouses that no longer attract holiday-makers have gained a second wind as multi-occupied rooming houses for those who can afford nothing better. The West End, in particular, is full of such accommodation and it has been identified as one of the most deprived areas in the Northwest.

Morecambe's decline as a holiday resort is epitomised by the succession of closures of its major tourist attractions: the Winter Gardens, the Frontierland amusement park and the Bubbles swimming complex. There's now nothing to include on the brown 'tourist attraction' signs on the M6. There's also the sad story of the Mr Blobby theme park (officially called Crinkley Bottom, but more popularly known as Blobbyland). Happy Mount Park was, and remains, a pleasant enough seaside park, with a model railway, an area of spouting fountains and some lovely traditional swing-boats. But in the 1990s, someone from Lancaster City Council had the bright idea of transforming it into a theme park featuring Noel Edmonds' inflated monstrosity Mr Blobby. A large amount of council tax-payers' money was invested in the scheme, which turned out to be a total fiasco. It seemed that Mr Blobby's sell-by date had passed, and the public stayed away.

But the town also has some positive features. There is the stunning view across Morecambe Bay to the Lake District mountains. There is a widely acknowledged architectural gem, the recently renovated 1930s art-deco Midland hotel, with its impressive Eric Gill murals. It has also recently been announced that a second Eden Project, similar to the one located in Cornwall, is to be sited in Morecambe. And the iconic Winter Gardens, once the venue for political party conferences (including the legendary acrimonious Labour conference of 1952) has recently been partially re-opened, after years of neglect, due to some effective lobbying and fundraising by a local community group. There is every sign that Morecambe is on the up.

However, in the unlikely event of a survey being commissioned to discover what the general public know about Morecambe, my guess is that by far the most dominant response would be the tragic death on a freezing cold February night in 2004 of twenty-three (or, possibly, twenty-four) Chinese cockle-pickers, who were caught unawares by the incoming tide, which moves in with deceptive swiftness over the bay. Their families had paid substantial sums of money to dubious entrepreneurs to fund their journey to England as illegal immigrants, in the hope that they would find work and be able to send money back home. What happened, however, is that they were exploited by unscrupulous Liverpool-based criminal organisations, who housed them in squalid overcrowded rooming-house accommodation in Liverpool, transported them each day to the bay and paid them a pittance. The 'British dream' was never going to happen for them.

There exists a small memorial to the cockle-pickers on Morecambe promenade, but you could easily pass it without noticing it, unlike the statue of Eric Morecambe which is unmissable further along the promenade, closer to the town centre. The memorial consists of a poem inscribed on a metal sheet on a small concrete post. It is clearly a sincere and deeply felt tribute, but there should surely be a more substantial memorial that not only recognises the awful circumstances of the cockle-pickers' deaths – the terror generated by the awareness of the rising water is incredibly painful to think about – but also acknowledges the wider context of the disaster. Some tragedies are unavoidable, caused by an unfortunate combination of circumstances that no one could have reasonably foreseen, but this was not the case for the cockle-pickers. There had been several previous near-misses; it was a disaster waiting to happen. The circumstances in which they perished were as much the result of criminal exploitation, lack of proper regulation and flagrant neglect, all of which should have no place in a civilised society, as they were to do with the perils of the movements of the tides on the bay. Whatever is built to remind future generations of this disaster, and to act as a point of pilgrimage for the bereaved families, should not neglect the underlying causes of the disaster.

The residents of Morecambe would, no doubt, like their town to be known for other things beyond the cockling disaster, and identity has been an important issue in recent decades. Morecambe used to have a local council of its own, until the 1974 local government reorganisation merged it with the adjacent but very different city of Lancaster. There was understandably a good deal of resentment about this loss of identity in Morecambe, particularly as it became clear that the town was being marginalised when it came to investment. The Morecambe Bay Independent Party was formed and went from strength to strength, becoming the largest party on the council in 2002.

Morecambe is similar to many towns in Britain, in that the reason why it was established and grew from Victorian times onwards has disappeared, and it is struggling to find an alternative identity. This is a problem faced by the Lancashire cotton towns, East Coast fishing ports, many holiday resorts, most places dependent on steel (like Consett or Corby), and numerous mining towns and villages, amongst many others. The economic raison d'être has gone, but the town remains.

I first watched Morecambe FC in 1997, their second season in the Conference after promotion from the Northern Premier League in 1995. We'd recently moved from Gateshead to Kendal, and I was looking for a football club within reasonable access of home. I'd already – perhaps unfairly – rejected Kendal Town as a possibility. Morecambe's Christie Park was a mere thirty-five minutes' drive away, so I thought I'd give it a go. In the first game I saw, Hayes were the visitors and came away with a 4-2 victory, aided by two superb long-range strikes. The quality of the football was excellent, and the crowd (just over a thousand) was big enough to create a lively atmosphere. If this is the Conference, I'll settle for it, I thought. Much more convenient than Carlisle or Preston.

Over the next ten years I saw far more of Morecambe than any other football club. I came to enjoy the relaxed atmosphere of Christie Park, and later the Globe Arena. I witnessed the growth in ability and confidence of midfield dynamo David Perkins, later to play a key role for Rochdale, Barnsley, Blackpool and Wigan Athletic, amongst others, and appreciated the talents of Justin Jackson, Gary Thompson and Brian Hardy, all of whom later moved to League clubs. My experience there heralded a shift in interest from the Premier League and the Championship to Leagues One and Two and the Conference, which I have increasingly come to relish.

Having made it to the Conference in 1996, thanks to the fact that the ground of Northern Premier League champions Marine was deemed inadequate, Morecambe prospered. They were always up there with the leaders from 2000 onwards, reaching the play-offs twice, in 2003 and 2005 respectively. In 2003, they were within five minutes of reaching the final, only to be denied by a late goal from Dagenham and Redbridge's Mark Terry (brother of the more famous John). I watched this game with my ten-year-old son, Callum, who, unfortunately for me, was cold and fed-up by fulltime, when the score was 2-2 on aggregate. We missed extra time and the penalty shoot-out from which the visitors emerged victorious. In 2005, Morecambe went out 4-3 on aggregate to Hereford United. But by then, the previously unlikely prospect of Morecambe making it to the Football League was emerging as a distinct possibility. And in 2007, they did just that, beating Exeter City 2-1 in a memorable final at Wembley, thanks to a superb run and shot from the leg-weary Danny Carlton, five minutes from time. I would have been there, had it not been for Karen having inconveniently organised her fiftieth birthday celebrations for that very day.

Since then, against the odds, Morecambe have survived in League Two, even making it to the play-offs in 2010, although a 6-0 defeat in the first leg at Dagenham and Redbridge put paid to any hope of further progress. Every season, the pundits in *When Saturday Comes*, and the like, predict relegation for Morecambe – and why wouldn't they, given the club's relatively modest financial resources and meagre crowds, which average 1,500 in a good year? And every season, Morecambe, with a mixture of free transfers, youngsters, loanees and a few seasoned old hands, confound the pundits and survive. Accrington Stanley and Dagenham and Redbridge have typically also been viewed as likely candidates for the drop, for similar reasons. But they, too, have refused to bow to the inevitable (except that it isn't), although Dagenham and Redbridge, after twelve years in the League did finally drop back to the National League in 2016.

What is the secret behind Morecambe's unlikely 'decade of survival' in the League? My view would be 'managerial stability'. Admittedly, Morecambe's recent managers can't compete with the longevity of Sir Alex Ferguson and Arsene Wenger, but there were only three of them between 1994 and 2019: Jim Harvey (1994–2005), Sammy McIlroy (2005–11) and Jim Bentley (2011–19). Jim Harvey's term of office was interrupted by a heart attack, and Sammy McIlroy was brought in on a caretaker basis, but so impressed the board (and the players) that his status was made permanent after a year. Understandably, Jim Harvey was not well pleased and the rift between the two erstwhile friends was never healed. Seven years later long-term centre-back and club captain Jim Bentley moved seamlessly into the managerial role, where he became the longest-serving manager in the League, until he left for AFC Fylde in 2019. Derek Adams took over at Morecambe.

Jim Bentley deserves huge credit for managing to ensure the club's survival, year after year, when all the odds were stacked against it: small budget, meagre crowds and the difficulty of recruiting players, who often don't fancy signing for a club so far from the south, nor indeed from the social hubs of the Northwest, such as Manchester. Jim was with the club for nearly twenty years; he signed from Telford United as a central defender in the early 2000s and captained the side for many years, including the occasion of the play-off win in 2007. A gruff Liverpudlian who always says what he thinks, the antithesis of the many evasive, bull-shitting Premier League and Championship managers, he has used his Liverpool connections to recruit players from the Merseyside area, who probably wouldn't otherwise have been prepared to sign. He should be awarded the freedom of Morecambe, if there is such a thing.

Until 2016, Jim Bentley benefitted from stability of club ownership, but early in the 2016–17 season the board decided to sell the club to a Brazilian businessman called Diego Lemos. Why would a Brazilian businessman want to buy a small club like Morecambe? That was the question puzzling many of the club's supporters. A sense of uncertainty about the club's future began to develop, which was more than justified when it was revealed early in 2017 that players and staff, including the manager, had not been paid for several weeks. The confusion and uncertainty were amplified when a second businessman, Joseph Cala, claimed to have bought the club from Lemos, an assertion contested by the latter. For good measure, a third party, accountant Graham Barnard, also claimed ownership. For a period of several weeks, it was not clear who really did own Morecambe FC. What on earth was happening to our homely, small-town club? The matter was clarified, up to a point, when a finance company called G50

Holdings, into which Lemos's assets had been transferred, took over the responsibility of paying the players and staff, who had soldiered on valiantly throughout the period of financial uncertainty. By the start of the 2017–18 season, this development had restored a degree of stability.

MORECAMBE v STEVENAGE
League Two, Saturday January 13th, 2018

Morecambe came into this game on the back of two successive League wins, the first time they'd managed this all season, which had lifted them to 20th position, seven points clear of 23rd-placed Chesterfield. A win today against Stevenage would enable them to reach the (illusory) security of a mid-table place – there were nineteen more games still to play.

I arrived early at the Globe Arena, purchased a seat in the comfort of the Peter McGuigan Stand, to shelter myself from the bitter north-west wind, bought a programme, and made my way to Morecambe's West End. In Regent Road, I passed a large 1930s dwelling which housed the Dance Factory – ballroom, and possibly tap, I conjectured from the traditional appearance of the place. I later discovered that there were as many as twelve such establishments in Morecambe, which boasts a population of less than fifty thousand. Was this a throwback, I wondered, to the days when Morecambe was a hotbed of seaside entertainment, during the summer months? Presumably the chorus lines in the shows at the Winter Gardens and the pier employed local recruits, who would have needed somewhere to develop their dancing skills. But given that this is no longer the case, one can only assume that it is a historical tradition that has survived against the odds, despite the current lack of job opportunities.

I moved on to where the gridiron pattern of the terraced streets of the West End begin, symbolised by the decaying grandeur of the Park Hotel. Then came the rows of rooming houses and bedsits with the multiple (and probably non-functioning) door-bells, the tatty sagging curtains and the naked light bulbs; a close approximation to John Cooper Clarke's 'Beesley Street'. There were numerous boarded-up retail establishments and those that had survived were dominated by charity shops, second-hand fur-niture stores, and cheap takeaways, all meeting the needs of the poverty-stricken inhabitants of the area, many of whom had been decanted from Manchester and Liverpool. There was one particu-larly poignant empty shop, Joy's Toys. No doubt at one time it did good business, a magnet for the children of the holidaymakers from Bradford and beyond. But they stopped coming long ago. Around the corner was another relic of the West End's better days, the Clarendon Hotel, which I visited a few years ago, to be served by an elderly lugubrious waiter in a dinner jacket, another echo of the town's former glories. At least the Clarendon was still open for business, although I did wonder how many people now stayed there.

I made my way back to the Globe Arena, where I purchased one of the establishment's justifiably renowned meat and potato pies. Morecambe's new purpose-built ground, to which they moved from Christie Park in 2010, is lacking in atmosphere, which per-haps helps to explain Morecambe's abysmal home record since they moved there. Before the teams emerged, there was a dancing display from a group of girls in cheerleaders' attire (perhaps they were schooled at one of Morecambe's twelve dance academies). The youngest and smallest of the group couldn't quite get her movements in sync with those of the others, but that somehow added to the appeal of the display.

Morecambe's starting line-up included three long-serv-ing veterans: Kevin Ellison, aged thirty-eight, captain Michael

Rose (thirty-five) and goalkeeper Barry Roche (thirty-six). Gary Thompson (also thirty-six), who had been a regular for Morecambe in the 1999–2007 period and scored the equalising goal in the Wembley play-off final against Exeter City, before moving on to a range of other clubs, was now back at Morecambe, and on the bench. Otherwise, it was the usual mixture of youngsters, including Callum Lang, a twenty-year-old loan signing from Wigan Athletic, alongside mid-career professionals who had moved around a lot, and would no doubt continue to do so.

The tentative early exchanges revealed contrasting styles. Stevenage played the better football, building attacks methodically from the back, but showed little penetration in and around the penalty area. Morecambe's football was less pretty, but equally ineffective, relying on long balls out of defence, typically aimed at the head of lone striker Vadaine Oliver, who was generally able to out-jump his marker, but whose flicks-on rarely found a colleague. Then, in the twenty-third minute, the game came to life with a Morecambe goal. Following a rare coherent inter-passing move down the left, the ball reached Kevin Ellison in the penalty area, and he scored with a crisp first-time low shot. His exuberant celebration, as always, reflected the enthusiasm and commitment of a player twenty years younger.

Ellison joined Morecambe in 2011, when he was already over thirty, and has become something of a local legend. He has consistently scored goals, including many crucial ones, such as the injury-time winner in the 4-3 epic with Yeovil Town a couple of weeks previously. In a game against Rochdale in 2014, he scored one of the best goals I have ever seen in over sixty years of watching football at all levels. He was standing in midfield, equidistant from the halfway line and the penalty area, when a cross came over from the right at knee height. He hit it first time, and his shot's formidable velocity propelled the ball high into the net before anyone (including the Rochdale keeper) quite realised what was happening.

Ellison's goal helped to settle down his team, and they looked comfortable for the remainder of the first half, without ever looking likely to add to their lead. The second half continued in similar fashion to the first, with Stevenage having more of the play, but Morecambe's well-marshalled defence never looking in real difficulty. Vadaine Oliver continued to win almost every lofted ball delivered to him, nodding it down into a space where you might reasonably (but wrongly) have expected a teammate to be lurking. It seemed to me a missed opportunity. Oliver must have been winning balls in the air all season. You would have thought that a routine could have been devised whereby someone could have routinely positioned themselves in close proximity, to take advantage. One of Morecambe's previous strikers, Jack Redshaw, would have been an ideal foil for Oliver, but he was now with Salford City. But there must be others in the current squad who could play the role.

Just when it looked like Morecambe would hold out for a 1-0 win, and thus secure an unexpected but very welcome run of three successive League victories, Stevenage substitute Fraser Franks hit a spectacular volley from the edge of the area to secure a deserved point for the visitors. The annual struggle against relegation was looking likely to continue to the end of the season, which would at least maintain interest – particularly as Barnet, Forest Green Rovers and Chesterfield, all below Morecambe in the table, were due to appear at the Globe Arena in the next few weeks. Bring them on!

ACCRINGTON

Unwanted dumplings and useless wingers

The town of Accrington in East Lancashire, and its heroic football club Accrington Stanley (the club that refused to die) have had a profound impact on the development of my interest in football as a spectator sport. The way it happened was this. In 1952, when I was nine years old and my sister Cathy was six, we were taken to my Uncle Arthur's to meet some friends of his who were visiting and who had a son, Howard, of around my age. They lived close to Accrington in the village of Huncoat, three miles to the east of the town itself. Howard and I got on well, and the two sets of parents (and Uncle Arthur) hatched a plan. My dad and Uncle Arthur would take us from Manchester to Huncoat, one Saturday when Accrington Stanley were playing at home. Then we'd all go to the match, except Cathy who would remain at home with Howard's mum. Dad and Uncle Arthur would then return to Manchester, leaving Cathy and I with Howard and family for what would now be called a sleepover (but wasn't in 1952). My parents would then drive over on Sunday afternoon to pick us up. A month or so later the favour would be returned, and Howard would stay with us in Manchester.

The opponents on the day of our visit early in February were Chesterfield. Accrington Stanley were alive and well at the time (it was ten years before their untimely, if temporary, demise). On reflection, they were perhaps not so well in February 1952, hovering close to the foot of the Third Division North table, whereas Chesterfield were positioned comfortably in the upper half of the table. New Brighton had been kicked out of the League in 1951, a decision that sent shockwaves amongst the Third Division strugglers the following season. There was a good deal of pressure on Stanley to win.

As far as the sleepover went, the visit of the Leach children was a disaster. We were both faddy eaters, and when we were served with an evening meal of stew and dumplings, panic set in. Dumplings were unheard of in our middle-class culinary world. I managed to eat about half of what was on the plate (but not the dumplings); my sister hardly managed a mouthful. Howard's mother must have been in despair – whose idea had it been to invite these impossible children? Then neither of us could get to sleep until well past midnight. The next day was wet, so the proposed outing was truncated. By the time our parents arrived in the afternoon to collect their offspring, who had had enough and couldn't wait to get home, fog had descended on Accrington. During the car journey across the West Pennine Moors, the fog thickened, and the pace of our car slowed down to a crawl. As we got closer to Manchester, the fog acquired a yellow tinge; the early 1950s was the heyday of smog, that lethal mixture of fog and smoke emanating from the coal fires, which were the dominant form of winter heating back then.

But if the visit to Huncoat was a fiasco, the football match at Peel Park was a revelation. Up to that time, my visits to football grounds had been limited to those of the two Manchester clubs. Peel Park was another world, but in its way, equally mesmerising. There was an intimacy between spectators and players that was not apparent at Maine Road or Old Trafford, or at least not from where we used to stand. At Peel Park, you could hear the players shouting at one another. You could hear the reactions of the crowd to the players' efforts, and the advice they offered, both provided liberally. There was a strong sense of spectator involvement in the proceedings, enhanced by the size of the crowd. These were the heady days of the post-war boom in attendances. There were over seven thousand there at Peel Park for a routine Third Division North match.

The main target of the crowd's reactions and advice was Accrington's hapless, not to say hopeless, right-winger, whose name was Des Collins. In 1952, there was a greater rigidity of role and function within football teams. It was the job of a full-back to take goal-kicks, a wing-half to take throw-ins and a winger to take corners. Centre-forwards stayed up-front in the middle of the pitch and scored goals (or didn't). Wingers were expected to stick close to the touchline, run with the ball towards the opposing full-back, neatly side-step his tackle, and then make for the goal-line before dispatching dangerous crosses into the penalty area. Sadly, Collins proved manifestly incapable of making any progress beyond the initial run. Time after time, he received the ball and approached the full-back. Time after time, the full-back halted his progress. The crowd's reaction changed from frustration to abuse to ridicule, as Collins's self-confidence diminished exponentially. I'd be surprised if he ever played for Accrington again.

Chesterfield scored in the first half, but the home team's perseverance paid off with a late equaliser, which I celebrated joyously with those around me. It was probably a rather mundane match, but I remember it as being compelling from start to finish. If this was lower-league football, I wanted more of it, a wish that was fulfilled when I started watching Stockport County five years later. Stanley finished the season in 22nd position, three points above bottom-placed Workington Town (who were re-elected).

I returned to Peel Park in 1959 with my friend John Davies to see Stockport County achieve a streaky 2-2 draw (in a season when County were relegated from the Third Division to the newly established Fourth Division). Accrington remained in the Third Division until 1961, when they joined County in the Fourth. But not for long! In the spring of 1962, burdened by debt and unable to pay utility bills, they resigned from the Football League.

Encouraged by the money that flowed into the club after this announcement had been made, they withdrew their resignation, or at least tried to. Faced with lack of support from Bob Lord, the chairman of nearby Burnley, and the opposition of Alan Hardiker of the Football League, their plea for reinstatement was rejected and their thirty-three-match playing record expunged. Had the same problem been encountered by a team thirty years later, it would have simply 'gone into administration' and had points deducted from its playing record. But it would survive, as numerous examples over the past thirty years confirm. Accrington were unlucky in presenting a test to the football authorities that they had not faced since before World War Two, and which they did not have a strategy for dealing with. Stanley played in the Northern Premier League for the next four seasons, but finally folded in 1966. Accrington Stanley were one of the twelve founding members of the Football League in 1888 (they finished sixth and fifth in their first two seasons), but now they ceased to exist.

To characterise Accrington Stanley as 'the club that refused to die' is not strictly accurate. They did indeed die in 1966, but were resurrected two years later, the prototype of what have come to be known as 'phoenix clubs'. Since then, their progress from the lower reaches of the non-league pyramid to League One has been truly remarkable, a powerful illustration of how much football teams can mean to the towns in which they are situated. Former player Eric Whalley was an influential figure in rebuilding the club and master-minding the move up the non-league hierarchy. In 2006, the club finished top of the Conference and returned to the Football League after a forty-four-year absence. It is highly appropriate that the main stand in Stanley's new home, the Crown Ground, was named after him.

The managerial team of John Coleman and Jimmy Bell were also instrumental in inspiring Stanley's return to the League.

Coleman was appointed as manager by Eric Whalley in 1999, with Bell as his assistant. Since growing up together in Kirkby on Merseyside, they have proved inseparable in their careers as players and managers. They left in 2012, when the club was (to quote John) 'in turmoil – three people thought they owned the club, and they were all fighting against each other' (a situation replicated at Morecambe FC in the spring of 2017). After brief spells at Rochdale and Southport, the duo returned in 2014, after which the club exceeded expectations, narrowly missing out on automatic promotion in 2016. A win in the final game of the season, at home to mid-table Stevenage would have sent Stanley up, but they froze on the big occasion, only managing a goalless draw, and then lost out in the lottery of the play-offs. A late run in the 2016–17 season put them within striking distance of the play-offs, but they couldn't sustain it, and finished mid-table. In the 2017–18 season, they were up with the front-runners from the start.

One of the ingredients of the club's success has been the ability of the managers, in the close season, to identify out-of-contract players with potential, and to persuade them to come to Accrington (which can't be easy!). The 2017–18 season saw the arrival of the successful striker Kayden Jackson, who had previously enjoyed a low-key career with the likes of Wrexham, Tamworth and Swindon (Swindon Submarine, that is, not Swindon Town). Billy Kee, a consistent leading scorer for Accrington, had one productive year with Burton Albion in 2012 but had otherwise moved between a variety of non-league clubs. Sean McConville, an influential midfielder, previously played for Chester, Barrow, Stockport County and Stalybridge Celtic. There is little in the career histories of any of these players which would have motivated most managers to sign them, but the good judgement of Coleman and Bell was well illustrated by the major contributions of these players in the 2017–18 season.

ACCRINGTON STANLEY v PORT VALE
League Two, Saturday January 20th, 2018

I was on my way to Accrington to watch them take on Port Vale. It was the first time I had been back there since my last visit to Peel Park in 1959. The train from Preston passes through Church and the delightfully named Oswaldtwistle – both contiguous with Accrington itself, but fiercely independent settlements – before arriving at Accrington station. The borough that Accrington dominates is named Hyndburn (after a modest river flowing through the town), a title which resulted from pressure from the likes of Church, Oswaldtwistle, Rishton and Great Harwood not wanting the council named after their dominant neighbour.

Oswaldtwistle is a family joke in our household. Living on the edge of the Lake District, as we do, we often encounter straggling processions of earnest-looking, middle-aged, kagoule-clad, rucksack-bearing walkers wending their way along a local footpath. 'Oh no,' we groan, 'here come the Oswaldtwistle Ramblers again.'

Beyond Accrington station there is a lovely curving viaduct that supports the train on its journey towards Burnley and beyond. A viaduct can provide an impressive element in the townscape, as it does here and in Stockport, Mansfield and Berwick-on-Tweed. But Accrington, an old cotton-weaving town, has other impressive visual qualities. Rows of terraced streets of grey millstone grit-constructed houses rise steeply to the north-east of the town centre, until they peter out on the edge of the West Pennine Moors, which were snow-covered on this damp, dank, bitterly cold January day.

Accrington is best known outside its boundaries for four attributes: first, its cotton mills (of which one or two remain, but none are operational); second, 'Accrington brick', a shiny and durable example of the brick genre, the material for which came from a local quarry (now also out of action); third, the 'Accrington Pals', a group of local lads who volunteered enthusiastically for action when World War One broke out in 1914, and were formed into a separate battalion (865 Accrington men perished in the mud of Flanders – there's a memorial to them in the town centre with an old photograph of a contingent of the pals, looking cheerful as they assembled for the journey across the Channel, not knowing what kind of hell they were being transported into); and fourth, there is the rebirth of Accrington Stanley, the club that refused to die.

If you are an admirer of Jeanette Winterson's work, you will know that she was raised in Accrington by her adoptive parents. Her semi-autobiographical novel, *Oranges Are Not the Only Fruit*, is set in the town, and her autobiography, the intriguingly titled *Why Be Happy When You Could Be Normal?*, reflects on her time there, before moving away to university. In a recent *Guardian* article, she noted that in its heyday, Accrington was a proud industrial town, with its cotton mills, engineering works and the famous NORI brickworks. Sadly, all three industries have long since disappeared, and Accrington is now a town with no recognisable economic base. Winterson discovered her own vocation by reading English literature in the 'Prose A–Z' section of the Accrington public library. But she no longer goes back to Accrington.

The town centre is uninspiring (although at least it's pedestrianised), and it bears all the hallmarks of impoverishment: unoccupied shops, obese shoppers and a large Poundland store. I made my way up Whalley Road, towards the football ground, passing on the way a United Reform church with a thought-provoking notice outside: 'Need Exercise? Walk with the Lord.' *What kind of pace does he set?* I wondered. Further along the road is the Crown Hotel, which gave its name to Stanley's ground, before it became known as the Wham Stadium. Disappointingly, this is not a tribute to the renowned pop group of the 1980s, but rather a reference to its sponsor, a local firm specialising in plastic storage, houseware and garden products.

In the programme, which hadn't quite got the balance right between adverts (too many) and football-related material (not enough), there was notice of a 'Lancashire Night', organised by the Supporters' Club. It was to be compered by 'the wonderful Stanley Accrington', and the main attractions were 'the one and only Oldham Tinkers'. I don't remember Stanley Accrington being particularly wonderful when I saw him at the Fleetwood Folk Festival in the early 1990s – he was an unassuming and mildly amusing purveyor of unremarkable folk songs, but maybe he had improved since then. However, the Oldham Tinkers were, and no doubt still are, a class act. They had unearthed, or in some cases composed, a range of evocative songs about life in the Lancashire mill towns, including the following gem, a verse from the song 'We Were Eatin' Parkin':

Me an' t' wife an' t' family o' three
went to Royton by the sea.
We watched t' clog dancers and we listened to t' band
and then we played on Royton sands.

To those who lack the relevant local knowledge, Royton is a mill town a few miles north of Oldham. It's nowhere near the sea, and hence there is no sand of the seaside variety, although there used to be a publicly accessible expanse of quarried sand, which accounts for the song's lyrics.

I last saw the Oldham Tinkers in Droylsden (east Manchester) in 1986. They are part of a rich tradition of industrial folk song (mills, mines, clogs, Wakes Weeks, etc), which has been resurrected in Lancashire since the early 1960s, and which acts as a welcome contrast to the dominant rural tradition of English folk song associated with Cecil Sharp (harvests, hunting, ploughing, country wenches, etc). I didn't realise they were still performing – well worth seeing, if you get the chance.

The Wham Stadium (which I don't think George Michael would have seen as a fitting tribute) has the appropriate ambience of a National League North ground. It reminded me of the Lamb Stadium at Tamworth and the equally low-profile grounds of Alfreton Town and Braintree Town. The main stand, where I located myself, had about six rows of seats, making any kind of bird's-eye view of the play difficult. But it was possible to move unencumbered into a covered terrace behind the goal (reserved for the home supporters), which is what I did at halftime. Visiting fans are accommodated on the terrace opposite, which is open to the elements. The ground's capacity is just over five thousand, the smallest in the Football League, but more than adequate for Stanley's needs. The home support averages out at around 1,200. Today, that figure was augmented by five hundred travelling supporters, braving the elements in the open end.

Accrington were on a good run. They had won their previous three League games, without conceding a goal. Admittedly, this followed a sequence of four consecutive League defeats, but they were now in third place, which, if sustained, would guarantee promotion. Port Vale, after a dismal start, and a managerial change (Neil Aspin in for Michael Brown) had improved steadily in recent weeks and were now sitting (reasonably) comfortably in 18th position, well clear of the two relegation slots.

In the third minute, Port Vale took the lead, in their first serious attack: a cross from the right found the head of prolific striker Tom Pope, whose header squeezed past Stanley's keeper, Aaron Chapman. The home side came back strongly, creating several good chances, including a header from defender Ben Richards-Everton, which went close. They looked a well-organised side, alternating between long balls to Billy Kee or Kayden Jackson and building up inter-passing movements from the back. It was good to see the deployment of a traditional winger. Sean McConville stuck to the left touchline (although he was always ready to chase back) and was prepared to take on the full-back, with a lot more success than his predecessor Collins had enjoyed in 1952. But just before halftime, Port Vale went further ahead. A free kick from a central position just outside the penalty area was taken by Michael Tonge, and it found its way through a crowd of players into the net, with Chapman appearing unsighted.

Things didn't look good for Accrington. They had played well enough, but Port Vale had taken advantage of two of the few opportunities they'd had, whereas the home side hadn't. Could they turn it round in the second half? I moved behind the goal they would be attacking, close to the noisy cheerleaders amongst their fans, one of whom sought to encourage his team by frequent thumps on a large drum. This may (or may not) have been influential in Stanley pulling a goal back seven minutes into the half, when Kee held the ball up well in the area before teeing it up for McConville, who scored emphatically from close range. Two minutes later, they were level. Jackson hit a fast, low cross from the left, and Kee was well positioned to head home from close range. The Port Vale players were convinced that Kee had handled the ball, or so their gestures to the referee indicated. There was a unified vehemence about the protests that suggested they might have some justification, but neither the referee nor the linesman had seen anything amiss, and the goal stood. My view was also impeded, so I am unable to resolve the dispute about its legitimacy.

Port Vale were still looking dangerous on the counter attack, and a close-range header by defender Danny Pugh was brilliantly tipped over the bar by Aaron Chapman. Stanley came storming back, and following a well-worked move involving Callum

Johnson and Billy Kee, McConville found space in the area to smash the ball past Vale's keeper, for his second goal, which turned out to be the match-winner. This was the cue for a burst of euphoria from the Accrington fans behind the goal, who had been magnificent in their support throughout the game. It was one of those occasions when it really felt that this might just have made a difference to the result. Certainly, McConville thought so. 'It was like the crowd were sucking the ball into the net,' he said in a post-match interview.

I scuttled down Whalley Road to catch the train back to Preston, unnecessarily so, as it turned out – the train was twenty-five minutes late. Accrington station is not the pleasantest place to be stranded on a bitterly cold January evening, but I didn't mind. The match had been riveting and uplifting. I was full of admiration for what John Coleman and Jimmy Bell had achieved, particularly the team spirit and level of commitment they had engendered in their squad, with what was probably the smallest budget in the whole of the Football League. I very much hoped they would secure promotion.

CARLISLE

The lucky soup and other football rituals

Carlisle: a cathedral city, the county town of Cumbria, and gateway to Scotland, but a place where the local accent is more redolent of Tyneside than the rural drawl of the Lake District (there are those under the misapprehension that Carlisle is in the Northeast). It's the nearest big shopping centre to Kendal, where I now live, and much as I dislike shopping, if I am required to look for something we can't get in Kendal, I'm happy to settle for Carlisle. I like the spacious, traffic-free city centre, and the way in which the new shopping development (The Lanes) has been sensitively integrated into the existing shopping area, rather than created as a one-off in-your-face expression of some architect's overblown ego. There's an impressive second-hand bookshop, full of nooks and crannies, and a peaceful tearoom attached to the city's red sandstone cathedral. And there's one of my favourite pubs, the Howard Arms, of which more shortly. What's not to like about Carlisle!

One thing that is very much not to the liking of many Carlisle residents is the vulnerability of parts of their town to flooding. One such 'high risk area' is adjacent to the point where the Rivers Petteril and Eden merge, close to Brunton Park, the picturesque old-fashioned stadium that is the home of Carlisle United. In the wake of Storm Desmond on December 6th, 2015, one of the most poignant images in the media was of the houses in the Warwick Road area appearing as an archipelago of islands in a sea of floodwater, which also inundated nearby Brunton Park. It was the second time in five years that flooding had hit this area. The houses had to be evacuated (again) for periods up to a year and rarely less than six months. It must now be well-nigh impossible to sell property around there.

On the day of the flood, the Carlisle United squad returned from administering a 5-0 thrashing to Welling United in the second round of the FA Cup, only to discover their cars submerged in the flooded Brunton Park car park. It was almost two months before they played another fixture there. Other clubs generously made their grounds available for Carlisle's home fixtures, until January 23rd, 2016, when York City were the first visitors to experience the re-laid playing area. It turned out to be a special occasion, not due to the attractiveness of the opposition (York were then bottom of League Two), but because of the outpouring of gratitude from local people for the time and effort put in by the Carlisle players in helping residents deal with the devastating consequences of the flooding. Once they'd recovered from the shock of the sight of their waterlogged cars, they put in many hours of voluntary 'community work', displaying genuine solidarity with the plight of those affected by the flooding, which seemed to me to provide a vivid illustration of the positive relationship that often exists between a football club and its local community. The players were given a tumultuous welcome by a crowd, three thousand above the average, as they emerged for the pre-match warm-up, and again when they trooped out for the game itself. York City managed to scrape an undeserved draw, but that didn't detract from the sense of celebration.

Since we moved to Kendal in 1995, Brunton Park has been second only to Morecambe's Christie Park (and Globe Arena) as my most frequently visited football venue. But the club and ground were familiar to me much earlier. In the early 1970s, my friend Bill Brown moved to Rockcliffe (near Carlisle), and John Davies and I were regular visitors. His move coincided with an unprecedented rise in Carlisle United's fortunes. After spending most of their Football League life since 1928 (when they were first elected) in the Third Division North and then the Fourth Division, they began in the late 1960s to move up the divisions, and finally and unbelievably achieved promotion to the First Division in 1974 (Bill Shankly described it as the greatest achievement in the history of the League). This was the era in which, every now and then, a small-time club such as Carlisle managed to climb to these lofty heights. Northampton Town, Leyton Orient and Oxford United provide other examples. None of them lasted very long in the top flight, but their brief sojourns (typically a single season) at this level have long been celebrated in the collective consciousness of the clubs and their supporters. It rarely happens nowadays, although Bournemouth's recent rise from obscurity to the Premier League (and Wigan's similar achievement the decade before) shows that it is still possible, which is something for which all football enthusiasts should be grateful.

Even more improbably, after three games, all of which they won, Carlisle headed the First Division table in 1974. I was present at the second of these games, a 2-0 win at Middlesbrough. Sadly, they couldn't maintain this early impetus, and although there were other highlights scattered throughout the season, including a 2-1 home win against the mighty Arsenal, witnessed by Bill, John and I, they were few and far between, and Carlisle duly returned to the more familiar world of the Second Division, before sliding down to the even more familiar world of the Third Division a couple of seasons later.

All clubs have their revered iconic former players. Carlisle's include Ivor Broadis, who was appointed player-manager at the age of twenty-three in 1946, before transferring himself to Sunderland. He later spent a few years with Manchester City, where I was full of admiration for his ball-playing skills, before leaving for Newcastle and then returning for a second spell at

Carlisle. In 2018, aged ninety-five, he was still living in the same semi-detached house in Carlisle that he had purchased during his playing career.

There was also Jimmy Glass, a not particularly distinguished goalkeeper, newly signed from Swindon Town on an emergency loan deal, whose winning goal in the fourth (and last) minute of injury time of the last game of the 1998–99 season against Plymouth Argyle averted relegation to the Conference and sent Scarborough down instead.

Outside Brunton Park, there is a statue of Chris Balderstone. Chris, as well as being a Carlisle legend, was a remarkable individual in many ways. He was one of the decreasing number of sportsmen who combined careers in professional football and county cricket. He joined Carlisle United from Huddersfield Town in 1965, and stayed there for eleven seasons, making over four hundred appearances and becoming club captain at the time they achieved promotion to the First Division in 1974. Indeed, it was his penalty against Tottenham Hotspur in the third game of the season that gave Carlisle a 1-0 win and put them briefly top of the table.

When Chris first moved to Carlisle, the crowd gave him 'a bit of stick': 'I wasn't the quickest player or the hardest tackler,' he has said. 'I used to think I made up for it with speed of thought and control of the ball. I won them over and they were very good to me.'

They were indeed. I saw him on several occasions in his last two seasons at Carlisle, and the crowd clearly loved him. His own assessment of his strengths and weaknesses is accurate. He always seemed to have time on the ball and showed great vision in his use of it. He ended his football career in the late 1970s with Queen of the South, where I once saw him. Then in his late thirties, he 'paced himself', which is perhaps the kindest way of putting it. He occupied a stationary position on the left wing, hardly moving forward or back, waiting for the ball to come to him. But when it did, he was still capable of great things, in particular defence-splitting passes.

His cricket career started at Yorkshire, from whence he moved to Leicestershire with Ray Illingworth in 1970. On one famous occasion in September 1975, he became the only sportsman ever to play first-class football and cricket on the same day (not even the legendary Dennis Compton ever managed that feat). Having ended the second day of the Derbyshire / Leicestershire game at Chesterfield on 51 not out, he dashed over to Doncaster to appear (and score) in an evening League game. He returned to Chesterfield the next morning, and later completed his century and took three Derbyshire wickets into the bargain.

Chris appeared twice for England, in 1976. He was unfortunate to come up against the West Indies in the days when they had a formidable pace attack, including Andy Roberts and Michael Holding, and only managed a total of 39 runs in four innings. He did take a wicket, though. His sense of humour was apparent in his response. A huge hit from Collis King off his bowling was caught shoulder-high by Mike Selvey at long-on. Balderstone rushed over to congratulate him. 'That,' he said, 'has put them in the shit.' West Indies were, at the time, 647 for 7!

In the 1970s and '80s, when Balderstone was playing, there were still a handful of cricketing footballers around: Jim Cumbes (Lancashire and Aston Villa); Ted Hemsley (Worcestershire and Sheffield United); Alan Ramage (Yorkshire and Middlesbrough); and, briefly, Ian Botham (Somerset and Scunthorpe United). But Balderstone was arguably the most impressive example of this species, which now appears to be extinct. Maybe Ben Stokes should be encouraged to take up football; I can just see him as a combative midfielder!

CARLISLE UNITED v FOREST GREEN ROVERS
League Two, Saturday January 27th, 2018

Since 2013, I have been going to Carlisle home games every six weeks or so with Harry Pearson, regular contributor to *When Saturday Comes* and author of the classic book on Northeast football, *The Far Corner*. There's a ritualistic pattern to our meetings, but I make no apologies for that; in these troubled times, we need our rituals and fixed points. Harry catches a train from Hexham, I catch one from Oxenholme. We meet at the Howard Arms, a small traditional friendly pub in the town centre, which is always bustling on match days, with visiting supporters often in evidence. We each have a pint and a half of Theakstons or Wainwright draught bitter, and a bowl of homemade vegetable soup. There are plenty of other tempting options on the menu, but our preference for the soup goes back to the time when Carlisle lost every time either of us had something other than the soup. So the Howard Arms' vegetable soup became our (and Carlisle United's) 'lucky soup'.

Football abounds with examples of bad (or good) omens, good luck charms and the like. Many a programme has included an interview with the midfielder who reveals that he always puts on his left boot first, has sausage and chips for his pre-match lunch, and scratches his left ear twice before emerging from the dressing room. It's all nonsense, of course, but it helps fill the pages. I suspect such practices are now on the decline – players are more likely to kiss whichever tattoo (partner, ex-girlfriend, previous manager, favourite rock group) they find most inspiring, assuming they can reach it.

One of the positive features of watching Carlisle is that they can usually be relied upon to sustain the interest of their supporters through to the end of the season, by challenging for promotion (or at least a play-off place) or struggling against relegation right to the bitter end. Take the 2016–17 season, when, for a long time, automatic promotion looked on the cards, following Carlisle's record-breaking seventeen-match unbeaten run in the autumn. Thereafter, their home form took a nosedive, and a play-off place began to look uncertain. But they recovered in time to achieve this outcome. After a thrilling 3-3 draw with Exeter City, at Brunton Park, Carlisle were within seconds of taking the second leg into extra time (and penalties), when Exeter's Jack Stacey put paid to that, with a late winner. Whatever else, the season had not been boring. You feel for the supporters of Oldham Athletic, in League One for twenty-one seasons, with rarely a sniff of promotion (but there have been plenty of battles to avoid relegation – a battle they finally lost in 2018). During the same period, Carlisle zigzagged between the Championship, Leagues One and Two and (briefly) the Conference.

But the 2017–18 season had proved different. Late in January, Carlisle were becalmed in mid-table, having won ten, lost ten and drawn eight. They were twelve points clear of the relegation positions, but nine points short of the total accumulated by the club in seventh place (Mansfield Town). Was their season effectively already over? This is the stage of the season when, as a spectator, motivation sometimes becomes a problem. If your team holds a mid-table position, with little realistic prospect of promotion nor danger of relegation, then it matters much less whether or not they win. If the team they are playing is similarly placed, then the game can become metaphorically (though not literally) pointless.

Was this the situation Carlisle was in? If they beat Forest Green Rovers today (probable) and Mansfield lost at Morecambe (unlikely) the gap would be down to six points, and a good run of results would take United into play-off contention. The problem was that, this season, consistency had proved elusive. Impressive away victories (5-0 at Crewe Alexandra) had been followed by inexplicable home defeats (2-0 to Stevenage). Carlisle had been consistent in their inconsistency. As we walked from the Howard Arms to Brunton Park, Harry and I agreed that relegation was highly unlikely, but managed to convince ourselves that if Forest Green Rovers were defeated today, promotion was still a possibility. So, a make or break game for Carlisle, rather than a pointless exercise.

Harry and I always stand in the Paddock in front of Brunton Park's main stand, opposite the new stand, constructed during Michael Knighton's controversial and unstable period of ownership. He was the businessman who was going to take over the ownership of Manchester United in 1989 when the Edwards family were seeking to sell up. Unfortunately (or perhaps fortunately for United), the deal fell through. He then turned his attentions to the (much) more modest world of Carlisle United, which he purchased in 1992, and relinquished, to the heartfelt relief of the club's supporters, in 2002.

The great thing about the Paddock is that it is high enough to give you a good sense of the pattern of the play, if you stand near the back, as we do. Standing areas in front of main stands are a rarity nowadays, and would be greatly missed at Brunton Park, if Carlisle ever reached the lofty heights of the Championship and had to transform their ground to an all-seater stadium. But that doesn't seem very likely at present.

Forest Green Rovers are perhaps the most unlikely club ever to find their way into the Football League. Forest Green is an unremarkable suburb of Nailsworth, a small town in the Cotswolds whose total population is a mere seven thousand. Fleetwood, the next smallest host town in the League, is four times more populous. It sounds like a romantic dream from the pages of the *Boy's Own Paper*. But the reality behind the dream is the existence of a wealthy club owner, namely Dale Vance, whose company (Ecotricity) is flourishing due to its 'alternative' wind-sourced energy provision. As a result, the Rovers have much more money to splash around then many of their League Two colleagues. Dale Vance has 'big plans' for the future of his adopted club, involving relocation to a new wooden stadium, close to Junction 13 of the M5, three miles west of the small town of Stonehouse. Personally, I think this is a thoroughly bad idea. Forest Green Rovers have been around for over fifty years, acquiring a small but devoted local following during their eighteen-year spell in the Conference. Nailsworth has no affinity with Stonehouse (eight miles away), nor with Junction 13 of the M5. The club would lose all connection with its roots, in effect becoming transformed into 'Middle of Nowhere Rovers'. But there are precedents: Bolton Wanderers made a similar move, eight miles west on the M61 to the small town of Horwich.

The visitors turned out in their all-green strip (would we have expected any other?). Their starting eleven included Reuben Reid, recently signed from Exeter City, and leading scorer Christian Doidge. Carlisle started with two recent signings up front, Cole Stockton (from Hearts) and Kris Twardek, on loan from Millwall. So recent were these signings that their names did not appear in the programme team sheets. I was doubtful about the wisdom of playing them both. Neither would be familiar with the other's game, nor indeed with those of any of their new teammates. But then the previous strike force of Richie Bennett and Hallam Hope had not been impressive, managing a mere eight League goals between them. So maybe it was worth taking a chance with the two newcomers.

Carlisle started with a swirling wind at their backs, something they failed to take advantage of (as is so often the case at this level). Long balls intended for the new strike force sailed or bounced aimlessly into touch or beyond the goal-line. The two newcomers were certainly charging around enthusiastically, although on the rare occasions a ball reached Stockton, it tended to bounce off different parts of his anatomy into no-man's land. Forest Green were relying more on an inter-passing game, which produced some pretty patterns that usually petered out on the approach to the penalty area. Indeed, the first twenty-five minutes was singularly devoid of incident or interest. Then, after a rare coherent Carlisle move down the left, the resulting cross found its way to Jamie Devitt, and he volleyed the ball home confidently. Devitt had been playing well; unlike most of his colleagues, he seemed able to find time to use the ball productively. I'd seen him with two previous clubs: Grimsby Town (in 2013) and Morecambe (2014–16), and regard him as a rare creative talent, but one who would struggle if Carlisle were to make it to League One. He has found his level of competence (unlike Richie Bennett, who has moved beyond it).

Devitt's goal led to an increased sense of purpose in Carlisle's play, and they created further chances. After the interval, they continued to look the more threatening side, despite having less of the possession. Kris Twardik's enthusiasm and readiness to chase lost causes were beginning to endear him to the home crowd, and after dispossessing a Forest Green defender, his cross found unmarked midfielder Luke Joyce, whose goal-bound shot was fortuitously diverted for an unproductive corner.

The advantage of a 1-0 scoreline as the last quarter of the game begins is that it sustains interest. One slip-up from the side holding the lead, and three points could become a measly one. Carlisle continued to create chances, but the second goal that would seal the win eluded them, and there was always the chance that Forest Green might snatch an undeserved equaliser. But the home fans needn't have worried; the visitors' pretty football continued to go nowhere. The *Football League Paper* the next day indicated the absence of a single Forest Green shot on target, which doesn't equate with my recollection of a feeble header near the end, easily caught by the Carlisle keeper. But maybe whoever keeps tally of such things felt it was so pathetic as to be not worthy of record.

As Harry and I made our way along the cold Warwick Road (it always seems to be cold in Carlisle) to the station, we felt that Carlisle's season was still just about alive, despite the fact that Mansfield had, as expected, won at Morecambe, and so the nine-point gap to the play-offs remained. But if the game the following Saturday away to Wycombe Wanderers, who were currently on a roll, were to end in defeat, it would be difficult to sustain such optimism.

WIGAN

Pies, the pier and fantastic fanzines

Wigan, both as a place and a football team, inspired my affections relatively late in life. I visited Wigan Town Hall a couple of times in the 1990s in my capacity as a local government expert. However, I never came to know the place well until 2015, when I embarked on my epic study of the contrasting fortunes (as it turned out) of Wigan Athletic and Blackpool during the 2015–16 season, for my book *Tangerines and Pies*. Both teams had been relegated from the Championship the previous season. Wigan went straight back up, whilst Blackpool descended into the murky depths of League Two. Whereas I developed no great affection for Blackpool, particularly the club, which was then still in the hands of the much-despised Oyston family, I warmed to Wigan as a town and to the Latics as a football club. I appreciated its family-centred ethos, and the friendliness of the women in the ticket office. I enjoyed reading the excellent fanzine, *Mudhutter*, and meeting its editor Martin Tarbuck. My understanding of the recent history of Wigan Athletic was greatly facilitated through conversations with Martin, who started supporting his hometown club in the late 1980s, while still at school, only ten years after they gained admission to the Football League. In the town itself, I discovered the delights of Galloways' succulent meat and potato pies and enjoyed the pre-match buzz (and the real ales) at the Bird I' th' Hand (known locally as the Henhole).

A joint interest in football provides a wonderful stimulus to conversation. Many an uneventful train journey of mine has burst into life as the result of a discovery that the bloke sitting opposite me is a supporter of Grimsby Town (or wherever). Such discoveries at social gatherings can lead to one's wife/partner quickly scurrying to another part of the room to talk to someone (anyone!) she's not seen in ages. That's fair enough: football is one of those things that you either get or you don't. There's no halfway house!

A chance meeting of this nature with Tony Siney provided me with insights into the club's history going back even further in time to 1963, when the Latics were in the Lancashire Combination. I first met Tony outside Oxenholme Station (Kendal) on a cold January evening in 2017. I was on my way back from Carlisle, where I'd watched the home side go down to a 3-1 defeat at the hands of Grimsby Town. I was waiting for a bus outside the station, which never turned up (I'd forgotten that it was a bank holiday). A lady who was waiting for someone from a northbound train kindly offered me a lift home. On the way into Kendal, her passenger mentioned that he'd just come from Wigan. 'That's interesting,' I said, 'I've just written a book about Wigan Athletic.' 'Have you now?' was his response. 'Well, I've just been to the DW stadium, and I've supported the Latics for fifty-four years.' The result of this chance encounter was a series of meetings in a Kendal pub, where Tony shared with me memories of his years of dedicated support.

In 1963, when he was eight, his dad, a long-term rugby league fan, took his son to Central Park for the first time. Tony was not impressed: 'Thirteen big fat buggers colliding with thirteen other big fat buggers,' was how he described it to me. The very next Saturday, he asked his dad if he would take him to see Wigan Athletic, then in the Cheshire County League, despite not being in Cheshire. 'Just the once!' was his dad's reply, aghast at his son's heretical request. One visit was enough to convince the lad that this was the game and the team for him. The players were 'slim, agile and fast', unlike their rugby league counterparts. Tony recalled how a defence-splitting pass from left-half Dave Roberts struck him as a 'thing of beauty'. He was hooked and told his incredulous father that he was now a Wigan Athletic supporter. From then on, he made the two-bus journey from his home in Ashton-in Makerfield to Springfield Park as often as he was allowed. In 1975, he purchased his first season ticket, which he has renewed every year since.

Tony's period of dedicated support can be differentiated into three distinctive phases. In 1963, they were one of the most successful non-league clubs in the country, with some impressive FA Cup achievements dotted throughout their history (including a 2-2 draw with Newcastle United at Springfield Park in 1954). They were then playing in the Cheshire County League (although they'd been in the Lancashire Combination), which had been the case since 1931, when Athletic's undistinguished predecessor Wigan Borough went bust, and its hastily reformed successor was denied re-entry to the Third Division North. Opponents in 1963 would have included the likes of Great Harwood, Stafford Rangers, Netherfield (who later became Kendal Town) and Horwich RMI – so, not the quality of opposition to get the pulses racing, but I guess if that is what you'd been used to, you made the most of it. But in the 1970s, Tony, by then a teenager, became increasingly frustrated by Wigan's failure to gain election to the Football League, which they had applied to join every year since 1931. There was even an abortive attempt to join the Scottish League in 1975 (there was the precedent of Berwick Rangers' membership, but they were much closer to the border than Wigan).

But at last, in 1978, came the long-awaited and well-deserved election to the Football League, at the expense of fellow Lancastrians Southport. The fifteen years of watching teams such as Rossendale United were over. Welcome to the Uniteds of Carlisle and Hartlepool! Wigan didn't exactly set the Fourth Division alight, but they finished a respectable sixth position in each of their first two seasons there. Twenty-five years of ups and downs followed. They were not a well-off club and survived financially by selling their most successful players (Warren Aspinall being a prime example), which may have made financial sense but didn't help in keeping together their more successful squads. There was a worrying end to the 1993–94 season, when the Latics were in real danger of relegation. Tony well remembers a home match against Northampton Town, who were propping up the table, three points behind Wigan. The visitors went ahead in the second minute, through a fortuitous own-goal. There followed an eighty-five-minute bombardment of the Northampton goal, with nothing to show for it. Then, with time running out, Wigan equalised and maintained their three-point safety cushion. At the end of the game, many of the crowd were in tears – of relief – with an added ingredient of emotional exhaustion. Tony remembers the way his hands were shaking with tension, and how, when he arrived home, he was unable to speak for half an hour. Such is the power of football to generate emotional extremes in us: exhilaration, utter despondency, profound relief and physical/mental exhaustion.

Tony's job as a Barclays bank manager, at a time when Barclays were sponsoring the Football League, meant he was often able to get free tickets and, on one such occasion, he travelled down to Hereford, where Wigan were outplayed from the start, and were 3-0 down at halftime. This was during the brief and undistinguished managerial reign of Kenny Swain, who remained on the visitors' bench throughout the whole interval, with his head in his hands! No halftime pep talk, no encouraging expressions of belief that 'we can still turn this round'. You wonder what the lads in the dressing room made of it. It wasn't that he'd 'lost the dressing room' – he just never got around to re-entering it!

Then, in 1995, David Whelan purchased Wigan Athletic and

expressed his intention of taking the club into the Premier League within ten years. There was a strong element of incredulity in the reaction of supporters, including Tony. After all, Wigan were languishing in the fourth tier, and the average home attendance the previous season had been a paltry 1,845. But Whelan delivered. In 2003, Wigan gained promotion to the second tier, and two years later they made it to the Premier League. After fifteen years of watching non-league football and then a further twenty-five years in the lower regions of the League, the golden years had begun, and lasted until 2013, when the club was relegated to the Championship. It is always a source of great satisfaction to supporters when, after years of under-achievement, a club of modest means finally achieves lift-off. This is how it was for Wigan between 2003 and 2013; and how it had been for the long-term object of my affections Stockport County, between 1996 and 2001.

Although what outsiders are most likely to remember about Wigan's glory years is the FA Cup victory against Manchester City in 2013, the highlight for Tony was the quarter-final at Everton a few weeks before, when Wigan were 3-0 up at halftime, having played their illustrious opponents off the park.

Life has rarely been boring for a Wigan Athletic supporter. The last twenty years have seen promotions, relegations, play-offs and an FA Cup win and semi-final the following season. Even during their eight years in the Premier League, their survival at that level was always in doubt until late in the season, apart from 2008–09, when they finished eleventh. Wouldn't Oldham Athletic be grateful for a recent history as exciting as this?!

Listening to Tony's account of his years of following Wigan really brought the club's history alive. My account of the interviews with Tony first appeared in issue 62 (April 2017) of the Wigan Athletic fanzine, *Mudhutter*. Fanzines are now much more of a rarity than they used to be. In the 1980s and '90s almost all clubs had one, sometimes more. They have gradually been replaced by the more fragmented, less analytical and often superficial world of social media. Those that have survived are always good for a hype-free account of the team's strengths and weaknesses, not to mention those of the owners, the manager and tea ladies. Unlike official programmes, which are often unrealistically upbeat about the team's recent performances, and unconvincingly optimistic about their prospects, fanzines are honest, with words un-minced and shortcomings fearlessly exposed. I applaud the fact that they express an often emotional commitment to their club and that they are a product of the local community, rather than the club itself.

But at their best they achieve much more than this. They sometimes include material that is not specifically concerned with the current performance or the recent history of the team in question, nor indeed with football issues of wider concern (such as the increasing dominance of big business in the Premier League, or England's chances in the next competition), but cover non-football issues: for example, articles about the town or city in which the club is located; its culture, politics, famous sons and daughters. In the long-forgotten catchphrase of the *News of the World*, 'all human life is there' – although admittedly seen through the eyes of white males of a certain age (old enough to have wives and children, but young enough to still attend a selection of away games, and with the capacity to down copious amounts of beer).

Mudhutter is a particularly impressive example of a fanzine with wide-ranging contents. It celebrates Wigan as a place as much as it does Wigan Athletic as a football team. Recent editions have included the following contributions: 'Barge-spotting' (Wigan has a plethora of canals, reflecting its strategic location in the early days of the Industrial Revolution); a celebration of 'council teas', which develops into a witty account of the author's childhood culinary experiences; and a piece on the history of Haigh Hall, a stately home, now owned by Wigan Council ('one of the jewels in Wigan's crown'). There is an evocative article on Frank Randle, a Wigan-born comedian, whose career flourished between from the 1930s to the 1950s before being cut short by an untimely death in 1957, caused by excessive alcohol and nicotine intake. The author of the fanzine article clearly prefers him to 'that gormless grinning toothy banjolele-plucking twerp George Formby' (also from Wigan).

But *Mudhutter* contributors often stray beyond the boundaries of their hometown. There have been tributes to the Temptations on their 57th anniversary, and an imaginative evocation of the football match on Christmas Day 1914 in the no-man's land between the British and German trenches in Flanders. Most topics are treated with humour, as well as insight, but there are some that are wholly serious: one about a former work colleague who developed Alzheimer's, and the author's attempts to maintain a relationship with him as the disease worsened; the other a moving personal account of a struggle with depression (there are, of course, several examples of well-known footballers who have suffered from this illness). Not what you'd expect to find in a fanzine, but all credit to *Mudhutter* for including them. I would be surprised if there are any other publications in Wigan that include such an interesting blend of football-related, Wigan-related and more general topics on a regular basis. *Mudhutter* is providing a valuable service to the town, which I hope is appreciated.

WIGAN ATHLETIC v ROCHDALE
League One, Saturday February 24th, 2018

I decided to make my way to Wigan on the Saturday after their memorable and totally unexpected win over Manchester City in the fifth round of the FA Cup, five days before, depriving their illustrious visitors of the chance of an unprecedented 'quadruple' (Premier League title, the two domestic cups, and the Champions League). The statistics tell a remarkable story: City enjoyed 82% of the possession and rained twenty-nine shots in the direction of the Wigan goal (five on target), compared with Wigan's paltry 18% and five shots (two on target). But the one shot that counted was Wigan's solitary second-half opportunity, which Will Grigg confidently steered past the approaching Claudio Bravo. I'd been watching the game on TV, but unfortunately chose that very moment to leave the room to make a cup of tea, rushing back, after hearing a mighty roar, to see Grigg being embraced by Max Power. Even the introduction of Kevin de Bruyne could not rescue the match for City. As a former City supporter who lost faith in them when they became an 'oil-rich' outfit, and someone who became a (fair weather?) Wigan fan during their 2015–16 promotion season, I was utterly delighted at the outcome.

This unlikely victory made it three out of three recent FA Cup victories for Wigan over a club with infinitely more resources, and a playing staff that must have cost at least thirty times more than Wigan's current squad. There was the famous FA Cup final victory in 2013, with Ben Watson's 89th-minute header sealing it, the 2-1 quarter-final win the following year in Manchester ... and now this, arguably the most remarkable and meretricious win of all, given the fact that City were virtual certainties to secure the Premier League title. I wondered whether a chant of 'Can we play you every week?' might have been heard from the home supporters towards the end of the game. But that would have perhaps been overstretching the imagination; they wisely stuck to 'Will Grigg's on fire', which indeed he was.

Today's opponents were, appropriately enough, Rochdale, also underdog FA Cup heroes, following a 2-2 draw with Tottenham

Hotspur at Spotland the previous Sunday. I wanted to be there to cheer both teams on to the field. What a fine advert they had proved for League One, bottom-placed Rochdale as much as third-placed Wigan. They had together helped keep the magic of the FA Cup alive, when, in the earlier rounds at least, it has long appeared to be diminishing.

Having arrived at Wigan North Western station, I embarked on my usual Saturday Wigan match day ritual: a walk up Wallgate to Galloways for a meat-and-potato pie (highly recommended) and on to Springfield, a nostalgia-inducing un-redeveloped working-class area of terraced streets, where Wigan's previous ground was located, before the move to the DW Stadium in 1999. En route, I noticed that what had once been the Colliers Arms had been transformed into Mr Wang's Chinese and Japanese Restaurant (Eat as much as you like for £15.99). Then I made the customary visit to the Henhole for a pint of Wainwrights, served by the friendly and efficient young barmaids (everyone seems to be friendly in Wigan), quaffed whilst watching the lunchtime game on Sky, which on this occasion was an uninspiring clash between the Cities of Leicester and Stoke. Finally, there was the short walk under the railway bridge and over the canal to the ground itself.

The attendance for the City game had been 19,200, of which 4,600 were from Manchester. Today, it looked like the crowd was back to the usual eight thousand (plus around four hundred visiting Rochdale fans scattered around the North Stand, which holds ten times that number). It was apparent from the programme notes that this outcome would prove disappointing both to manager Paul Cook ('Those who came back for the Manchester City game, we need you to stay with us') and captain Dan Burn ('If those supporters could get to the League games as well, I'm sure it would give us a massive boost'). However, it was back to reality, on a bitterly cold February afternoon, with bottom-of-the-table

Rochdale the much less glamorous visitors.

When the teams were announced, it became apparent that the game we were about to see was in effect one between Wigan Reserves and Rochdale. Of those who'd started the City game, only four were in today's starting line-up, with a further three on the bench. Several of the Wigan players had hardly appeared in the first team at all. There was Donervon Daniels (three starts early in the season), Jamie Walker (two appearances as sub), Jay Fulton (five appearances as sub) and James Vaughan (likewise). This struck me as a risky approach. Wigan had dropped to third place in the table, following two consecutive League defeats, both in the week before the City cup-tie. It was true that they had three games in hand over Blackburn Rovers and Shrewsbury Town (who were three and two points ahead of Wigan, respectively), but those games needed to be turned into points, and anything other than a win today would set the alarm bells ringing. The epic cup run had been exhilarating, but it would be a shame if it got in the way of automatic promotion, which a month ago had looked virtually certain.

This sense of unease appeared unfounded when in the thirteenth minute, following Wigan's first coherent attacking move, Michael Jacobs found space in the area and steered a left foot shot past Rochdale's Josh Lillis – a strike not unlike Will Grigg's match-winning effort against City. Rochdale were constructing some neat inter-passing moves, which belied their lowly League position, but lacked penetration. Without looking particularly impressive, Wigan were creating the better chances, two of which fell to Jamie Walker, but neither resulted in goals (one felt that Will Grigg would have put at least one of them away). Otherwise, the youngster was doing well, contributing more than the largely anonymous Vaughan and Fulton.

At halftime, I chatted to Martin Tarbuck who had (of course) been present at the Manchester game. We discussed whether the fact that City had had a player controversially sent off just before halftime (Fabian Delph, for a sliding tackle on Max Power) had been a decisive factor in the result and agreed that it hadn't. Manchester City were even more dominant in the second half than in the first; it doesn't seem to make a lot of difference to a team of that quality whether they play with eleven or ten.

Back to today's game, and if the first half had been mediocre, the second proved even worse. I realised that it had probably been a mistake to come to this match. The desire to celebrate two memorable cup performances should perhaps have been tempered by an awareness of the likely impact on the teams involved. Both would have been drained by their efforts a few days earlier (so maybe Wigan's much-changed starting line-up did make sense). Rochdale's minds would be on the following Wednesday's replay against Spurs at Wembley; whilst Wigan had two tough away games at Bristol on Tuesday and at League leaders Blackburn the following Sunday. Today's game was never going to be a classic. Rochdale needed the points, but the fleeting glory of a Wembley appearance beckoned. Wigan also needed the points, but their attitude seemed to be 'what's the minimum we need to do to win them?'

Ryan Colclough put in a couple of lively runs on the right but was then unaccountably substituted. The first-teamers on the bench (Grigg, Massey and Perkins) were all brought on, but not, it transpired to add to the goal tally and make the game safe, but rather to introduce fresh defensive energies as Wigan's midfield sank ever deeper. Rochdale began to dominate possession but found the massed ranks of Wigan defenders impenetrable – if Manchester City couldn't find a way through, what hope was there for Rochdale? There were the odd moments of inspiration, as when Max Power hit the bar with a well-placed free-kick ten minutes from the end, but they were few and far between. The game petered out, ending with Rochdale in serious trouble at the bottom of the table, and Wigan having maintained the status quo at the top of the table (Blackburn and Shrewsbury both also recorded victories). No doubt both clubs were left reflecting on the age-old dilemma of the respective merits of lucrative and euphoric FA Cup runs vis-à-vis the longer-term benefits of securing promotion or avoiding relegation.

MACCLESFIELD

Living on the Edge

My mum and dad spent their retirement in Macclesfield; not the town itself, but a particularly affluent corner of the borough, named Alderley Edge. Dad joined the British Engine and Boiler Insurance Company in 1924 at the age of fourteen and ended up as assistant general manager before he retired in 1975. As his career prospered, so the family moved further and further away from central Manchester, which is where he worked: a common pattern of movement for the professional and managerial class of that city. Dad was brought up in Rusholme and Mum in Moss Side, both now part of the inner city, although in the 1920s both were on the edge of the city's built-up area, with access to open countryside. Their first home after their marriage in 1937 was a flat in Chorlton-cum-Hardy, now a favoured location for trendy BBC executives working in Salford Quays. After that, they moved to Fallowfield, now a popular student location, where I spent the first three years of my life. Then, in 1945, there was a further move to a 1930s semi-detached house in West Didsbury (with a sign on the gate that read, *No hawkers, canvassers or circulars*). In 1956, they moved to Heaton Moor, north of Stockport, before they finally made it, when Dad retired, to the highly desirable small town of Alderley Edge (although it still thinks of itself as a village), where they bought the ground floor flat of a spacious Victorian residence, five minutes' walk from the town (or village) centre.

My sister Cathy and I were fortunate with our parents. They were loving, supportive and tolerant. The absence of tensions in their own relationship contributed to a peaceful home environment, punctuated only by the occasional inevitable dis-agreements with their teenage children. But even when these occurred, they acknowledged our right to think and act differ-ently to the way they did. Cathy and I both became committed supporters of the Campaign for Nuclear Disarmament in the late 1950s, and although Dad profoundly disagreed with its aims, he tolerated our unilateral predispositions, and never tried to pre-vent us from going on Aldermaston Marches in the early '60s. Although physical punishment of children was considered normal at the time, Dad only once ever administered a beating on my backside – I had persistently refused to go to bed when ordered to do so. He later told me it had upset him so much that he never contemplated repeating it. And Mum, bless her, ignored the conventional wisdom of the time regarding baby care. It was advocated that babies should be put outside in their prams for at least a couple of hours every day, whatever the weather; and that if they cried or demanded attention between the specified four-hourly feeds, they should be ignored, and left to howl. She was not prepared to impose either of these barbaric practices on us, which I am sure helped avoid subsequent adult hang-ups of various kinds. Nor were we required to eat 'whatever was put in front of us'. Both my sister and I were faddy eaters, but our parents accepted our choosiness, for which I am also extremely grateful, although I acknowledge that there are different views about the wisdom of this kind of laissez-faire approach.

Neither Mum nor Dad found it easy to display emotion overtly, which has no doubt contributed to my own emotional reticence. Such behaviour was the norm in middle-class households in the 1950s and '60s – the stiff upper lip syndrome. I only ever saw Dad in tears twice, both times towards the end of his life: once, when listening to a piece of classical music by Schubert song; another, when reminiscing about Mrs Pattinson's farmhouse in Borrowdale, where he used to stay in his Lake District rock-climbing days with his older brother Arthur. Mum would, I think, have been more emotionally expressive if it not been for Dad's reticence. But she did share his distaste for rows and overt expressions of anger. Our various houses were mercifully free of such disruptive behaviour.

In 1975, the year my parents moved to Alderley Edge, there was a celebratory atmosphere about the place. The town/village, together with the larger settlement of Wilmslow to the north, had just escaped from becoming part of the Greater Manchester area, under the jurisdiction of the newly formed Greater Manchester Council and an enlarged Stockport Borough Council. As far as the residents were concerned, Alderley Edge was part of Cheshire, and that was the way it should stay. The reality was that, just as in Victorian times, a large proportion of the professional middle-class population of Alderley Edge and Wilmslow caught a train in the morning, bound for Manchester, fifteen miles to the north, which is where their offices were located, and which provided their livelihood. The place was, and remains, unquestionably part of the Greater Manchester journey-to-work area. But as a result of some effective lobbying, not least by the pompous and ponderous local notable Sir Walter Bromley-Davenport, whose stately home was nearby Capesthorne Hall, the Conservative government of the time disregarded the recommendation of the Royal Commission involved and retained Alderley Edge within leafy Cheshire, placing it within the newly extended district council of Macclesfield. And Macclesfield is where it stayed until 2009, when as a result a further reorganisation, Macclesfield was merged with Congleton and Crewe and Nantwich to form a new super-council, Cheshire East, which stretches from Handforth in the north to the fringes of Stoke-on-Trent in the south. Cheshire East is a totally arbitrary concoction, unlike Macclesfield District Council, or indeed its predecessor Alderley Edge Urban District Council, both of which represented real places with which local people identified.

You might think all this local government stuff is irrelevant, not to say boring. But you'd be wrong. If support for a football club is an expression of community identity (which it typically is), then so also should be the designation of local authorities, so that they too represent the towns and cities with which people identify. In some cases, that is still the case; no problems with the congruence between Manchester, Sheffield and Liverpool City Councils, and the football teams of the same names that have long been seen as representing those cities.

But look further afield to the names of other football teams, for example, Huddersfield Town. Is there a local authority based on the town of Huddersfield? There used to be, until 1974, when Huddersfield Council was merged with Batley, Dewsbury and other miscellaneous bits and pieces to form the new metropolitan district council of Kirklees. Who would have a clue where Kirklees was, if they didn't live there (and even to some residents, the name must be something of a mystery – where or what exactly is Kirklees?). There are similar problems for West Bromwich Albion (now located within Sandwell), Scunthorpe (now part of North Lincolnshire) and Shrewsbury (now swallowed up within a Shropshire-wide council), amongst many others.

On the day of my visit to watch Macclesfield Town, I fitted in a visit to Alderley Edge to see how much it had changed in the twenty years since I had last been there. Had it been transformed by the reported influx of millionaire footballers and their WAGs? The train journey from Manchester Piccadilly to Alderley Edge takes twenty-seven minutes. It is one I have done many times before, when visiting my parents, and it proved to be steeped in nostalgia. Soon after departing from the first station stop (Levenshulme), I noticed Ross Place Primary School, whose football team my school (Old Moat) beat in our illustrious cup run of 1954. Just beyond Ross Place lie the football pitches of Cringle Fields, the home ground of Parrswood Athletic, the team I helped set up in 1966. Then on to Heaton Chapel station, close to where we lived in Heaton Moor, before crossing the viaduct in Stockport that straddles the Mersey valley to Edgeley Station, on leaving which, you can see Edgeley Park, home of Stockport County. The train line then skirts Adswood, before stopping at Cheadle Hulme, where I used to attend Stockport Youth CND meetings at Hulme Hall School. Next station stop is Handforth, close to the Mermaid pub, where Parrswood Athletic recorded a memorable 4-0 win against the pub-based team in 1968. Then it's on to Wilmslow and finally Alderley Edge.

Alderley Edge, as we know it today, was created by the coming of the railway in the 1850s. Before then, it really was a village, but once the railway arrived, its potential as a high-class residential area, with easy access to Manchester, was quickly recognised and exploited. The 'Edge', after which the town is named, is a pleasant wooded sandstone ridge, a spur of the Pennines jutting out into the Cheshire plain, on the south side of the town. It is the first bit of raised ground that you encounter travelling south from Manchester: a prime location for the burgeoning class of wealthy entrepreneurs working in the city. The Edge itself was soon colonised by such people, who commissioned large, ornate detached houses, in spacious grounds, with the indigenous trees retained, as far as possible, to ensure privacy. 'The residence of the merchant princes of Manchester' is how the *Baddeley's Guide* of the time described it.

Katharine Chorley's book, *Manchester Made Them*, is an evocative portrait of life in Alderley Edge, where she grew up in the years before the First World War in 'Ferns', one of the big houses on the Edge. The political ambience of the place is well summarised as follows:

Our neighbours had one common and dominant characteristic – their acceptance of the economic system which produced Alderley Edge. Indeed, acceptance is too passive a word, for they believed positively in the system; it was for all of them a fundamental article of social faith. A socialist was unthinkable in that company and had he got there, he would have been treated with a mixture of distrust, contempt and fear.

I suspect these attitudes are still dominant. Nowadays, there is a small council estate on the edge of the town (although many of the dwellings there are now privately owned). Of all the places to be a council house tenant, Alderley Edge must be one of the most depressing, with so much unattainable conspicuous wealth on your doorstep.

From the station, it is only a short walk to my parents' old house, a ground floor flat in a spacious yellow-brick Victorian semi-detached residence, close to the parish church. Katharine Chorley was not enamoured of the yellow-brick variety of local mansion. She preferred the 'gritty pleasant-hued local sandstone' to the 'custard-yellow brick', when it came to building materials. But I liked that kind of brick, which on my parents' house, was of a discreetly pale shade of custard. Brookside had changed very little. The large front garden, to which Dad devoted much of his spare time and around which a one-year-old Callum trundled his trolley, was much as I remembered it, although a few tasteful garden accessories had been added. I was reassured that the Victorian character of the place had not been spoiled by inappropriate extensions.

I walked across to the small park where four-year-old Callum had his first experience of a zip line, and on to the De Trafford Arms (which looks as posh as it sounds), at the south end of the town, before travelling the length of the main street, back towards the station. The place had indeed changed; it had become even more opulent and exclusive in its range of retail outlets than it was when my parents were alive, twenty-five years ago. There were five estate agents, and house prices were exorbitant. The only house I saw that we could have afforded was a two-bedroom ex-council house, priced at £240,000.

Unexpectedly, there were four charity shops on the main street. But the quality of the clothes on sale was unprecedented. The Oxfam shop had a sign outside: *Gucci. Chanel. Tyrell Baker. Louis Vuitton. Maybe? You never know what you'll find at Oxfam!* The ambience of Alderley Edge is well illustrated by what the shops there choose to call themselves. There was Margaret Dobbs (London), offering a range of anti-ageing treatments and promises of 'your new feet'. There was Cedric's Health and Beauty Pharmacy, Pascha's Gentleman's Grooming, Tuula (Scandinavian fashion), Running Bear (for all your exercise needs), The Style Lounge, Beauty Works and SieMatic Arthouse Creative Interiors. But the town was best epitomised by a hair and beauty salon that called itself ENVY. That's Alderley Edge for you! An hour there was more than enough.

When Mum and Dad lived there, the level of ostentation that exists today was much less apparent. It suited them well as a retirement location, and they made some good friends. I used to enjoy visiting them there, but that was before it became a trendy venue for millionaire footballers. I was happy to move on to Macclesfield.

Macclesfield Town had been stalwarts of the Cheshire County League and Northern Premier League for many years, before joining the Conference in 1987. They finished as champions in 1995 but were denied promotion to the Football League because their ground (the attractive sounding 'Moss Rose') was deemed not to be up to League standards. Two years later, they were again champions and having judiciously made the requisite improvements, were promoted to the League, where they went on to enjoy fifteen seasons, typically in the lower reaches of the fourth tier. They had one promotion to the third tier in 1998, where they were joined by Manchester City, no less, but went straight back down again (City went in the other direction). In 2012, they were back in the Conference.

I'd last been to the Moss Rose Ground in 2012, to watch the Town take on Newport County. Newport made it back to the League that season. Macclesfield didn't, and hadn't really looked like doing so since, apart from 2014–15, when they narrowly missed the play-offs. But in 2017–18, under new manager John Askey, they had been up with the leaders from the start. This was an impressive achievement. Town were not one of the 'big clubs' in the National League, either in terms of attendances (which average at around 1,400) nor in terms of finance. The owners, the Iraqi-based Alkadhi brothers, although no doubt very well-off, had not been inclined to divert their riches in the direction of Macclesfield Town. Indeed, only a week or so before today's game, the players and other staff had not been paid. That was soon rectified, but it raised questions about the financial stability of the club.

MACCLESFIELD TOWN v BARROW
National League, Saturday March 10th, 2018

The second Saturday in March. The 'Beast from the East', which caused major disruptions over the previous ten days, not least to the football fixture list, had mercifully buggered off to create mayhem elsewhere. The end of the season was approaching, and with it, crunch time for those clubs involved in promotion or relegation battles. The two clubs on view today faced very different varieties of crunch. Macclesfield Town were sitting on top of the National League, two points ahead of their nearest rivals, Sutton

United, and with a game in hand. Barrow, in contrast, were a mere two points ahead of Solihull Moors and the four relegation places. They too had games in hand over their partners in distress, but hadn't managed a home win since October, relying on a much stronger away record to keep them afloat.

I made my way southwards from the station towards the ground, before arriving at a road junction, where I couldn't remember which fork to take. But I needn't have worried. Ahead of me, along one of the options, was a group bedecked in blue-and-white scarves and hats (Macclesfield's colours) who presumably knew where they were going. I followed them. Five minutes later, they came to a halt and began to consult mobile phones. By the time I caught up with them, they were deep in conversation with two locals, who were busy explaining that this was not the way to the Moss Rose ground. I then realised my mistake. Barrow also play in blue and white (though they wouldn't be today). I'd been following a group of away supporters who were clearly struggling to interpret the maps on their smartphones.

Fortunately, there was still time to retrace our steps, and reach the ground in time for kick-off, although only just. I located the ticket office, and was just about to join the queue, when I was approached by a young man who asked me if I was about to buy a ticket. I said I was. He then offered me one. 'What do you want for it?' I asked. 'Nothing, my friend can't use it' was his reply. This was my third recent experience of the generosity of strangers, and the camaraderie of football supporters in such circumstances. The same thing happened to me at Lincoln in 2013 and at Bury in 2015. The other side of the 'ticket tout' coin!

The programme had a sombre note to it. The Macclesfield line-up in the list of today's teams included, at squad number 21, the poignant entry 'retired in memory of Richard Butcher', a popular defender who died suddenly in 2011 at the age of twenty-nine.

Elsewhere in the programme the 'eight-year anniversary of the tragic death of manager Keith Alexander' was remembered ('Time might have moved on, but Keith will never be forgotten at the game'). There was also reference to a more recent tragedy: the sudden death at the age of forty-one of former Town player Kieron Durkan. I remember him well from when he played for Stockport County. He was a key member of the squad that won promotion to the First Division (now the Championship) in 1997; a muscular, combative midfielder, who went on to score County's first goal at that exalted level the following season, at Bradford City. He then spent three productive years at Macclesfield before moving elsewhere. There were no details of the circumstances of his death.

My free ticket was in the pitch-length stand facing the older, much smaller main stand from which the teams emerged. The Barrow fans – always a noisy lot – were gathered at one end of it. They certainly made their presence felt when, after eleven minutes, the visitors went ahead, thanks to a piece of individual brilliance from Forest Green loanee Luke James, who weaved his way past a couple of defenders before dispatching an exquisite angled left-foot shot past the Macclesfield keeper. Barrow were playing with a confidence which belied their lowly league position, and could have gone 2-0 up a few minutes later, when James again broke clear, but this time Jamal managed to block his effort. For a while, it looked like a shock away win might be on the cards. But Macclesfield began to dominate the exchanges, playing some lovely football in the process. Their tactics were an astute blend of composed inter-passing, with passes side-footed firmly and precisely to their desired locations, and well-judged long balls out to the wings, where, on the right, Elliot Durrell threatened danger every time he gained possession. The pressure began to build, forcing two fine saves from Barrow's keeper, Steve Arnold, one from a point-blank diving header by Mitch Hancox.

But Macclesfield could not be contained for much longer. Ten minutes before halftime, the ball fell to Hancox just outside the area, and he blasted a superb volley into the top corner. That energised the previously subdued home fans, and on the terrace to my right, a chant developed, the words of which I couldn't at first identify. Then the penny dropped. It was 'Come on you silkmen'. Macclesfield's industrial heritage was silk manufacture. No silk has been produced here since early in the twentieth century, but it lives on in the nickname of the town's football club. It is not unusual for such names to provide reminders of industrial history – there are the Hatters (Stockport and Luton) the Saddlers (Walsall) and the Cobblers (Northampton), to name but three.

The home side continued to dominate. I admired the way there was always a predisposition to move forward, either via inter-passing movements or from individuals surging forward and taking on defenders. But Barrow's defence held firm, and at halftime it remained 1-1. It had been an engrossing half, and the game was still wide open.

The home side resumed their domination after the interval, again playing some delightful, creative football. But Barrow continued to look dangerous on the break, and Luke James again found himself in the clear on the right. His fierce cross-shot from an acute angle flew past the keeper, but also cleared the right-hand post. As was the case in the Barrow/ Solihull Moors game I saw in December, Grant Holt's contribution to the proceedings was negligible, apart from occasionally haranguing one of his teammates. Despite being a supposed goalscorer, he had not registered a single goal since coming into the team in November. Maybe if you're on the coaching staff you're allowed to select yourself?

Then, with twenty minutes left, there came the decisive breakthrough. Mitch Hancox bustled his way into the penalty area and was brought down by Barrow's Jack Bartram. It looked like a clear penalty to me, and (more importantly) the referee was of the same opinion, although the Barrow bench of course thought otherwise. Danny Whitaker converted the spot-kick emphatically. Then came another flowing move, culminating in an astute through pass from Scott Wilson, which Man of the Match (and recent National League Player of the Month) Elliot Durrell slid past the encroaching keeper.

It was one of those games where you come away feeling exhilarated. I couldn't recall seeing a better team performance than Macclesfield's in all the National League games I have seen in recent years. But Barrow had made a game of it and, until Durrell's late goal, could easily have come away with something. They looked too good to go down. Macclesfield looked too good not to go up. I hoped they would; on today's evidence they would grace League Two with their presence.

The club's strapline is 'Your town, your club, your passion'. That, to me, is what football is all about, and there was certainly an abundance of passion in evidence at the Moss Rose ground today.

BOLTON

Stephen! Blackrod is calling your name!

Bolton featured in my childhood and adolescent years in two ways. At Manchester Grammar School, I played for the various school football teams and, each year, we paid a visit to Bolton School, a game we usually won, on a pitch cut into a hillside. Later, there were occasional visits to Burnden Park, which was unique in having a railway embankment at the top of the open terrace on the north side of the ground. I can still picture the locomotives billowing steam as they made their way along it during a match. I was there for a game in the 1965–66 season, when Manchester City were tormented by the speedy winger Francis Lee, who was instrumental in securing a 3-1 victory for the Wanderers. The following year he was transferred to Manchester City, and the rest, as they say, is history.

But my main connection with Bolton results from my time at Birmingham University in the early 1960s. In my final year as a sociology student, my tutor was Charles Madge, then approaching retirement. I remember those tutorials well; if none of the three students present could think of any response to one of his observations or questions, there would be a silence – sometimes a long one – which he didn't feel it necessary to fill. I found this most disconcerting, and typically sought to come up with something – anything – that might be remotely relevant.

The silvery-haired Charles ended up making a significant contribution to my later academic career. To pursue such a career, you needed at least an upper second degree. A major contribution to the classification awarded was the dissertation. Charles was my supervisor and was instrumental in enabling me to transform a sub-standard piece of work (on green belts) into something much better. That helped me get my 2.1. So many thanks, Charles, I wouldn't be where I am today (or rather, *was yesterday*, now that I've retired) without your help.

Charles Madge's standing in the world of sociological academia stemmed from his role (together with anthropologist Tom Harrison) in setting up an organisation called Mass Observation in 1937. Mass Observation was a pioneer in developing large-scale investigations into the habits, customs and daily routines of 'ordinary people', which transformed sociology from an esoteric academic discipline into a topic of much wider interest. It became one of the defining cultural phenomena of Britain in the late 1930s. And here's where the Bolton connection comes in: its first and most famous project was a community study of Bolton (which they called Worktown). It was Tom Harrison who was the project leader in Bolton. Although Charles made frequent visits 'up North', he remained based in Blackheath, with his wife, the poet Kathleen Raine, and their family. His main role was to encourage people all over Britain to keep detailed diaries of their daily lives, and to send them on a regular basis to Blackheath for analysis.

Tom Harrison's team of volunteers – some local, some from the London area –lived collectively in a terraced house (85 Davenport Street) just north of the town centre. As David Hall's book *Worktown* vividly illustrates, conditions within the house were squalid and chaotic. Harrison was a slovenly and disorderly individual at the best of times, and others took their cue from him: empty bottles, cigarette ends and greasy fish-and-chip papers were typically strewn around the place. There was a local pub, the Royal, conveniently situated at the end of the street, where members of the team were often to be found.

Some of the volunteers were from Bolton itself, including Bill

Naughton, who later found fame as a novelist (he wrote that epitome of the Swinging Sixties, *Alfie*). The local volunteers would have had little difficulty blending into the background of the pubs, shops, markets and churches where they were dispatched to carry out observations. But the visitors from the south, such as socialite Zita Baker (later married to Labour cabinet minister Dick Crossman), photographer Humphrey Spender and film-maker Humphrey Jennings must have stood out like sore thumbs amongst the cotton-spinners of Bolton; indeed, they were often regarded with suspicion and questioned as to what they were doing there.

Although the project did unearth a good deal of fascinating and potentially useful information, some of the observations team members were asked to make seem bizarre. For example, in pubs, they were required to record not just how long it took drinkers to finish their pints of beer, but also how many individual swigs they made in the process. It's hard to see, with the benefit of hindsight, what helpful interpretations could be based on such data! A few years later Mass Observation were commissioned by the government to carry out a much more relevant project: a survey of public attitudes and morale during wartime.

In my visit to Bolton in 2018, I wanted to see if 85 Davenport Street was still there and, if so, what it was like. Would there be a commemorative plaque? To reach it, I had to walk from Trinity Street Station, through the pedestrianised town centre, which turned out to be a more rewarding experience than I'd anticipated. First, you pass the Town Hall on your left, which is in the classical style rather than the more customary gothic and is located within a Bath-like crescent. Next you encounter a statue of the steeplejack Fred Dibnah, a minor TV celebrity in the 1980s who hailed from Bolton (no doubt he'll be joined by Peter Kay, in due course). Close by, enclosed in a large perspex container is a refurbished steam engine, of the type that was produced in large numbers in Bolton in its industrial heyday. Then, on the right, is the Market Hall, which is no longer a market hall in the traditional sense – it is the main shopping centre of Bolton. All the usual suspects are there, including Debenhams, River Island and an establishment called Men, to which I followed a sign, under the mistaken impression I would find the gents' toilets there! But this was no ordinary shopping centre. The external fabric of the old Market Hall had been imaginatively retained, including the sloping glass panels of the ceiling. It still felt like a market hall. What a refreshing contrast to the shiny, overheated Arndale centres of this world (many of them now well past their sell-by date). I am a reluctant shopper at the best of times but I could imagine enjoying shopping here.

Having passed through the town centre, I made my way towards Davenport Street, passing the impressive-sounding Redeemed Christian Church of God (RCCG): Breakthrough Church, Bolton. Not a denomination I'd come across before, but it certainly sounded dynamic, if perhaps somewhat exclusive (unredeemed Christians not welcome here?). Passing the Spinners Hall, a relic of the town's long-lost cotton-spinning economic base, I finally reached Davenport Street, which was still there. Sadly, the terrace in which the Mass Observation team had lived no longer existed, having been replaced by modern low-rise housing. But the ornate Royal Hotel was still there, though its peeling paintwork gave the impression of neglect, and directly opposite was the Union Mill, which must have served as a helpfully convenient source of research material for the team. I closed my eyes and imagined Tom Harrison walking unsteadily back from the Royal to 85 Davenport Street, arm-in-arm with Zita Baker (to whom he was devoted), followed by a strange mixture of locals and London toffs.

Passing the Union Mill and thinking of the mill girls who would have been working there, I remembered that in my late teens, at a time when I was rebelling against all things middle class and identifying strongly with 'the workers', I decided I would like to marry a mill girl, and hence become an honorary member of the working class. Unfortunately, mill girls were in short supply in Heaton Moor, an affluent suburb of Stockport, where we lived at the time, so my plan never came to fruition.

I was on my way to the Macron Stadium to watch a crunch game between Bolton Wanderers and Birmingham City, both struggling to stay in the Championship. Bolton had enjoyed a good run recently, but remained perilously close to the three relegation slots, one of which was currently occupied by the visitors, who were showing signs of a revival under new manager Garry Monk. If Bolton won this evening, it would put a six-point cushion between them and Birmingham. If Birmingham won, the two sides would be equal on points.

Bolton had, in fact, recovered well from a truly abysmal start to the season. Newly promoted from League One, it was not until October 14th that they recorded their first League victory. Prior to that, their record was 'played eleven, drawn two, lost nine'. September was a particularly barren month; Wanderers lost all six League matches, without registering a single goal. Relegation was looking like a foregone conclusion. Since then, however, there had been a marked improvement. Nine League wins had been recorded, mostly at home, the last five by 1-0, which said a lot about where Bolton's newfound strength lay.

Bolton Wanderers would be seen by many as a 'fallen giant', a club that was at one time amongst the elite of the land but has since experienced hard times. That, however, would be a misleading characterisation. Bolton's past achievements have mainly been in the FA Cup, which they won in 1923 (the first Wembley final),

1926, 1929 and 1958, the final where Nat Lofthouse clattered into Manchester United's keeper Ray Wood for a goal that would certainly be disallowed nowadays. There were defeats in 1894, 1904 and 1953, a game etched in the memory of every football fan now over seventy-five – a 4-3 defeat at the hands of Blackpool, in the final in which the legendary Stanley Matthews won his first and only cup-winner's medal. And that's about it, in terms of major trophies. They've never won the League; fourth in 1958–59 is the best they've managed since the 1920s. And although they were First Division regulars between 1935 and 1964, for the following thirty-five years they struggled, alternating between the second and third tiers, with the occasional brief visit back to the top level, and in 1987–88, a season all the way down in the Fourth Division. Then came the arrival of Sam Allardyce, and a promotion to the Premier League in 2001, where they survived for the next eleven seasons, achieving 6th position in 2005. For a while they were back amongst the elite. But it wasn't to last. In 2012, they were back in the second tier, and have never looked like making it back to the Premiership since.

As the cotton towns of Lancashire have declined, so have the fortunes of their football clubs, with the notable recent exception of Burnley. The achievements of Preston North End, Blackburn Rovers, Bolton Wanderers and Bury (yes, they too are past FA Cup winners – twice) became sparser from the 1960s onwards, with only few exceptions since, including Blackburn Rovers' unexpected Premier League win in 1995. But the importance of the football club as a symbol of local pride in such towns remains. Bolton continue to attract big crowds, and at a ground nine miles away from the centre of Bolton. And their FA Cup record should not be undervalued: it was a much bigger deal in the pre-war years and the two decades following it than it is now.

BOLTON WANDERERS v BIRMINGHAM CITY
The Championship, Tuesday April 3rd, 2018

This was my first ever visit to the Macron Stadium. Well, that's what it used to be called. It's now, I gather, the University of Bolton Stadium. It's confusing the way so many grounds change their names nowadays, as their sponsors change. The name of Burnden Park, Bolton's previous ground, survived happily for nearly a hundred years! I arrived an hour before kick-off time at Horwich Parkway station and walked the short distance to the ground. The place was buzzing with activity, even at this early stage. The coaches from Birmingham were already piling into the spacious car park. There was clearly going to be a lot of vocal support for City.

The fact that the stadium is adjacent to Horwich Parkway station provides a clue that the Wanderers have indeed wandered some distance from their Bolton base. Horwich is not a suburb of Bolton; it's a separate town, which used to have a football team of its own, with the bizarre name of Horwich Railway Mechanics Institute (or Horwich RMI, for short), who played for many years in the Lancashire Combination. Well, I suppose it makes a refreshing change from the commonplace 'Towns', and 'Uniteds'. They were later transformed into Leigh RMI, and had two or three seasons in the Conference, watched by sparse crowds at Leigh's rugby league ground, Hilton Park, before disappearing from sight.

I'd booked in at a hotel on the edge of Blackrod, a bleak former mining settlement on the A6, which I remember from my childhood. In the pre-motorway days, we passed through it on route to our holidays in the Lake District. I'd made the reservation, as usual, through a travel website, and a few weeks later I received an email from them headed, 'Stephen! Blackrod is calling your name!' I suspect it's been a long while since Blackrod called anyone's name. Vienna, Venice or Barcelona, perhaps – but Blackrod? On my map, the hotel looked closer to the ground than turned out to be the case; I only just made it in time for kick-off.

The stadium is situated in the centre of a business park, which is not my favourite location for a football ground. I much prefer a walk through an area of terraced streets, with a pub on every other corner, which is how Burnden Park used to be, with a few cotton mills thrown in for good measure. But surroundings aside, Bolton's stadium is a cut above most new stadia, both when viewed from the outside, and when you're inside it. Externally, it resembles a saucer: it's easy to imagine a giant cup of tea being placed on top of it. But it's a strangely satisfying shape. Inside, the four identical stands are convex-shaped, with the length of the rows of seats continually narrowing, as you move higher; again, a pleasing design. And the atmosphere was electric. One end was totally filled with Birmingham fans already in full voice with their familiar anthem:

Keep roight on tew the end of the road
keep roight on round the bend
though the way be long let yer 'earts be strong
keep roight on to the end.

The Bolton fans, although equally noisy, had nothing to match that. The programme included an advert for 'An Evening with Gazza' (tickets from £65). Very much a high-risk investment, I would have thought.

Given how much was at stake, it was not surprising that both sides started cautiously. There was a good deal of passing the ball around in pretty patterns in midfield, but few signs of any shots – neither team was getting close enough to their opponents' goal to justify trying one. Bolton were playing a single striker, the much-travelled Adam le Fondre, who sounds like a French import, but isn't; he hails from Stockport. When the ball is played on the ground to his feet or at chest height, le Fondre has always been adept at creating a modicum of space and making good use of it. But standing at a mere 5'9", if balls are lofted towards him at head height, he is always likely to be outjumped by taller defenders. So, what was the point in hoofing high balls in his direction? It was hardly worth his while jumping, although he always showed willing and did.

If these pointless tactics were attributable to the manager, Phil Parkinson, then the voluble and outspoken bloke sitting next to me had his own criticisms of the manager's approach. 'Will Buckley hasn't touched the ball for twenty minutes – take him off!' he yelled. And there were, in his opinion, two midfield players with duplicating roles, getting in each other's way. 'Come on, Parkinson,' he bellowed, 'change your tactics!'

Birmingham were looking marginally the more dangerous, particularly down their left flank, where Jacques Maghoma was prepared to take defenders on, and five minutes before halftime, they broke the deadlock. A free kick from the left was met with a first-time volley from Lukas Jutkiewicz, and the ball thundered into the net, to the delight of Birmingham fans at the far end. The one minute of added time was sponsored by Fitness Co, or so the big screen informed us. That, in my view, is taking the concept of sponsorship to ridiculous lengths.

When I lived in Birmingham in the late 1970s and early 1980s, it was a time when players from foreign lands were beginning to appear on the scene. The familiar chant of 'One Bobby Charlton, there's only one Bobby Charlton' (or whoever) was having to be applied to more challenging surnames. They managed fine at St Andrews, to which I was a regular visitor at the time, with 'One Tarantini, there's only one Tarantini' (City's newly acquired

Argentinian full-back). Earlier, at the Hawthorns, 'Krzywicki' proved more of a challenge, but the fans were equal to it. As the numbers of foreign imports have grown, this particular chant has understandably begun to die out. At today's game, 'Jutkiewicz' would certainly present problems, and Dacres-Cogley (a substitute) would just sound silly!

The visitors seemed content to operate a policy of containment after the interval. That choice became a necessity when, with half an hour remaining, Birmingham striker Ché Adams upended Craig Noone with a palpably dangerous tackle and was rightly sent off. But little changed as a result. Bolton continued to dominate possession, but rarely demonstrated the ability to make effective use of it. So few were the openings they created that the only way an equaliser seemed possible would be through a penalty. The home fans in the stadium felt that they should have been awarded one, if not two, but in both instances, it was a case of the ball striking the hand of a defender from close range. If you can't get your hand out of the way in time, it shouldn't be a penalty. But that wasn't the way the Bolton faithful saw it.

A strange atmosphere developed in the stadium: a mixture of anger and passion. In what turned out to be the biggest crowd of the season (over twenty-two thousand), five thousand Brummies happily sang their way through their limited repertoire at one end of the ground. On the other three sides, there was a barrage of splenetic verbal aggression directed equally at the referee and the home side, in response to the shortcomings of the performance of both. They don't mince their words in Bolton! It wasn't a lack of effort that was the problem, rather the sheer lack of imagination in their creative play.

The game petered out to its predictable conclusion. Bolton had managed not a single shot on target, whilst Birmingham managed a mere three, one of which was the one that counted.

The Birmingham fans departed happily for the coach park, still singing. The Bolton fans made their way morosely back to Bolton, eight miles down the road (or, in a few cases no doubt, to Horwich, or even Blackrod). It had been one of those games that, although short on quality, had been surprisingly full of interest. I had certainly relished the 'big-time' atmosphere of the stadium; it had made a welcome change from the small grounds (and small crowds) to be found at Morecambe, Barrow, Accrington and Macclesfield, much as I love them. As a result of their victory, Birmingham had escaped from the relegation positions and were now equal on points with Bolton. Both were five points clear of Barnsley, who had a game in hand. With six games to go, it was clearly going to be a stressful few weeks for both clubs.

As I left the ground, I paused to admire the statue of Nat Lofthouse, probably Bolton's most revered former player, and to gaze perplexedly at a sculpture in the centre of a nearby round-about, which was the shape of a tall thin funnel bedecked with sparkly bits, and with a jagged top, where it looked like a piece had been broken off. It turned out to be 'The Spirit of Sport'. Hmm. Then past lines of static cars towards Blackrod, which may (or may not) have been 'calling my name'.

CHESTER

The dire warnings of Mr Suspicious

I moved to Chester in 1969, having been appointed as a planning officer at Cheshire County Council. I was twenty-six at the time, and the move felt like a big step into the unknown. I had left home in 1961 to go to Birmingham University, but I frequently came back to Stockport, and returned to take a job with Manchester City Council once I'd obtained my degree in 1964. Chester was different – I was on my own, with just a handful of acquaintances, needing to find a place to live and a social world in which I felt at ease.

I lived in and around Chester for the next seven years, although I stayed only two years with the county council, before moving into the world of academia as a lecturer in the Department of Town Planning at Liverpool Polytechnic. It proved to be an unstable period in my life, as I was struggling to 'find myself' (to use the parlance of the early 1970s). I lived in seven different houses, two of which I was required to leave (for reasons I won't trouble you with) and one of which – Wildholme - I still shudder when I think about. Wildholme (or Kings Buildings) was a group of three or four contiguous Georgian terraced houses that had been amalgamated and modified (but certainly not modernised) to provide accommodation for single men. There were sixty-seven bed-sitting rooms and a communal lounge, which was rarely used; I think most of the residents felt a sense of shame that they'd ended up there – I certainly did. Each room had minimal cooking facilities, and the bathroom and toilet facilities were communal. The whole place stank of stale air and loneliness. I tried to capture the essence of Wildholme in a poem. One stanza reads as follows:

Wildholme is a front-door bell ringing at four in the morning
Echoing along the endless corridors
Which wakes sixty-seven solitary men, alone in their little cells
But no one answers it.

It was the most depressing place in which I have ever lived, and I still have the occasional nightmare about it.

My relationships with girls (as they were called by those of us in our mid-twenties at the time) proved as unstable as my places of residence. I enjoyed (or in some cases, didn't) a series of largely unsatisfactory liaisons. I was a confused young adult, floundering around in pools of romantic love and sexual desire, and often confusing the two, at a time when the 'permissive society' was gathering momentum. With the benefit of hindsight, I lacked the maturity and self-confidence to cope with the opportunities and pitfalls of this brave new world.

There were two overlapping social worlds that I discovered, and which helped me retain a tenuous hold on sanity. The first was the world of St Theresa's FC. Someone at work, who knew of my burgeoning football career, mentioned that there was a new football club starting up in Blacon, a large council estate to the east of Chester's town centre. St Theresa's was a Catholic church, which was apparently happy to welcome non-believers on to their football team, provided they were sufficiently talented. I went along to training sessions and was judged to be up to the mark (this is the Chester and District Amateur League Division Four we're talking about).

St Theresa's FC's first opponents were Runcorn Boys Club Reserves. We lost 4-1 before a crowd of over a hundred enthusiastic but ultimately disappointed supporters. The second game was a local derby against Blacon Youth Club Reserves, which we lost 6-0. After that, although our form and results improved, our support dwindled to a nucleus of girlfriends, and churchgoers with nothing better to do on a Saturday afternoon. It was a world I really enjoyed. At twenty-seven, I was the experienced old hand in a team otherwise composed of final-year schoolboys and young workers at the Vauxhall factory in nearby Ellesmere Port. We played in various picturesque Cheshire villages, such as Bunbury, Whitegate, Helsby and Mickle Trafford. I appreciated the social club attached to the church, where the beer was cheap, and on Saturday evenings, St Theresa's teammates could usually be found, enjoying the odd post-match pint or two (or three or four).

Playing for St Theresa's led to one of the few achievements of my modest playing career. In our second season, we reached the final of the Cayzar Shield, which was, and possibly still is, a knock-out competition for the teams in Divisions Three and Four of the Chester and District Amateur League (our version of the Checkatrade Trophy, or whatever it's called nowadays). Our opponents were St Werbergh's, one of the leading clubs in Division Three: a battle between the two principal Catholic churches in Chester. We were very much the underdogs. For some reason I can't recall, I was moved from my customary midfield position to that of one of the centre-backs, or perhaps the only centre-back, it being 1971. I was totally out of my depth. Not being particularly tall, the ball sailed over my head to onrushing St Werburgh's forwards time after time. Not being a particularly good header of the ball, I was beaten in the air on numerous occasions. I can't understand how we didn't lose by a cricket score. But that wasn't the outcome; we lost 1-0, due to a disputed penalty, and we had a goal controversially disallowed into the bargain. I proudly stepped forward for my medal, which held pride of place on various mantelpieces, until it went missing in one of the many house-moves I made during the next few years.

The other social world in which I became involved was the Chester folk music scene, in particular a folk club called Black

Diamonds, located, as folk clubs generally were, in the upstairs room of a pub, the Crossfoxes, on the edge of the town centre. The early 1970s was a fertile period for the development of folk music, with a mixture of traditional singers like Martin Carthy, groups such as the Watersons and electrified 'folk rock' bands, like Mr Fox, emerging onto the scene. There was a resident group at the Crossfoxes, superficially resembling Peter, Paul and Mary, but more traditionally inclined. They played every Friday evening and brought in some excellent guests, including Nic Jones (before his disabling accident), Jeremy Taylor and Barbara Dickson (before she became famous). I went along with friends from St Theresa's. Other guests included Mike Harding and Jasper Carrott, who were in the process of transition from folk singers to stand-up comedians. Amusing though their numerous jokes were, the folk club audience was there to listen to folk songs rather than jokes, or at least we wanted an emphasis on the former rather than the latter. Shouts of 'Sing another song' would sometimes be heard from those irritated by a prolonged anecdote.

It was a source of great delight to me when my elder son, Callum, discovered folk music in his early twenties; it meant that, for the first time, we shared a common musical interest. We started going to gigs together, of which two stand out, both at the Brewery Arts Centre in Kendal. The first was a performance by the reformed early-1970s group Fotheringay. It was only a partial reformation; Sandy Denny had died in the 1980s and her husband, Trevor Lucas, was back in his native Australia. But lead guitarist Jerry Donahue and the original rhythm section of Pat Donaldson and Gerry Conway had recruited three new members, and together they were able to recreate the authentic Fotheringay sound, or at least a close approximation to it. They played the full content of the second album by the original line-up, which had only just been released, following a long-term struggle on the part of Jerry

112

Donahue to rescue it from the vaults of the record company.

The second occasion was equally memorable, but more poignant. Callum had become enthusiastic about the music of Bert Jansch (he can play a passable version of Jansch's classic rendition of *Blackwaterside* on his own guitar). Jansch had died in 2012, but his close friend and fellow-blues guitarist, John Renbourn, was still on the scene, and we went to see him playing with another 1970s legend, Whizz Jones, in Kendal in 2016. Although somewhat unsteady on his feet as he walked on stage, he and his fellow guitarist gave an inspirational performance; his gait may have been unsteady, but the quality of his guitar-playing was as good as ever. A few days later, I read in the *Guardian* that John Renbourn had been found dead in his home in the Scottish Borders. We had witnessed what was probably his final performance.

Callum had earlier had his own brief moment of fame at the Brewery, when he was part of the warm-up act for Dave Swarbrick's group, Lazarus (so-called because of a premature obituary of Swarbrick in the *Daily Telegraph* the previous year). Callum provided guitar accompaniment for a very talented young fiddle player. Unfortunately, it was before his interest in folk music had developed, and his reaction afterwards was 'I'm not doing that again; it's not good for my image.'

In Chester in the early 1970s, it was music and football that helped to keep me going (or perhaps distracted me) during a period of personal instability and self-doubt, as they have continued to do since. The move to Chester also meant I had a new set of League clubs to attend: not just Chester, but also Wrexham, fifteen miles to the south, and Tranmere Rovers in Birkenhead, a similar distance to the north. Regular visits to Sealand Road, the Racecourse Ground and Prenton Park were punctuated by visits back to Maine Road to watch Manchester City, for whom the early 1970s was a time of attractive football but limited success.

Chester FC's football history is undistinguished, but when I was around, they experienced a rare purple patch. After playing in the Third Division North and later the Fourth Division, they were promoted to the Third Division for the first time in their history in 1975. But what brought them to wider public attention in the 1974–75 season was a spectacular run in the League Cup, which saw them defeat Leeds United, then amongst the leaders of the First Division, 3-0 and Newcastle United (then mid-table) 1-0, both at Sealand Road. I was at both games together with large numbers of Cestrians who had developed a sudden enthusiasm for their local team, which dissipated as soon as the cup run ended, which it did in the semi-final, Chester going down (bravely, of course) 3-2 on aggregate to Aston Villa, the eventual winners. After that successful year, they survived in the Third Division for seven seasons, narrowly missing a play-off place in 1978, when under the management of former Manchester City midfielder Alan Oakes. But in 1982 they were back in the Fourth Division.

Since then, things have not gone well for Chester. The move to the Deva Stadium heralded a period of instability, with the club oscillating between five levels of senior football, ranging from the fourth tier of the Football League to the Northern Premier League Division One North, in which they were placed by the FA after going into liquidation in 2010 (and having their 2009–10 record in the Conference expunged). They made it back to the Conference in 2013.

CHESTER v TRANMERE ROVERS
National League, Saturday April 7th, 2018

The Chester/Tranmere game was a local derby and, with Tranmere one of the best-supported clubs in the National League, it was not surprising that it had been made an all-ticket affair. I had booked my ticket over the phone, a few days previously. A rather suspicious official wanted to know which club I supported.

'Well, I guess I'm a neutral,' I replied. 'But I used to live in Chester many years ago, and I often watched them then.'

'You're not a Tranmere fan?' Because if you are, you'll be ejected from the ground – no transfers, no refunds.'

I assured him that wouldn't be a problem. His tone became somewhat more conciliatory. 'I've got to ask,' he explained. 'We had a lot of trouble at this fixture last season.'

I had travelled by train, via Warrington, a familiar journey from my time with Cheshire County Council. Emerging from Chester station, I noticed an old sign at the entrance to the old stables adjacent to the Queens Hotel: *Carriages and post horses for hire*. Not much call for that sort of thing nowadays, I'd imagine. In the town centre, I was surprised to see a man standing on the pavement, holding a board advertising a tattoo parlour, and displaying an arrow which helpfully pointed down the side street in which it was located. It had been a long time since I'd seen this personalised form of advertising, perhaps the prime example of an unskilled job – no previous training, experience or skill required. Presumably the milling throngs of tourists in Chester convinced the proprietor it would be a worthwhile endeavour.

Chester is always busy, particularly at weekends. It is undeniably and attractively 'historic', with its unique 'rows' (ancient wooden walkways above street level, with shops opening on to them). But it always seems to me to have an air of unreality about it: like a film-set, constructed to accommodate crowd scenes in an historical drama. My aim was to seek out places in the town that held strong memories for me. Commerce House, behind the old town hall, was where Cheshire Planning department was located in the 1970s, but it had been demolished and replaced by something: a cinema. I then turned into King Street, passing an old hostelry called The Punch Bowl on the corner, where the solitary tenants of Wildholme (including me) could often be found. Kings Buildings, which had housed that dreadful place, had been restored in 1984, so a plaque on its frontage informed us. That meant that Wildholme had continued to provide accommodation for lonely single men for a further fourteen years after I gratefully moved out in 1970. It had now been transformed into a set of up-market apartments.

Moving on, along Watergate I stopped off for a pint at the Customs House (now called Ye Olde Customs House, I regret to say) where I used to meet my friends Ray and Gill (to whom I shall ever be grateful for rescuing me from Wildholme). Across the road is the ancient Guildhall, where I attended a celebration of Ray's life, following his untimely death in 2005. Then a quick detour to the Cross Foxes on Boughton Road, home of the aforementioned Black Diamonds folk club, which had retained its unpretentious ambience (but didn't host folk music any longer), before it was time to commence the long walk to the Deva Stadium.

Even in my seventies, I still get excited about the prospect of attending a game at a new football stadium. In 1992, Chester had moved from the familiar though uninspiring Sealand Road ground, their home since 1906, to a new purpose-built ground, the Deva Stadium (named after the fort which the Romans established in Chester). It is located right on the edge of the city boundary; indeed, the greater part of it overlaps the border, and finds itself in Wales. So, watch out for a trick pub quiz question such as 'how many senior football clubs play in Wales?' and remember to add Chester to Cardiff, Swansea, Newport and Wrexham.

The Deva Stadium turned out not to be the most imaginatively designed new ground I'd come across, but it did have the advantage of a standing terrace at one end (the Harry McNulty Terrace, named after an illustrious former player), which is where

I'd chosen to buy a ticket from Mr Suspicious. Barring an unlikely purple patch and help from other threatened clubs, relegation was looking almost certain for Chester. They had started the season badly, sacked their manager Jon McCarthy and replaced him with the highly rated Marcus Bignot in September. But he had proved unable to turn the club round, experiencing only five League victories in his thirty-two games in charge. He had been told earlier in the week that his contract would not be renewed at the end of the season. The *Chester Chronicle* also reported a major falling-out within the board of directors, all of whom are elected by the City Fans United supporters' trust. I was saddened by this development; in my view, supporter-owned clubs represent the ideal ownership model. But I guess whatever form of ownership there is, you're going to get such disagreements, particularly given the passion such involvement generates.

In contrast, Tranmere Rovers were on a roll. Widely tipped as promotion front-runners, they'd had an inconsistent start to the season. When Chester hung on for a 0-0 draw at Prenton Park in October, Rovers were marooned in mid-table. Since then, they'd had one of the best records in the League, winning fourteen and drawing five of the twenty-four games played (only Macclesfield Town could beat that). Although there was probably too much ground to make up to catch Macclesfield, the League leaders, a play-off position was looking increasingly likely. A win today would keep up the momentum and could put them in the top three. That was no doubt what the two thousand Rovers supporters in the stands were expecting. Chester, on the other hand, were playing mainly for their pride.

When the teams emerged from the dressing rooms, I recognised a familiar figure. Central defender Steve McNulty made his debut for Luton Town in a 1-0 defeat at Dartford, which I witnessed in 2013. He had (and still has) the build of a sumo wrestler.

The Dartford crowd christened him 'Chunky McNulty' and the Braintree fans, where I saw him again later in the season, called him 'The Tank'. But Chester had their own answer to The Tank: Ryan Astles, also a central defender, had a physique to match McNulty's (well, approaching it). I looked forward to seeing how they would deal with each other during set-pieces.

Tranmere dominated play in the early stages, with some crisp passing movements. But Chester were by no means outclassed and put together some fluent approach play of their own, which rarely resulted in a shot on (or indeed off) target. They were playing two speedy wingers, Dominic Vose and Craig Mahon, both of whom were prepared to take on defenders. It was good to see that both sides were eschewing the 'long ball' approach, typically a recipe for tedium in my experience. The visitors were proving much more incisive and, twenty minutes into the half, hit the woodwork twice in quick succession. Ben Tollitt, who also played on the wing, looked dangerous every time he received the ball. Just when it looked as if the sides would remain level at halftime, Tranmere made their breakthrough. In added time, a corner from the right found leading scorer Andy Cook just outside the six-yard box, and his well-placed header looped past the Chester keeper.

During the first half, I'd noticed a young ball-girl, rather than the customary boy, and I was impressed by how composed she was. When the ball went out of play, she'd run to fetch it, her long hair blowing in the wind, with a minimum of fuss. When not required, she followed the game intently from her makeshift seat. She looked delighted to be there, doing that job, and I thought how exciting it must be for a nine-year-old, who was enthusiastic about football, to be making a real contribution to the flow of the game; more so, I would guess, than being a mascot for the day, when you have your moment of glory before kick-off, and that's it.

Both sides continued to try to play creative football after

the interval. But ten minutes into the half, Tranmere made the game safe when James Norwood (ex-Forest Green Rovers) was put through on the left and slipped the ball neatly past Andrew Firth from a difficult angle. There was no way back for Chester, although in the 70th minute, they did create their first clear-cut chance, duly squandered by James Akintunde. The visitors could have scored more but appeared content to defend their two-goal lead, which they did without trouble.

Towards the end of the game there was a distraction that we could have done without. Two burly, tattooed, middle-aged men made their way to the far right of the Harry McNally Stand and started shouting abuse at the Tranmere contingent in the adjacent stand. I hope it didn't adversely affect the ball-girl's enjoyable afternoon. Thankfully, the visiting fans declined to rise to the bait, and refused to take the two loudmouths seriously, which was certainly the best reaction. Their responses were laced with humour, some of it incomprehensible (to me, anyway). Why, for example, did they burst into a chorus of 'One Harry Potter; there's only one Harry Potter'? But I guess when you're 2-0 up and on your way to the play-offs, you can afford to be magnanimous.

The defeat, and the way results went elsewhere, meant that by five o'clock, Chester's relegation was confirmed. At least they could now relax in their remaining four fixtures, the last vestige of hope having disappeared.

On the way out of the ground, I noticed a sign at the back of the main stand. It read, *Our City, Our Community, Our Club*. That is very much the ethos behind this book.

KIDDERMINSTER

The renowned cuisine of Brian and Joan

Every now and then, the past has a habit of re-emerging and slapping you in the face. It was as a result of just such an occurrence that I was on my way to Kidderminster to watch Kidderminster Harriers play Stockport County. It all goes back to my three years as an undergraduate at Birmingham University in the early 1960s.

In 1961, my parents dropped me off at 479 Gillott Road, a lodging house owned and run by the formidable Mrs Smith (a widow, whose first name we never discovered), in a distinctly down-market part of Edgbaston. I shared it with five other students, one of whom was called Roger Perrin, who hailed from Kidderminster. Roger was instrumental in inspiring me to change my course of study. I'd started out doing chemistry, without being convinced it was the right choice. It soon became clear that it wasn't. I found it increasingly boring and regularly failed to successfully complete the laboratory experiments – it was highly likely that I would have failed the year. Roger was studying social science and really enjoying it, and he encouraged me to transfer to his faculty. The prospect of such a move tied in with my growing interest in politics and current affairs and I took his advice, a decision I have never regretted.

Roger and I and the other occupants of 479 Gillott Road spent an enjoyable year doing what students typically do: drinking in local pubs or the students' union bar, watching football matches and attempting, with little success, to persuade various female students to succumb to our sexual advances (this was 1961 – the permissive society had not yet arrived, or at least, not in Birmingham!). On one occasion, whilst walking home along the

Bristol Road late one evening, he and I were set upon by a gang of youths. I escaped with a few bruises and scratches, but Roger was less fortunate; he suffered a broken nose, which had to be re-set the next day in hospital. The incident made the headline story of the prize-winning university newspaper, *Redbrick*, probably because Roger was a close friend of its editor, Chris Buckland, who later became a renowned journalist. After graduation, I returned to Stockport, whilst Roger went back to Kidderminster, where he took over responsibility for the family building firm, following his dad's sudden death. Despite intending to keep in touch, we failed to do so.

Fast forward fifty years to 2015. My book *Conference Season* had been published the previous year and had included a chapter on Kidderminster Harriers, who ended the 2012–13 season unfortunate not to be promoted; they finished second, a point behind the champions, Mansfield Town, and way ahead of third-placed Newport. But they lost to Wrexham in the play-off semis, an outcome that I felt instinctively at the time was unjust. But that's the play-off system for you.

Dan Perrin, Roger's son, was trawling the internet, looking for something to buy his dad for Christmas. He happened upon *Conference Season*, noticed that it included a chapter on Kidderminster, and knowing his dad was a long-term supporter of the Harriers, bought it for him. Roger failed to recognise the name of the author, but as he read through the book, began to wonder 'do I know this guy?' There are references to Birmingham and its university in the early 1960s, and to a 'Sunday league team of staggering ineptitude', for which I (and he) made a few guest appearances. Eventually the proverbial penny dropped; yes, it is *that* Steve Leach, the one who shared his experience of being beaten up by a gang of youths on Bristol Road. He contacted me and, a month or so later, we were sitting together in the old main stand at Aggborough (where he he'd had a season ticket for many years), watching the Harriers take on Eastleigh. Such is the power of a shared interest in football to re-unite long-lost friends.

For long-term season ticket holders, the social dimension of match attendance is often as important as the quality of the match itself. In the seats adjacent to Roger's and in the row in front, there was a group of regulars with a long tradition of lively discussion, both before the match and during it. The bloke sitting next to me had been at Borehamwood the previous Saturday (an admirable example of dedicated support) to witness a rare Harriers win. He shared his generally positive impressions of his visit with the regulars around him.

Kidderminster were, at the time, rock bottom of the Conference, but you wouldn't have thought so. They fielded several talented youngsters and were two goals up by halftime. In the second half, Eastleigh scored twice to level the score, in both cases through James Constable, previously a Harriers favourite. But the home side came back to win the game, five minutes from the end. The match had been highly entertaining and its outcome stimulated talk amongst the regulars of the possibility that the tide was turning (two wins in succession was unprecedented that season), and that relegation might – just might – be avoided.

But there was too much ground to make up, and too few fixtures remaining. Kidderminster went down to the National League North, where they found themselves in the company of Stockport County, the club I have supported since the 1950s. The clash between these two giants of non-league football was the obvious choice for the next meeting with Roger in Kidderminster. The hosts were firmly entrenched in a play-off position at the time, with Stockport on the fringes of the play-offs. It was an even, closely contested game, which Kidderminster won 2-0. They went on to reach the play-offs, where they went out to a rugged Chorley side. Stockport did not, as a result of conceding a late goal to Gloucester City on the final day of the season.

I was back in Kidderminster in April 2018 for the much-postponed League match between the two sides. Kidderminster is a pleasant laid-back West Midlands town with one foot in the West Country. For a couple of centuries, its basic industry was carpet-making. Carpets are still made in the town at the long-established firm of Brintons. But the industry now employs a fraction of the workforce of its heyday, when it really was a 'carpet town'.

The town centre operates within the straitjacket of a ring road, most of it a dual carriageway and difficult to cross, which separates it from its inner residential areas. You might think that's the fault of 'those planners', but believe me (as a former town planner), it isn't; it's 'those highway engineers' who are really to blame. The local council really ought to be called Kidderminster – councillors from the town constitute by far the largest group on the council – but it isn't. The idea of calling the council 'Kidderminster' proved unacceptable to councillors from the smaller towns of Bewdley and Stourport, when the new borough was created in 1974. Instead it is called Wyre Forest, after a largely uninhabited part of the borough to the west of the River Severn. Local loyalties die hard, here as elsewhere.

On our second trip to Aggborough, Roger and I compared our own personal football histories. We were both members of successful primary school teams, and we can both recall the names of all of our fellow team members. But Roger could go one better: the members of his primary school team still met every year (or at least, those still alive did – we are talking about a group of seventy-five-year-olds here).

At the time of his primary school years, Kidderminster were in the Southern League, probably then the strongest non-league entity. Whereas my football-watching history was facilitated by my dad, who took me along to Old Trafford or Maine Road from time to time, Roger's dad wasn't interested in football. Roger went with groups of mates from school to watch the occasional Kidderminster game, typically the more interesting ones against local rivals such as Worcester City and Wellington Town. But as with most eleven-year-olds, the lure of the 'big name' clubs proved stronger than that of those in the Fourth Division or the Southern League. At the time, football in the West Midlands was in a much healthier state than it is now. Wolves, West Bromwich Albion, Aston Villa and Birmingham City were all in the top tier. Wolves were then a formidable team; it was the era of Bert Williams, Billy Wright, Bill Slater, Peter Broadbent and Dennis Wilshaw, all of whom Roger remembers seeing, when he was taken there on a Cubs outing. Later when at secondary school, he started making occasional visits to either Molineux or the Hawthorns (both only twelve miles from Kidderminster) with friends. At the latter he saw the legendary Stanley Matthews in action when Blackpool were the visitors. When we were both at Birmingham University between 1961 and 1964, we would pick out whatever was the most attractive Saturday fixture on offer (always a choice of two) and go to that.

When Roger left university, he took over the family business, and had little spare time for watching football. Even if he had, he probably wouldn't have given much thought to Kidderminster – by the 1960s, they had found life in the Southern League too expensive and had voluntarily moved down to the Birmingham League. Local derbies against Stourbridge and Halesowen would have had little appeal when you'd become used to watching Billy Wright and Stanley Matthews.

But over time, Roger's attitude changed. By the late 1970s, he felt he wanted to give something back to his town, and so began to organise Cubs football teams. At the same time, his interest in the Harriers, who in 1983 had been promoted to the Conference, was re-ignited. He started taking his son to home games from time to time, and even attended the occasional away game, when assignments in the company car took him close to a town where Kidderminster had an evening fixture. In the mid-1990s, he took his support further and purchased his first season ticket, which he has renewed every season since. As it happened, the timing proved to be excellent. In 1994, Kidderminster emerged as Conference champions, but were denied promotion to the Football League because of the wooden seats in the main stand (this was five years after the devastating fire at Bradford City's ground).

But the Harriers eventually made it to the Football League in 2000, under the management of Danish international and Liverpool midfielder Jan Mølby. Appointed in 1999, he proved an inspired choice, drawing both on his links with Liverpool and the Denmark football scene to attract players to Aggborough that other managers couldn't have hoped to do. But there was another key factor: money! Local businessman Lionel Newton became chairman and bankrolled the club for a time, enabling Mølby to buy players that would have been beyond the financial reach of other managers at that level. Under the Mølby/Newton regime, 2000–05 turned out to be the golden years of Kidderminster football. It was true that they never looked like progressing any further upward (10th was the best position they achieved, in 2002). But simply to be in the Football League felt like a major achievement, and hosting teams such as Hull City, Cardiff City and Blackpool would have seemed unthinkable a few years previously.

It wasn't to last. Mølby departed for Hull City in 2004 and there followed a period of instability. Kidderminster were relegated back to the Conference in 2005, and Lionel Newton withdrew his investment in the club, only to be succeeded by a series of local businessmen who thought they could match his achievements but lacked the resources and know-how to do so. Good players who emerged during the season would be sold at its end to raise money. Managers came and went: twelve in a fourteen-year period, several on a 'caretaker' basis. There was a major financial crisis in 2010, when the club was faced with insolvency. This outcome was avoided at the last minute, thanks to the efforts of large numbers of ordinary fans. There was a crowdfunding initiative where fans asked everybody they knew to send a pound; many contributed much more than this. It's another heartwarming example of how important football clubs are to local communities.

Despite this instability, Kidderminster only just missed out on a play-off place in 2009, 2011 and 2012, and, as noted above, had an excellent season in 2012–13, finishing second to Mansfield Town. But further instability and changes of ownership followed. In 2016, Colin Gordon bought out the existing owners and, after a brief period where he also operated as caretaker-manager, installed John Eustace (ex-Derby County) as manager, since when there has been a more stable ambience around the club, with a play-off position achieved in 2017 and 2018. But given its recent history, it would be a mistake to assume that this encouraging state of affairs will last.

The history of Kidderminster's ups and downs over the past fifty years is typical of that of so many clubs in the lower leagues. So much depends on the credibility, commitment and financial clout of their owners, the good judgement (or lack of it) in the managerial appointments made, and the outcome of crucial matches at the end of the season (including play-offs), on which promotion or relegation issues are decided. In the case of Kidderminster, the fortuitous coming together of Lionel Newton and Jan Mølby gave the Harriers their five years of glory in the new millennium. The inflated egos and unrealistic agendas of Morton's many successors served to set the club in reverse, a process temporarily halted by the appointment of Steve Burr as manager in 2012, which would have returned Kidderminster to the Football League in 2013, had it not been for the phenomenal run of success of Mansfield Town in the second half of the season, and the injustices of the play-off system.

KIDDERMINSTER HARRIERS v STOCKPORT COUNTY
National League North, Tuesday April 10th, 2018

Aggborough is justly famous for the quality of the pies served by Brian and Joan Murdoch. Were they still there, I wondered? They were indeed, and what's more had extended their pie repertoire since my last visit, when the choice was between a cottage pie and a cheese and onion pie (both excellent). Now there were ten options, including five non-pies, such as sweet and sour pork and chicken curry. I'm sure their standards have been maintained across the board, but there was no way I could have sampled any of them, having recently consumed a delicious Moroccan lamb casserole, cooked by Roger's wife, Penny. But it was good to know Brian and Joan were still delivering the goods.

Before the teams emerged, I was introduced to a former West Bromwich Albion player, David Rimmington, who, unlike many of his playing colleagues from the 1980s, has prospered as a businessman since his retirement from the game. He was now part of Roger's tight-knit group of fellow-supporters, sitting below the press box. The group included two elderly ladies in the row in front, who fortified themselves throughout the game with sips from a metal flask, the contents of which were, I suspect, rather stronger than tea.

I noticed that Lee Vaughan was in the Harriers squad but was not playing tonight. I remember being greatly impressed with him in the Kidderminster/Telford match in January 2013 I attended when writing *Conference Season*. 'Remember when you see him playing in the Premier League in a couple of seasons time that you first saw this outcome predicted here,' I confidently wrote. Well, it didn't quite work out like that for Lee. He was indeed destined for higher things; but only as far as Cheltenham Town, which hardly qualifies as the 'big time'. Cheltenham joined Kidderminster in the Conference in his second season there, after which he moved to Tranmere, also in the Conference, and then back to Kidderminster. I asked Roger why he wasn't playing tonight. 'Sent off a couple of weeks ago against Boston', was the reply.

With four games to play, both Kidderminster and Stockport were comfortably placed in play-off positions. The visitors had won all their previous six games, the Harriers four of their previous six. It was apparent from the start that both teams were out to play attacking football. Defenders and midfielders surged forward at every opportunity. Chances were created even before Joe Ironside, Kidderminster's leading scorer, found space on the edge of the area in the fifth minute and his deflected shot wrong-footed Ben Hinchcliffe in the County goal. But it was not long before Stockport equalised; some inspired inter-passing between Jimmy Ball and Rhys Turner on the left led to an opening for Ball, which he converted confidently from a tight angle. There were around three hundred visiting County fans present (not bad for a Tuesday evening) who roared their appreciation. Ten minutes later, an astute through-ball found midfielder James McQuilkin in space and his well-placed shot past the advancing keeper, putting the Harriers back in front. But Stockport responded positively and carved out several more scoring opportunities. Three weeks previously, the Harriers had drawn 4-4 with League leaders Salford City and, earlier in the season, had beaten Blyth Spartans 5-4. Was this to be another goal bonanza? It certainly had that feel about it, as both sides continued to attack. It was proving to be an exhilarating game. Sometimes at this level (or indeed higher), there seems to be very little space in midfield and passing movements regularly proceed sideways and backwards rather than forwards, to the frustration of the crowd. There was little sign of such negativity today. Halftime came with no further goals, but the game still seemed wide-open.

After the interval, the game continued to be open and entertaining. I lost count of the number of chances created, but it must have already been more than a dozen to both sides. Then, in the 60th minute, a County attack broke down when defender Harry Winter lost possession and the ball reached Harriers' striker Dan Bradley. He raced up-field to the edge of the County penalty area, and ignoring options to his right and left, went on to hit a powerful shot past Hinchcliffe. It was a goal worthy of deciding any match and proved to be the decisive moment in this contest. Although County (and indeed Kidderminster) continued to create chances, a two-goal deficit was always going to be difficult to overcome against a well-drilled defence. And so it proved.

As Jim Gannon, County's manager said afterwards, 'As a game of football it was a fantastic advert for the League and shows the quality of players emerging at clubs in the National League North.' He was right, on both counts. I'd seen worse games this season in the Football League. When the County players made their customary detour to the visiting fans at the end of the game, they received an enthusiastic ovation, and rightly so. It was no disgrace to lose to an impressive Kidderminster side that County (having created, as it turned out, seventeen goalscoring opportunities) had matched in everything but the sharpness of their finishing. The likelihood was that both sides would make the play-offs.

As Roger and I walked away from Aggborough, we agreed that football at this level could be just as entertaining as that in the

Premier League, at around a third of the price. We also welcomed the fact that there had been a female referee (Amy Fearn) – the first I had ever seen in action – who had controlled the game with a quiet competence. There was now a possibility that Stockport and Kidderminster would meet yet again this season, for the fifth time (including two games in the FA Trophy), if they could both find a way through to the play-off final. Unlikely, but you never know! Now that really would put our friendship under pressure.

STOCKPORT

The manager who keeps coming back

If South Manchester was the setting for my childhood, Stockport (and its environs) was the focus of my adolescence. We moved to Heaton Moor, a middle-class suburb of the town, in 1957 when I was fourteen, and not long out of short trousers. I was at Manchester Grammar School, with O-levels approaching, under the tutelage of the tyrannical and punishment-obsessed Billy Hulme – I attribute any subsequent psychological problems of mine to the two years I suffered with him as form-master, and French and German teacher. The year before we moved, I had been to Edgeley Park for the first time with my friend John Davies for my second introduction to lower-division football – the first had been Accrington in 1952. Stockport County were then in the Third Division North and played against Workington Town (yes, they were once a League club). It was early April, and both clubs were high enough up the division to have a chance of promotion, although this was admittedly remote; only one club was promoted per season at the time.

My second taste of Third Division North football was as compelling as the first. Again, it was a relatively undistinguished game. Workington, whose manager at the time was one Bill Shankly, won 1-0, thus extinguishing County's forlorn hopes of promotion for another season. But I loved being close to the players on the pitch, the intimacy of the atmosphere and the passion of the crowd. By the start of the next season, I'd moved to Heaton Moor and John and I became regular attenders at Edgeley Park, whilst continuing to watch Manchester City at Maine Road.

As it turned out, it was a good season to have attached myself to Stockport County. They embarked on a run in the FA Cup which brought them fleeting glory and the rare experience of a national profile. Having disposed of Hartlepool United 2-1 in the second round in the pouring rain, thanks to a late winner from a striker called Paddy Sowden, they were drawn at home to Luton Town in the third round. Given Luton's recent history, this doesn't sound like a big deal, but in 1958, it certainly was. Luton Town were at the time fourth in the First Division and had the division's leading scorer, Gordon Turner, in their ranks. This cup-tie has become a key reference point in County's otherwise relatively undistin-guished history. After three minutes, Ken Finney (no relation to Tom), County's much-maligned and -barracked winger, made progress down the right and sent over a cross, which was met with a flying goal-bound header from inside-right Arnold Jackson, who had miraculously managed to find acres of space within the Luton defence. It is a goal frozen in my memory. I can still replay it at will. Jackson was a journeyman forward, with a reasonable goalscoring record, who later moved on to Shrewsbury Town. He was little heard of before or since, but this was his moment of glory. In the second half, at the far end of the pitch from where John and I were standing, the rather more famous Bill Holden (ex-Burnley) added two further goals to complete the giant-kill-ing achievement of the round.

Most football fans can recall the full line-up in crucial games of teams they support. I can do so for Stockport's side in the Luton match. It included:

- Goalkeeper Ken Grieves, who doubled as wicket-keeper for Lancashire County Cricket Club
- Centre-half Neil Franklin, an England international who had returned from a brief spell in South America

- Full backs Barrie Betts, who later became a Manchester City regular, and Willie Webb
- Wing-half Bobby Murray, whom County had signed from Inverurie Loco
- Player-manager Willie Moir, previously with Bolton Wanderers and who had brought himself into the team as soon as the third-round draw was announced, no doubt sensing a final bit of glory before finally hanging up his boots
- Centre-half Bill Holden, who had unexpectedly arrived at County after falling out with the formidable chairman of Burnley, Bob Lord.

I can also tell you the full line-up of the Old Moat Junior School football team that reached the quarter-finals of the Manchester Schools Cup in 1954: in goal, Damion Bentley; at right-back, Roger Pottage ... but perhaps we'll skip that one!

The second formative experience of my adolescent Stockport years was my involvement with Stockport Youth Campaign for Nuclear Disarmament (YCND). This happened when I was in the sixth form at Manchester Grammar School, studying chemistry, physics and maths (a big mistake, in every respect). A fellow member of my form was John Finney, later to become a prominent nuclear physicist. We had both become interested in politics, and he was already an active member of Stockport YCND. I had the same views on nuclear disarmament as he had and was readily persuaded to join. There was a strong element of self-preservation in my attachment to this cause. I didn't want my life to be cut short by the impact of a hydrogen bomb dropped by the Russians on Manchester, and I felt that this calamitous outcome was less likely if Britain declared that it was not prepared to deploy nuclear weapons. But there was also a genuine horror at the fact that there were nations prepared to contemplate their use. I wanted no part of that mind-set. I was also well aware, as a young man with developing left-wing leanings, that there was an internal battle raging within the Labour Party over whether it should adopt unilateral nuclear disarmament as a policy. I wanted to add my voice to those within the Labour Party who were pushing hard for it to adopt such a policy, which it finally did (with the help of the block vote of some of the larger trade unions) at the 1960 Scarborough Party conference. But they (and we in the CND) were then frustrated by the determination of Hugh Gaitskell (the Labour leader of the time) to 'fight, fight, and fight again to save the Party we love', in response to this conference decision. The following year he was influential in securing its reversal.

Stockport YCND met every month in Hulme Hall School in Cheadle Hulme, a location which may have had something to do with the fact that the father of one the group's leading lights – Elena Rogerson – was headmaster there. I fell in love with Elena (or imagined I did; I was a raw, impressionable seventeen-year-old) but soon transferred my affections to Gillian Smith, for whom I nursed an undeclared and unrequited passion for the next couple of years. We were an active branch. I remember thrusting leaflets into the unwilling hands of departing cinema-goers in Reddish, who had just watched a film adaption of Neville Shute's *On the Beach*, which vividly depicted the horrors of the aftermath of a nuclear apocalypse. Most of them were deposited in the nearest litter bin. We managed to get ourselves invited to local church youth clubs (including St Aidan's in West Didsbury, of which I was a member), where we endeavoured to convince those present that building up and being prepared to use a nuclear arsenal was incompatible with Christ's teachings. Our arguments usually suffered the same fate as the leaflets, falling on stony ground. And we attended events organised by the Northwest regional branch of YCND, the aim of which was to brief us on the evidence of the impact of a nuclear war, and to help fine-tune our arguments in seeking converts to the cause. It sounds like a religious crusade, and in a way felt like that. The events were usually held at the Friends' Meeting House in Cross Street, Manchester, with sympathetic local Labour MPs such as Frank Allaun, often in attendance.

But the highlight of my time with Stockport YCND was undoubtably the Aldermaston Marches, one of the iconic political phenomena of the late 1950s and early 1960s. I went on two of the Marches (1960 and 1961), probably the most demanding and committed political activity I have ever been involved in. In 1960, Stockport CND and YCND jointly travelled by coach to a site outside the nuclear research establishment at Aldermaston, from whence we marched the ten miles to Reading on the first day. Then on to Slough where we stayed at the end of the second day of the march, passing through Maidenhead, the constituency of Theresa May, who would have been a toddler at the time. The third overnight stop was in Ealing, before we finally made it to Trafalgar Square on Easter Monday.

We slept on the floors of school halls in Reading, Slough and Ealing; presumably the local authorities concerned were supportive of our cause, or at least tolerant of it. We marched proudly behind the Stockport YCND banner, which I took turns in holding aloft. In the towns and villages, crowds lined the route to observe us, often cheering and clapping as we passed through. There was a lot of music, mainly from brass bands, and contingents of Woodcraft Folk – a more right-on version of the Scouts – dressed in their green uniforms. At the front of the march were the CND celebrities, including: Michael Foot, then seen as an extremist but twenty years later leader of the Labour Party; A.J.P Taylor, the Oxford University historian and TV pundit; and Canon Collins ('Fire the Canon!' was a *News of the World* headline of the time).

There was a heartwarming camaraderie amongst the Marchers, a sense that we were all putting our feet where our mouths were (as it were) and possibly making history.

The most moving moment came when we were close to the centre of London. In 1960, the March had been planned differently from the previous year. Instead of a single march from Aldermaston to London, there were two strands to it, the other starting from Wethersfield, an American base in Essex where nuclear weapons were stored. Somewhere in the vicinity of Marble Arch, the two marching columns came together, in an atmosphere of exhilaration. We cheered the Wethersfield contingent, and they cheered us, as the two strands merged. People who had never met before hugged one another – an emotional coming-together, which is etched on my memory. The interwoven column then proceeded to Trafalgar Square, where we listened to a sequence of stirring speeches from our leaders, before dispersing, climbing aboard our waiting coach, and heading back for Stockport, exhausted but exhilarated.

The popular press had a field day. The Marchers were castigated as 'beardy weirdies' by Randolph Churchill in the *News of the World*; unfairly, I thought, because most of us were neither bearded nor (in our view) weird. If the term hippies had been in use then, no doubt that would also have been applied to us. Another paper claimed that there was 'widespread immorality' amongst the Marchers – shared sleeping bags and that kind of thing. Well, I didn't see much evidence of it, and in the highly unlikely event of my receiving an offer of this nature, I'd have been too knackered to take advantage of it.

Estimates of the numbers present in Trafalgar Square on Easter Monday varied considerably, depending on the political orientation of the paper concerned. The police estimate was, as usual with demonstrations of this nature, unrealistically low. I'm no expert at estimating numbers, but I can't believe that the crowds in and around Trafalgar Square wouldn't have filled Wembley stadium.

Did we make any difference? Although Hugh Gaitskell did manage to reverse the 1960 Scarborough Conference decision that had committed the Labour Party to a policy of unilateralism, the Conservative prime minister of the time, Harold MacMillan, later claimed that in negotiating a test-ban treaty with the Russians, he used the pressure he was under from the CND movement as an argument in reaching agreement. I'd like to believe this claim; it certainly felt at the time as though we were making history. I was back on the March in 1961, treading the same roads, a few months before enrolling at Birmingham University.

STOCKPORT COUNTY v AFC TELFORD UNITED
National League North, Saturday April 14th, 2018

After the setback of County's defeat at Kidderminster the previous Tuesday, I felt that they needed me to be there at Edgeley Park for the game against AFC Telford United. It looked like a straightforward home win. Telford were hovering just above the relegation slots, but there are no easy games in the National League North (possibly except against North Ferriby United – played thirty-eight, won three, drawn five and already relegated). The AFC prefix refers to the fact that the old Telford United went into liquidation in 2004, and on rising again Phoenix-like from the ashes, were required to change their name. It has become increasingly common in recent years. Clubs don't die anymore; they go bust, reform, get demoted two or three levels, and gradually, in most cases, work their way back up.

After arriving at Manchester Piccadilly, I caught the train to Stockport Edgeley, which (as its name suggests) is within easy access of the football ground. I'd left myself plenty of time to wander around Stockport's town centre, a familiar destination during my adolescent years in Heaton Moor. I wanted to check out how my favourite part of the town was faring. The main shopping centre, focused on Mersey Way, is uninspiring – full of the chain stores you find everywhere. But to the south, on rising ground, is the historic town centre: the Market Square with its impressive glass-roofed Market Hall (built in 1860) and Robinson's Brewery (which looks equally ancient) and close by, Little Underbank and St Petersgate, both with a range of quirky individual retail outlets, and not a chain store in sight.

I'd made a similar nostalgia-infused visit to the area in 2013. Despite the recent involvement of the 'retail queen and TV star' Mary Portas in an attempt to regenerate the area (and the allocation of a miserly pilot project grant of £100,000), it was then in a state of decline. The Market Hall had many empty stalls and few patrons. The stalls on the pavements outside offered various varieties of tatty second-hand goods and were also short of customers. There were some indications on Little Underbank of a move towards trendy specialist outlets aimed at young people, but there were numerous empty shops, and not much sign of young people – or anyone else, for that matter.

What a transformation five years later! Maybe Mary Portas's magic had slowly made the difference, although I suspect that the key transformation agent was Stockport Council itself. On a sunny early spring Saturday lunchtime, the area was buzzing, both inside the iconic Market Hall, and the surrounding pavements. I have childhood memories of a wonderful stall, Duerden's home-made fudge and toffee, which had not been there in 2013. It was too much to hope that it would somehow have miraculously returned, and it hadn't. But there was a stall selling an impressive variety of sweets, including some unusual varieties of fudge. Adjacent to the Market Hall was the Bulls Head, deserted and dilapidated when

I'd last seen it in 2013 and, though still closed, had clearly had a makeover and looked like a re-opening was imminent. Let's hope someone's kept the recipe for the pea and ham soup!

Little Underbank was quieter than the Market area, but also looked like it was on the up, with its eclectic variety of small shops. I climbed the steps to St Petersgate, delighted that it had proved possible to revitalise an area so full of evocative memories for me, and made my way towards Edgeley, where there is a small shopping centre, close to the football ground. In 2013, it had been in better shape than the Market area, but now the reverse was the case – there were far more empty premises and growing signs of dilapidation. Come back, Mary Portas, we need you here!

I enjoyed my customary lunchtime pint in a friendly local pub and watched Olivier Giroud turn a 2-1 Chelsea deficit at Southampton into a 3-2 victory. Then on to Edgeley Park itself. I purchased a seat in the old main stand, now called the Danny Bergera Stand, after the much-revered Uruguayan manager, who was instrumental in lifting County from the bottom of the Third Division to the upper reaches of the Second Division in the early 1990s. I usually locate myself here: it's been in situ since 1906, when the ground was constructed, and is redolent of County's history, unlike the spacious stand at the south end of the ground, which was built in 1995, just in time for the club's promotion to the second tier of the League.

The *Stockport Express* informed us that the previous home game, against Tamworth, was manager Jim Gannon's 380th game in charge, beating the previous record held by someone called Fred Stewart in the pre-World War Two era. If you also consider Gannon's 505 appearances for Stockport as a player, between 1990 and 2000, this represents a degree of loyalty to one particular club that is most unusual, and something to be celebrated and cherished. I can't think of many other players who have put in such long-term stints as player and manager with the same club. Jimmy Armfield, perhaps? Or Kenny Dalglish?

The evidence of Jim Gannon's track record, both as player and manager, suggests that he is not the easiest of people to get on with. There have been altercations with other players (Mark Stein, of Luton Town), other managers (Paul Ince, when with MK Dons) and he has often parted company with clubs in acrimonious circumstances (he took Stockport to an employment tribunal, claiming unfair dismissal in 2000). He comes over as Mr Angry on the touchline: his strident tones and gestures of frustration are often in evidence. But they love him in Stockport, and its right that they should, after his years of devoted service to the club.

He has been manager on three separate occasions. The first period was wholly successful; he saved them from relegation to the Conference in 2006, and by 2008 had masterminded the club to a respectable position in League One. Unfortunately, Stockport went into administration at the end of the 2008–09 season, and his contract was terminated by the receivers as a cost-saving measure. He returned in 2011, when County were in the Conference and again saved them from relegation. Things did not go well the following season, and he was sacked in January 2013, when County were hovering perilously close to the relegation zone. I saw the first game in which his replacement, Darije Kalezić, was in charge, a 3-2 win against Nuneaton Town. This proved a false dawn, and Kalezić lasted a mere three months, to be replaced by the equally ineffective Ian Bogle (previously with Gateshead). County went on to suffer the indignity of relegation, and it has always been my contention (to anyone prepared to listen) that if they'd stuck with Jim, he'd have pulled them through.

The game kicked off in bright sunshine. Despite the fact that the match was of crucial importance to both teams, the atmosphere at Edgeley Park was strangely subdued during the early stages.

This was probably a reflection of the lack of action on the pitch. County dominated possession and tried to build up play from the back. The problem was that as soon as the moves progressed close to the Telford penalty area, they ran out of steam: the final pass would be misdirected or intercepted, or a promising individual run would be halted by a timely tackle. Telford were well organised in defence, and seemed content to soak up pressure, without initiating more than the odd counter-attack; it began to look as if they had come for a point. County's prolific strike force of Jason Oswell and Matty Warburton (forty League goals between them so far this season) were hardly in the game. I can't recall either side having a shot on target in the first half. What a contrast with the excellent game at Kidderminster the previous Tuesday, when two attack-minded sides carved out over thirty goalscoring opportunities between them. Maybe it was the unexpected warmth of the weather, or maybe it was Telford's defensive game plan, but it just wasn't happening out there on the pitch today.

At halftime, I noticed that in one corner of the ground, close to the railway, there was an area of the old terracing, unchanged and long unused. I was amazed how shallow the steps were. It would have been impossible for any child or short-of-stature adult to see anything, unless they were right at the front. I know that in the 1950s Edgeley Park had a capacity of 27,000, and with an average home crowd of around a third of this figure, there would have been some room for manoeuvre. But for the big games – like the FA Cup replay against Liverpool in 1965 – there were a lot of frustrated spectators (including me).

I was hoping that Mr Angry's halftime pep talk might transform County's approach in a way that might at least create a few real chances. But there was little evidence to this effect as the second half progressed. Indeed, Telford were coming into the game more, perhaps realising that one breakaway goal could be enough to win it. County were relying more and more on long balls punted upfield by defenders, or the keeper, in the general direction of the two strikers. It's always depressing when teams resort to such tactics, which rarely deliver the goods and certainly weren't doing so today. A couple of substitutions were made, including the introduction of speedy winger Darren Stephenson. Little changed. With twenty minutes remaining, I turned to my neighbour and said, 'This game has got 0-0 written all over it.' Unoriginal, I know, and as it turned out, wrong! Four minutes later, after the only flowing attacking movement County had managed in the whole match, a cross from Warburton found Darryl Stephenson in the area. He scuffed his first goal attempt, but then swivelled neatly and struck a close-range shot past the Telford keeper. Relief all round and strains of 'I O County, County I O' echoed round the stadium.

County managed to hold on for the final minutes, and secured an invaluable three points. It was probably the least entertaining game I'd seen all season, but at least there was a positive outcome. The attendance was 3,546, which says a lot for the level of support County still attract, even in the National League North, where attendances in the hundreds are by no means uncommon at the likes of Brackley, Leamington and Curzon Ashton. A play-off place now looked highly likely. But promotion? Probably not, on this showing.

LIVERPOOL

The greatest game Anna ever saw

Although I've never actually lived in Liverpool, I did work there between 1971 and 1976 at Liverpool Polytechnic. The Town Planning department was situated in a converted printing factory on Victoria Street, close to where traffic descended into the Birkenhead tunnel. It was an appalling building, too hot in summer, too cold in winter. I recently returned to Liverpool to see if I could locate our premises, and failed to do so. That's the problem when one returns to a city centre after forty years. So much has changed that you wonder if you've come to the right city. There's a fair chance our sub-standard premises had been demolished. The planning course was discontinued some time ago, and there was no case for retaining the building on architectural or any other grounds.

The staff who taught at Liverpool Poly when I was there could be divided into two camps. There were the hard-nosed old-timers who had gravitated from the College of Building when the planning course was established, and who taught courses dealing with bricks, mortar, sewerage and that kind of thing. And there were the bright young newcomers, like me, who dealt with the social science-based stuff – the social and economic aspects of planning and other such subject matter. The former believed in making things as hard as possible for students, to sort out the men/women from the boys/girls. The latter were concerned about the stress experienced by students and sought ways of reducing it.

Amongst our group, it was common practice to inform students, in advance, of the topics coming up in the exam papers, as a means of facilitating revision and reducing stress. But one colleague decided to go one stage further. He was so concerned about the stress levels of our students that he decided to reveal to them the actual exam questions. Most of the newcomers felt this was unnecessary, but if that was what he wanted to do, so be it. No one was going to find out, were they? And that would probably have been the case, if one of the students who had benefitted from the lecturer's generosity had not complained bitterly to the invigilator, who happened to be one of the old-timers, that one of the questions they'd been assured would be on the exam paper hadn't actually appeared! All hell broke loose, with the shock waves being felt throughout the Polytechnic. A Committee of Inquiry was set up, before which all the town planning lecturers were required to appear. Surprisingly, although many admonitions were dispensed, no heads rolled.

My nostalgic return to Liverpool proved full of interest. I went to have a look at the Royal Albert Dock, immaculately restored and home to one of the regional establishments of the Tate Gallery. Worryingly, three weeks before Christmas, the Dock was very quiet, while the Liverpool One area, the other side of the Strand, was bustling. The retail outlets around the Dock were uninspiring: Liverpool-themed souvenir shops, gift shops and coffee outlets predominated. But the dock buildings themselves are magnificent; an evocative reminder of what Liverpool docks used to be like before they were overtaken and made superfluous by containerisation in the mid-twentieth century. I moved on to Pierhead, where a few months before, I had (unwisely) been eating a sandwich on a bench, admiring the view over the Mersey, when a seagull swooped down and bit a chunk out of it. There is an impressive statue of the Beatles close to the Liver Building: the Fab Four, looking incredibly lifelike, all gazing over to Birkenhead.

But the highlight of my trip was a visit to Doctor Duncan's, a pub close to Lime Street station. Dr Duncan was a hero of his time. Appalled by the squalor of the living conditions in the poorer areas of the fast-growing city, where mortality rates were high even compared with those of other industrialising cities, he joined forces with Edwin Chadwick to promote a Parliamentary Bill (a costly and laborious task in the 1840s) to improve sanitary conditions in Liverpool. The Liverpool Sanitary Act (1846) made a huge difference to the life expectancy of working-class people in the city. Not only that, but Dr Duncan abandoned his remunerative private practice to become the first Public Health Officer of the city, on a relatively modest salary. He was known as 'Doctor to the Town', a well-merited title. The pub that pays tribute to him has an excellent collection of real ales and is well worth a visit.

By the time I started work in Liverpool, the Beatles had moved elsewhere and were on the point of breaking up, and the remaining exponents of the 'Liverpool Sound', such as Gerry and the Pacemakers and the Merseybeats, were nowhere near the same quality. I did pay one sweaty visit to the Cavern to see Millie Small, of *My Boy Lollipop* fame, but its glory days had long since passed, a claim which could certainly not be made of the Everyman Theatre. I was fortunate to be around at the height of its creative period. Under the inspired direction of Alan Dossor (whose sister I went out with for a time in Manchester in the 1960s), the Everyman was a showcase for the burgeoning talents of Pete Postlethwaite, Julie Walters and Bernhard Hill, amongst many others who would move on to national recognition. A highlight was Pete Postlethwaite's performance in the lead role of *Coriolanus*, but there were many others.

There was also one memorable rock concert, which has developed a legendary status almost equivalent to Bob Dylan's 1966 tour. Having warmed to the gentle country-inspired songs of 'Harvest' (as had millions of others) I made a point of attending Neil Young's concert in November 1973 at the Liverpool Empire.

The support band was the Eagles. who were just beginning to break into the big-time, and who gave a professional performance of songs from 'Desperado', their first album. Then, after an interval, the stage lights went on to reveal a scene portraying a sleazy downtown Miami Beach bar, dimly lit by naked light bulbs. The band – the Santa Monica Flyers – shuffled on to the stage, Neil Young muttered something inaudible, and Nils Lofgren's piano set in motion a rendition of a bleak song of drug overdose and death, *Tonight's the Night*. The full contents of the album of the same name (at the time unreleased and unknown to those present) were then performed, with little in the way of introduction, to a bemused and less than enthusiastic audience. Just before the interval, Neil Young announced in a world-weary voice that they would finish the set with 'a song you've all heard before'. Expectations were suddenly raised. Would it be *Heart of Gold*? *Cowgirl in the Sand*? *After the Goldrush*? It was none of these classics; instead, the band launched into a louder more raucous version of *Tonight's the Night*.

What became apparent a couple of years later, when the album was finally released, was that the stage set at the Empire, and indeed the whole performance, was an attempt to recreate the ambience of the tequila-fuelled sessions at which the tracks of *Tonight's the Night* were recorded in the aftermath of the recent deaths of guitarist Danny Whitten and roadie Bruce Berry, caused by heroin overdoses. It has come to be regarded as a classic album, despite (or maybe because of) the rough-and-ready ensemble playing, Neil Young's out-of-tune singing and the rawness of the emotion and despair that pervade it.

Later in the concert, Neil Young did play a few old favourites, though not *Heart of Gold*, which (to coin a phrase of the 1970s) 'wasn't where he was at', at the time. But over forty years later, my elder son Callum and I went to see him playing with Crazy Horse at the Liverpool Echo Arena, where he did perform it, and we and four thousand Merseysiders sang along with every word of it. A magic few minutes.

* * *

At the time I was working in Liverpool, slum clearance was proceeding at a similar pace to what it had been in Manchester, where I had worked in the late 1960s, and with the same unjustified certainty on the part of the council's planners, architects, public health inspectors and highways engineers that this was the right approach. They took no account of the affection that the inhabitants felt for the terraced working-class areas of the inner city, such as Scotland Road, with their rich overlapping kinship and friendship networks. A local folk duo, Jacqui and Bridie, characterised this sense of loss in one of their songs: 'Don't want to go to Kirkby, don't want to go to Speke, don't want to go from all I know in Back Buchanan Street'. The most voluble critic of the slum clearance process was an outspoken local sculptor and community activist, Arthur Dooley. He used to refer to 'dose effete sociologists', who were ruining his city. But most of his venom was directed at town planners. I can't recall what terminology he used to describe them, but it can't have been pleasant!

I gained first-hand experience of conditions in Liverpool's inner city, including the infamous Liverpool 8, an area of decaying former middle-class terraced housing full of lodging-houses and rented rooms, occupied by those who couldn't find or afford anything better. This came about through my involvement as a volunteer in a welfare rights organisation called CHECK. My job was to advocate on behalf of those whose poverty and sub-standard living conditions led them to seek financial help through what was then called the Supplementary Benefits system. This was a kind of 'last resort' safety net for those lacking any other source of income. You could apply for exceptional needs grants to cover one-off expenses for basic but unaffordable items such as cookers and beds, or clothing grants. But this usually involved appearing before a tribunal of three local worthies, which was understandably quite a frightening prospect for many of the applicants. I would visit them in their homes, assess their circumstances and entitlements, and then represent them at the tribunal concerned. Ideally, my involvement should not have been necessary, but sadly it was. My most satisfying 'success' was to facilitate the reconnection of the gas and electricity supply of a family with three young children, a couple of days before Christmas. What was interesting was that the distinction made between the 'deserving' and the 'undeserving' poor was as dominant in the mindsets of the authorities then as it is now. It wasn't difficult to figure out in which category tribunal members were placing those appearing before them, and the way in which these judgements influenced their decisions. I don't know if CHECK, or a similar organisation is still operating, but I very much hope that it is. It will certainly be greatly needed in the 2020s, at a time when the welfare benefits system is much harsher than it was in the early 1970s, and many more people are dependent on it.

Beyond work and music, there was, of course, the football. I'd visited both Anfield and Goodison Park in the 1960s before joining Liverpool Polytechnic in 1971. The most memorable visit to Anfield was a third-round FA Cup tie against Stockport County, then bottom of the Fourth Division, in 1965. Stockport took the lead early in the first half when veteran striker Len White (ex-Newcastle United) scored in a rare County attack. The visitors then fought a heroic rear-guard action, before conceding a late equaliser from Ian Callaghan. The replay was an anti-climax, with Liverpool strolling to a 2-0 victory. I was also present for that game but saw very little of it because of that frustrating shallow stepping on the Edgeley Park terraces (see previous chapter). The frustration would have mattered less, of course, if County had won!

At Goodison Park in 1966, I had witnessed another memorable cup-tie. Manchester City were on their way back to the First Division, after three lean years in the Second. They drew Everton in the quarter-finals and held them to a 0-0 draw at Maine Road. My friend John and I, who were living in Manchester at the time, travelled over to Liverpool for the replay, and just managed to squeeze into a packed Goodison Park before they closed the gates. Again, City held the mighty Everton to a goalless draw, and although they lost the second replay, they had demonstrated their ability to hold their own against the highest quality opposition. Everton went on to win the Cup.

During my time at Liverpool Polytechnic, I paid occasional visits to both venues, though more often to Anfield, where Liverpool were flourishing, towards the end of the Bill Shankly era. Everton were going through a relatively lean period at the time, although they did move back into the limelight in the early 1980s under Howard Kendall. But the visits to Anfield that I remember best were those with my eleven-year-old stepdaughter, Anna, who became a committed Liverpool supporter when we lived in Birmingham. I don't know where that came from – certainly not from me – but I was happy to take her to grounds in Birmingham when Liverpool were the visitors. In the summer of 1982, we moved to North Lancashire, and visits to Anfield became much more feasible. Anna was fortunate; the limited number of games we saw included two 6-0 wins – Luton Town and West Ham United were the teams on the end of these thrashings. But let her describe the West Ham game in the words of her diary entry of the time:

Six-nil, six-nil, six-nil!!! Best game I've ever seen. Got up early, went shopping and bought tangerines and choc-dips for our picnic ... we had our picnic in Stanley Park and then walked to Anfield. Five minutes after we sat down Rush scored the first goal. We were only eight rows up (in the Kemlyn Road Stand), so we were really near the pitch, and saw the first goal clearly. By halftime we were 4-0 up, two to Rush, one to Dalgleish and one to Neal. Wark, Liverpool's new player, was quite good, always in the right place at the right time. Second half Souness scored two, but I could hardly see them, as they were at the other end. Grobbelaar was ace; he waved and pulled faces at the crowd. I waved and gave him a thumbs-up sign, and he waved back ... I'm sure it was me, because he copied everything I did, but Catherine said it was the lads below us (Lottie said she's just jealous!). Poor old West Ham, they looked really miserable, Liverpool made them look really crummy, but they're not. I bought a mini-LFC kit and a photo of Grobbelaar at the souvenir shop, and we had toffee apples on the way back. It was a GREAT match.

Anna's diary entry really captures the delight young people experience in watching a football match. Her enthusiasm for Liverpool lasted around two years and included seeing Ian Rush score five goals in the 6-0 defeat of Luton Town. Then she discovered horses, rock music and (later) boys, and Liverpool FC faded into the background. But it was good while it lasted. Some years later, my attempts to interest my two sons, Callum and Fergus, in watching football were less successful. But maybe Stockport County and Morecambe were not the most promising subjects for engendering enthusiasm.

I enjoyed my return to Liverpool. I'd always found it a friendly city, a perception that was confirmed when a local, seeing me looking perplexedly at my map, stopped and volunteered advice, which proved most helpful in locating the entrance to the Birkenhead tunnel. The city has a justifiable reputation for vitality, mixed, perhaps, with a significant element of the maudlin. I am unlikely to be returning to Anfield or Goodison Park, but I have many positive memories of my visits there in the 1960s and '70s. And I like the fact that the city centre has retained a good deal more of its character (including its old buildings) than its high-flying competitor forty miles down the East Lancs Road. In Manchester, there are many more cranes to be seen and new buildings going up (worryingly, many of them luxury 'investment' apartments). Personally, I feel more comfortable with the slower pace of change in Liverpool.

PART II

HOPES AND DREAMS

LEYTON

The new Shoreditch or the old East End?

I've always found London an exhilarating city. When I was at Birmingham University in the early 1960s, I used to travel down for concerts and football. At that time, if you wanted to watch Arsenal, Spurs or Chelsea, you just turned up. All-ticket games were mainly limited to cup semi-finals, finals and internationals. The stadia of the big clubs were then regarded as capable of holding crowds of sixty-to-seventy thousand, the vast majority standing on the terraces. In extremis, they would just close the turnstiles. So, I would turn up at Highbury, White Hart Lane or Stamford Bridge, usually when Manchester City were the visitors, pay my three-and-sixpence and stand on the packed terraces – there was no segregation in those days.

On one occasion, travelling by bus from central London to White Hart Lane, I found myself sitting directly behind A.J. Ayer, professor of philosophy at Oxford University, who was something of a minor celebrity at the time, as a result of a good deal of exposure on TV. He was engaged in an animated conversation with his travelling companion. I listened with interest. What would I learn of the relative merits of Bertrand Russell and Ludwig Wittgenstein? The answer soon became apparent – nothing. They were more concerned with the relative merits of Jimmy Greaves and Derek Kevan, the burly West Bromwich Albion striker, who Spurs were facing that day. Which team would come out on top? The answer turned out to be Spurs, courtesy of two goals from Greaves, countered by one from Kevan.

In more recent times, I have limited my trips to London to visit friends or relatives, or to see the occasional play or concert. One visit was to see Bob Dylan at the Royal Albert Hall in 2016, when he sang a string of Sinatra-type 'standards', to the delight of many of the audience, but not me. There were no cries of 'Judas', as there had been at Manchester's Free Trade Hall fifty years before. I was tempted to shout, 'Sing *Desolation Row!*' (or *Masters of War*), but of course I didn't. You can't dictate to artists of that stature what they should or shouldn't sing.

I've now no desire to visit Highbury, White Hart Lane or wherever. But I have been happy to watch Leyton Orient from time to time, with my old friend Tony Hogg, who lives in Walthamstow with his wife, Anne. Tony is the sole remaining school-friend from my Manchester Grammar School days. He was with me in 3A and 4A, where we both suffered under the oppressive regime of our form-master Billy Hulme. Quite apart from the over-the-top level of physical punishment he meted out, he used personal ridicule, which is not good news for a group of sensitive and impressionable thirteen-year-olds. I remember him lambasting Tony for some minor misdemeanour in the following terms: 'What are you, Hogg? You're a little piggy, that's what you are.' Another class member was named Eddie Bray, who was prone to be likened to a donkey. It's a miracle that, at some stage, I wasn't referred to as 'Leach, you slimy little bloodsucker'! 'Mouldy warp' was another favourite insult, if the offending pupil's surname didn't lend itself to wordplay. Many years after Billy Hulme's death, there was a reference to him in the *Old Mancunian* magazine, along the lines of 'what a wonderful character this bloke was'. In the next issue, I was pleased to see a rejoinder portraying him as a tyrannical bully, which was indeed the reality.

Like me, Tony is more interested in football below Premier League and Championship levels. Leyton Orient is his local club, located within the borough of Walthamstow. He has been watching Orient for around thirty years but characterises himself as a 'fair-weather supporter'. This description intrigued me. The reality is that there has been very little 'fair weather' at Brisbane Road over this period, with most seasons spent in the third and fourth tiers of the League, with a couple in the National League. They have achieved two promotions (2006 and 2019) and suffered three relegations (1996, 2015 and 2017). It has been rare for them to finish in the top seven; indeed, in the ten years prior to their promotion to League One in 2006, their average finishing position in the Third Division/League Two was fifteenth. I asked him whether, when it became apparent (as it often did) that Orient were going nowhere that season, he stopped going to see them. 'Not at all,' was his reply. 'I tend to go in late summer and autumn and spring, when the weather is better, and not bother in winter when it's wet and cold.'

Orient enjoyed a brief purple patch in the 1960s, gaining promotion from the Second Division in 1962, to reach the top level for the first and only time in their history. They only lasted one season but had the pleasure of defeating West Ham United. Otherwise, the ups and downs between the lower divisions experienced over the years of Tony's support have been typical of their record since they joined the League in 1905 as Clapton Orient (the name-change to Leyton came in 1946).

Before Brisbane Road's makeover was completed in 2005, Tony used to stand on the North Terrace, which was populated (in his words) by 'the nuttier elements of Orient's fan base and assorted solitaries like me'. The North Terrace was indeed a bleak inhospitable place in winter, as I can confirm from a visit I'd made to it in the late 1960s. It was a perishing cold winter evening, and the cold must have numbed my memory, because, untypically, I can't remember who they were playing, or what the score was. I can well understand the 'fair weather' nature of Tony's support, which is anyway a more admirable definition of the term than the more typical 'I only go when they're doing well'. Barring the winter months, Tony has been there for Orient through thick (occasionally) and thin (predominantly).

I certainly wasn't prepared for the transformation when I returned to Brisbane Road with Tony in 2011. It had been totally rebuilt over a ten-year period (completed in 2007), following the acquisition of the club by boxing promoter Barry Hearn. Uniquely, blocks of flats had been erected in all four corners of the ground, which no doubt helped to finance the makeover of the stadium itself. From some of their upper stories, there was a partial view of the pitch: was that an amenity for which extra rent was charged? (Or possibly a reduction when Orient were relegated to the National League.) Only the old Main Stand had survived from the 1935 facilities; the three new stands were covered, all-seated, and (with the exception of the South Stand) close to the pitch, which resulted in a febrile atmosphere once the game got under way; there was a sense of connectedness between the spectators, the pitch and the action.

In the spring of 2011, Orient had been well placed in League One, having recently enjoyed an unbeaten run of fourteen League games. A play-off position was looking a distinct possibility. Earlier in the season, a seventeen-year-old loan signing from Spurs had been in the side, name of Harry Kane. His five goals in nine starts can be seen (with the benefit of hindsight) as a portent of things to come. I was there to see Orient take on Notts County, then struggling in the bottom half of the table and managed by Paul Ince, whom the home crowd clearly did not like (but maybe they felt the same about all visiting managers). There were two Orient players who particularly impressed me that afternoon: Charlie Daniels, on the left-side of the back four who proved a potent attacking force down the left flank; and Dean Cox, a midfielder short in stature, but possessing a creativity and vision uncommon at this level. The crowd shared my enthusiasm. 'We've got tiny Cox,' they chorused at regular intervals, no doubt well aware of the innuendo involved. Orient won 2-0 but were one point short of the play-offs at the end of the season.

Tiny Cox was still there three years later, when I saw them thrash Gillingham 5-1. His thunderous volley contributed to Orient's 4-0 halftime lead. Dozens of disgruntled Gillingham fans, chanting 'You're a load of rubbish' at their team (they were right) departed at this stage for an early train. By this time, Charlie Daniels had been signed by Bournemouth, for whom he has been a regular throughout their Premier League years.

Orient came very close to promotion to the Championship that season. They led 2-0 in the play-off final against Rotherham United, but their opponents managed to pull it back to 2-2 and went on to win the penalty shoot-out. I had developed an affection for Orient and their passionate supporters and had made a point of going to see them that season, whenever they came up north: a 1-1 draw at Preston (on the day after Tom Finney's death) and a 1-0 win at Carlisle.

After their agonising penalty shoot-out defeat by Rotherham, long-term owner Barry Hearn sold the club to an Italian businessman called Francesco Becchetti. Leyton Orient's spell as a successful League One club came to a sad end with relegation at the end of the next season (2014–15), in which four managerial changes took place. In 2015–16, they finished in a mid-table position, with a mere three changes of manager. But 2016–17 saw them finish in bottom place, ten points behind fellow strugglers Hartlepool United, having lost eighteen of their twenty-three home games. Five different managers were involved (making twelve in three years, a turnover which it's hard to believe any other League club has matched in recent years). The season also saw the resignation of honorary president and previous owner

Barry Hearn in protest at the way Beccchetti was running the club.

Orient's final game of that shambolic season was at Blackpool. On that day the Blackpool Supporters' Trust (BST) had organised a pre-match march through Blackpool to protest about the way the club's owners, the Oyston family, were running their club, and had invited fans from other clubs with a similar problem to join the march. There were a surprisingly large number of Orient supporters who had made the trip, given that by then relegation was a certainty, but I guess if it's your team's last game in the Football League, you would want to be present. Many of them joined the march, together with equally disenchanted contingents from Blackburn Rovers and Coventry City. After the protest, the Orient fans made their way to the visitors' paddock. The BST members made their way home, as a result of a decision to boycott Blackpool's home games taken at the start of the previous season.

What the Orient fans didn't know at the time was that the end of the Becchetti era was close at hand. In the summer of 2017, he sold the club to local businessman and long-term Orient fan, Nigel Travis. Becchetti's press release on departure was revealing: 'Over the past two years, I have unfortunately not been able to dedicate myself to following the club as closely as I would have wished.' The words of an absentee owner! Why, one wonders, did he buy it in the first place? During his time in charge, the club dropped two levels and, for the first time in their history, were out of the Football League. The terms 'impulse buy' and 'plaything' spring to mind. 'I know what I'll do, I'll buy a football club'. Impulse buys are not too much of a problem if you're talking about T-shirts or garlic presses, but are potentially disastrous in relation to football clubs. The legacy of bitterness amongst Orient's fan base regarding Becchetti's period of ownership is totally understandable and justified.

LEYTON ORIENT v EBBSFLEET UNITED
National League, Tuesday August 7th, 2018

On a hot and humid Tuesday evening, early in August, Tony and I set out to walk to Leyton for Orient's first home game of the season against Ebbsfleet United. It had been a long hot summer, with barely a vestige of green remaining on the scorched grass. We walked along Walthamstow High Street, always teeming with social activity, where the street market vendors were beginning to dismantle their stalls. Then along Hoe Street, a relatively down-market retail area, where several of the shopkeepers were sitting out in front of their shops in the sun. As in so much of inner London, there was a cosmopolitan feel to the area, both the shops and cafés and the people on the street – a kaleidoscope of races and eating options. To me, this is one of the delights of London, providing evidence of the ability of different ethnic groups to co-exist harmoniously in the same location. I know interracial tensions have erupted from time to time, but on a hot summer's evening, the diversity seemed totally unproblematic.

We then came to the shopping centre known locally, Tony told me, as 'The Bakers Arms', reflecting the former presence of a large pub with that name. Further along Leyton High Road, we passed the former headquarters of Essex County Cricket Club, who moved there in 1885. The ornate Victorian pavilion remains, and the pitch is still used (though it was a parched light brown in colour today), but County Cricket was last played here in 1977, when the club moved to Chelmsford. It was a sad sight, as the residues of former County Cricket (and, indeed, Football League) grounds often are. You could imagine W.G. Grace playing there (as he did), and Tennyson once wrote a poem in honour of the ground (not one of his better efforts, apparently), but those days are gone and we are left only with the pavilion to remind us of former glories.

National League football does not come cheap at Brisbane Road: £20 for adults, £18 if you're a senior citizen. I've paid half that at other Conference venues. We opted for the Main Stand, which was built in 1935, when the ground was constructed on a piece of wasteland. Orient were coming into this game with a creditable 1-1 draw at Salford City under their belts (Salford City – the club adopted by Messrs Neville (G), Neville (P), Scholes, Giggs and Butt – were widely tipped for promotion). Ebbsfleet, who had made it to the play-offs in 2017–18, had started the new season with a 1-0 defeat at home to relegated Chesterfield. There was a lively pre-match atmosphere, enhanced by a sizeable contingent of Ebbsfleet fans, situated to our left. Leyton is their nearest thing to a local derby. Someone dressed in an inflatable red animal costume pranced aimlessly around the pitch before kick-off. 'What's that supposed to be?' I asked Tony. 'It's a griffin,' he said. 'A pair of them feature on the club crest.' Possibly the most unusual mascot I've come across!

Ebbsfleet started the more impressively and tore through the Orient defence with their first attack, which led to an unmissable chance for Darren McQueen … that he proceeded to miss. They continued to dominate, with crisp interpassing movements that reminded me of my visit to Macclesfield Town earlier in the year. Every time the visitors' midfielder Ebou Adams had the ball, a crescendo of booing resounded round the stadium. Bewildered, I consulted the programme, and discovered that Ebou Adams was a 'former Canaries man who had joined Orient on loan last season, appearing in sixteen League games, becoming a fan favourite in the process'. It certainly didn't sound like it. Why had they taken against him? Further perusal of the programme provided the answer: Adams's contract with Norwich had expired in the summer, and he had opted for Ebbsfleet rather than Orient. Traitor!

Despite being outplayed, Orient took the lead in their first coherent attacking move of the evening. After some incisive inter-passing on the right, in which veteran Jobi McAnuff played a key role, the ball reached striker Macauley Bonne on the left, and his pass provided an opening for midfielder James Brophy, which he volleyed home with assurance. After that the game became more even, although Ebbsfleet created more chances than Orient. Both teams were playing attacking football, and Ebbsfleet's Sean Shields looked dangerous every time he had the ball, whilst Brophy was a dominant force in midfield for Orient, despite being clattered by opponents on a regular basis.

Halftime came with Orient having maintained their unde-served lead. Looking around at my fellow-spectators in the well-populated Main Stand, I noticed the preponderance of middle-aged or elderly white males. There was little sign of the numerous ethnic minorities who now live in the area, and very few women or youngsters (although there may well be more of the latter at Saturday fixtures). Had Brisbane Road become one of the last remaining strongholds of the white working class in Leyton, the glue which continued to bind them to the community where they live? I shared this insight with Tony, who felt it had a degree of credibility, but pointed out that several of the white males in our vicinity looked distinctly middle class, with their baggy khaki shorts and trimmed white/grey beards. Tony's interpretation of this phenomenon was, I thought, plausible. Since the 1960s, there has been a steady exodus into Essex by those whose jobs have enabled them to afford to do so. Many of them will have had an attachment to the football club when they lived here and may well have been predisposed to continue their support, travelling from their new locations in Chigwell, Epping or Harlow. Indeed, this pattern of moving out of the city but staying with the club you supported when you lived there is, I suspect, widespread. How many of the inner-city residents of Manchester and Liverpool could afford season tickets at the respective Premier League clubs?

In the excellent match programme (entitled *E10*), the Director of Football, Martin Ling, argues that Leyton is becoming a very different sort of place than it was a few years ago. Gentrification, he suggests, is on the way: 'I believe Leyton will become the new Shoreditch, and we can tap into that.' Shoreditch is an inner London area that has moved up-market in recent times; both as a retail/eating-out venue and a desirable residential location. If that process were already happening in Leyton, then that would provide an alternative explanation for the presence of the 'khaki shorts and trimmed beards' brigade, although I could see little evidence of gentrification on our journey to the ground. I do hope that Leyton doesn't become a new yuppie-fied Shoreditch. I like it the way it is.

The second half continued in the same vein as the first, with lots of open attacking play and chances being created by both sides. Orient's tended to result from set pieces, whilst Ebbsfleet's came from open play. The visitors' keeper, Nathan Ashmore, exuded confidence and competence and dealt effectively with everything that came his way. The atmosphere continued to be lively; the Orient fans are well known for their passion, and the visiting Ebbsfleet fans were also making their presence felt, aided by the sound of frequent thumps on a large drum. We found out the next day that the attendance had been 4,710, which is not bad for the National League. Many a League Two side would be over-joyed with a crowd of that size; it's around three times the average attendance of my nearest League club, Morecambe.

The pressure from the visitors intensified in the final ten min-utes. Just when it looked like they would be returning to Kent with nothing to show for their impressive performance, a breaka-way down the left and a well-directed cross led to Corey Whitely slotting a precise left-footed shot past keeper Dean Brill. It was the least that Ebbsfleet deserved. Had I been an Orient fan, I'd no doubt have been bemoaning the late sacrifice of two valuable points, but as a neutral, I was pleased to see justice being done. Tony was phlegmatic about the outcome – 'It often happens like this' – but that's his nature.

The long-awaited rain had arrived during the match, and there was a fresher feel about this part of east London as we made our way back to Walthamstow. More rain was forecast; maybe the former home of Essex County Cricket Club would get its green surface back by the end of the cricket season.

GATESHEAD

Worm sandwiches and world-class stag and hen parties

I lived in Gateshead for just over two years, between 1993 and 1995. Towards the end of 1992, my girlfriend of the time, Karen, became pregnant. She was living in Gateshead, working as a probation officer in Newcastle. I was living in Silverdale, close to Morecambe Bay, but commuting every week to Birmingham, where I then worked. Six weeks before the baby was due (July 1993) I moved up to Karen's house in Gateshead. The due date came and went. Karen and I paid numerous visits to the excellent Tyneside Film Theatre to pass the time, waiting for something to happen.

I had not expected to become a father at the advanced age of fifty. I'd raised two stepdaughters, to whom I remain very close, but the prospect of becoming a biological parent felt very different and incredibly exciting. We furnished the (as-yet-unborn) baby's room with a cot and mobiles suspended from the ceiling. I remember finding it hard to believe that there would soon be a real live baby in that cot, looking up at those dangling animal shapes.

Two weeks after the due date had passed, Karen was to be induced, which didn't sound like a particularly pleasant experience. I accompanied her, of course, and stayed with her throughout the ordeal. By 1993, that was expected of fathers-to-be. I was about to experience something my dad had never experienced. I would be by Karen's side the whole time, massaging her back when requested, and generally seeking to be supportive, sympathetic or encouraging, as circumstances demanded.

Induction having been administered, we both expected the

birth process to follow swiftly. It didn't. The midwife assured us that a delay was perfectly normal. The morning passed and then the afternoon and still no progress. When, at last, things did start to happen, the meticulously prepared birth plan went out of the window. I did my best to support, sympathise and encourage, but felt increasingly like a helpless spare part.

I found the whole process increasingly nerve-wracking, particularly in the later stages. Maybe my dad was fortunate in being ordered to remain in the waiting room to await the news of my birth in 1942. The baby - a boy- did finally arrive shortly after 10.00 p.m. to the great relief of both mother and father, who, I regret to report, couldn't steel himself to watch the actual birth.

Karen was sure that the baby would be a girl. We were going to call her either Esme or Florence. Little thought had been given to a boy's name, so sure was she that it would be a girl, but we'd tentatively agreed on Callum (having recently been impressed by the film *Cal*). When the midwife told us 'You've got your Callum', Karen's response was, 'Are you sure? Can you have another look?' But Callum it was, and the experience of holding this little swaddled creature in my arms was the most magical of my life, before or since. I'll never forget the feeling of emotional exhilaration – this is our baby! – which lasted for months afterwards, and in a sense is still there with me, twenty-six years after the event. The appearance of his brother, Fergus, seven years later invoked a similar sense of wonder (and I did watch his birth!). But the experience of the birth of your first child has a special quality that can never be replicated.

It's not surprising that, in these circumstances, Gateshead should have a special place in my affections. We enjoyed Callum's first two years in Karen's terraced house in the area known as the Avenues. Saltwell Park, a lovely mid-Victorian example of the genre, was five minutes pram-journey away and, in the summer months, was frequented by large Jewish families (Gateshead has a long tradition of Jewish settlement). Callum made his first and (to date) only TV appearance in 1993, starring as a two-week-old baby in an adaptation of Catherine Cookson's *The Dwelling Place*. He (or rather we) were paid £60 for his role, which we passed on to him many years later. His name was unaccountably omitted from the credits, but the production is still available on DVD.

Gateshead has long been seen as Newcastle's poor relation, like Salford to Manchester, or Birkenhead to Liverpool. But this stereotype has had to be revised in recent years. An enterprising Labour council has managed to facilitate the location of Tyneside's new state-of-the-art concert hall – the Sage – south of the River Tyne, within the borough's boundaries. It has similarly established a new arts centre in a disused flour mill – the Baltic – close to the Sage. And in the south of the borough, there is the iconic Angel of the North statue, welcoming visitors from the south to Tyneside. Newcastle must be agonising over missed opportunities!

In my brief period of living in Gateshead, I watched a mind-numbingly boring 0-0 draw with Telford United in 1993, which discouraged me from further visits to the sterile atmosphere of the International Stadium. I returned in 2012, for one of my *Conference Season* visits, to witness a rather more eventful 2-2 draw with Macclesfield Town. Since then, there has been a good deal of talk of a move away from the International Stadium to a new purpose-built stadium, which might have come to something, had Gateshead made it back to the Football League in 2014, after a fifty-four-year absence. But having reached the play-off final at Wembley, they lost to Cambridge United. In the following seasons, they resumed their familiar mid-table status, strutting their stuff in front of six hundred or so diehards, to the sound of plaintive cries of 'Heed, Heed'.

Having been unceremoniously dumped out of the League in

1960 to make way for Peterborough United, Gateshead struggled for the next fifty years, changing their name twice after going out of existence in 1973 and 1977, only to be resurrected on each occasion (a double Phoenix club!). But after gaining promotion to the Conference in 2009, they became one of its longest-serving members.

I drove across the Pennines to Darlington and caught a train to Newcastle, where my friend John Davies had agreed to accompany me (without much enthusiasm, I suspect) to the fixture at the International Stadium: Gateshead versus Leyton Orient. As the train neared Newcastle Central, I was able to take a nostalgic glance at a series of parallel streets of Gateshead terraced housing, climbing the hillside to the east, at the top of which could be seen first of the Avenues (our house was in Windsor Avenue, the next one up). When we took Callum, then aged four, to see the house in which he had spent his first two years, he took one look at it and said, 'Can we go home now, please?' But it had a lot of positive memories for Karen and me.

John is my oldest friend. Our families lived on opposite sides of the local tennis club, and our mothers used to walk to the local shopping centre together, wheeling John and me in our respective prams. We both developed an attachment to Manchester City in the early 1950s, despite the lure of their more fashionable and successful neighbours at Old Trafford. A few years later, when both our families had moved to Stockport, we developed a similar attachment to Stockport County. In the early 1960s, we began to attend away matches together, many of which are etched in my memory: Stockport County at Peel Park (Accrington), the season before Stanley were kicked out of the League; at Valley Parade (Bradford City), where we stood on the vast open terrace on the north side of the ground; at Spotland (Rochdale), for a battle between relegation candidates (Stockport won, but they both went down); and at Haig Avenue (Southport), for an FA Cup third-round tie. In the season City won promotion to the First Division (1966), there were trips to Derby, Stoke, Bolton and Rotherham (the game where promotion was secured). One of the additional advantages of these excursions that we became acquainted with swathes of urban England (mainly in the north), which would otherwise have remained names on maps.

It's a minor miracle that my friendship with John survived our childhood years, given a traumatic episode, close to home, when we would have been nine or ten. The sequence of events remains vivid in my memory, over sixty years after their occurrence. What happened was this. By that time, I had developed an antipathy to worms – horrid, slimy little creatures – and this was well known amongst my closest associates. One summer's day, when the Leach and Davies children were scuttling between the two houses along the path through the tennis club, John approached me, an ingra-tiating smile on his face. 'I thought you might be hungry, Steve,' he said disarmingly, 'so I've brought you this sandwich.' 'Thanks, John, that's really kind of you,' was my response. I was just about to bite into it, when I thought I'd better check its contents. It was just as well I did, because squirming between the two slices of bread were two plump, glutinous worms. I threw the sandwich to the ground and ran, screaming, home to Mum. But I guess I must have been blessed with a spirit of forgiveness untypical of my years, because after a brief intermission, we resumed our friendship.

John and I had lunch in the Central Bar, which can be found once you emerge from the High Level Bridge into Gateshead. It is a beautifully restored piece of Victorian station architecture, no longer attached to a station (Gateshead Station was demolished many years ago) but having mercifully survived the disappear-ance of its raison d'être. The building is three stories high, built of substantial blocks of off-white stone and in the shape of a narrow oblong, with a modicum of convex curvature at its sides. Impressive as the external structure is, the building's exceptional qualities are to be found inside: the bars have retained an authentic mid-Victorian ethos. We imagined ourselves back a hundred and fifty years ago, observing bewhiskered Victorian entrepreneurs, waiting for their train out to Hexham, and enjoying a glass of best bitter, after a hard day exploiting the workers.

From the Bar's southern entrance, you can look up and see Gateshead's new town centre, which appears to be laid out on a pedestal, overlooking the Tyne. It really is almost wholly new, replacing the bulk of the old run-down centre, where Karen and I used to do our weekly shop at Tesco. The development, known as Trinity Square, didn't strike me as being particularly distinctive in design, and the shops within it were the usual fare. But I suppose it was an improvement on what it had replaced.

In *Conference Season*, I characterised Gateshead's High Street as 'surely the most down-at-heel, wretched, falling-to-pieces of any High Street in the land'. It was still there – just – but in a worse state than ever, with many of its shops closed and shuttered (at two o'clock on a Saturday afternoon). It can't be long before the demolition gang arrives, although the outcome may well be a derelict flattened site that no one can find a use for.

GATESHEAD v LEYTON ORIENT
National League, Saturday August 18th, 2018

John and I walked the mile or so from the town centre to the much-maligned International Stadium. For all I know, it's perfectly satisfactory as an athletics venue (which is what it was designed for), but it's not as the home ground of a National League side whose average attendance is around six-seven hundred. The pitch is too big, there is too large a space between it and the stands (a four-lane athletics track separates the two), and the fact that at least nine tenths of the available seats are unoccupied results in a profound lack of atmosphere, accentuated by the fact that all the home fans are in the Main Stand, well away from the action on the pitch.

There had been two minor changes since I was last there in 2012. A roof had been erected on the large stand opposite the Main Stand, which at least diluted the visual monotony of all those empty seats. But, more importantly, instead of being placed at one end of the Main Stand, visiting supporters were now directed to the newly roofed stand opposite. So at least home supporters have something across the pitch to look (and shout abuse) at. This change certainly generated an improvement in the atmosphere today, with over two hundred Orient fans making the long journey from East London.

Both teams had made reasonably good starts to the season. Gateshead had won their first three games, including one against the much-fancied Salford City, but had suffered their first defeat of the season at Bromley the previous Saturday. Leyton Orient were still unbeaten, although four of their six games had ended in draws, including the entertaining 1-1 draw against Ebbsfleet United I had witnessed (see previous chapter). Their squad was dominated by players who had been there the previous season, which is often not the case at this level, where it is not unusual for there to be a large turnover of players in the close season. Of the nineteen players in the Gateshead squad, fourteen were newcomers, a couple had played a handful of games at the end of last season, and only three had been with the club throughout 2017–18. There were two familiar names: Steve Rigg, a striker, who had a couple of relatively unproductive seasons with Carlisle United a few years ago; and J.J. O'Donnell, who I remember seeing in 2012 with Luton Town, then in the Conference, who was described in the Hyde programme for Luton's visit as a 'talented youngster'. Now, rather older and perhaps not having fulfilled his early promise, he'd ended up with Gateshead.

Throughout the first half, there was a marked difference in class between the two sides. Orient dominated the game, with some crisp passing movements indicative of a team that had been playing together for a while. Gateshead proved manifestly incapable of matching this fluency, indicative of a team that hadn't. In his programme notes, manager Steve Watson claimed that 'the lads know the system like the back of their hands, and they've proved that so far this season'. System? What system? Gateshead were reasonably tight at the back, but as an attacking force, 'the system' appeared to involve hoofing the ball into open spaces that Orient defenders invariably reached first or watched as the ball bounced into touch. Orient's midfielder Craig Clay had a golden opportunity when a clever dummy from Macauley Bonne, following Jobi McAnuff's cross, left him free in front of goal. He volleyed the ball high over the bar. But he nearly made amends a few minutes later when his goal-bound angled shot beat the keeper but was hooked over the bar by defender John Mellish. Orient deserved to be at least two goals up by halftime but went in on level terms.

It is interesting to speculate on what managers say at halftime, particularly when whatever it is that they've said turns out to make a big difference. Gateshead were a transformed side in the second half, playing with much more purpose and creativity and beginning to carve out chances in a way that they had failed to do before the break. The game changed from a one-sided affair to an even contest, with both sides creating scoring opportunities. An instinctive point-blank save from the visitor's keeper, Dean Brill, prevented Gateshead taking the lead. But not for long. Middlesbrough loanee Luke Armstrong (who'd already scored four goals in the opening games) latched on to Tom White's immaculate through ball, found a way past Marvin Ekpiteta's challenge, and placed the ball firmly past Dean Brill.

The Non-League Paper claimed that Ekpiteta had been responsible for Gateshead's goal, but we didn't think that was true – he had simply come off worse in a 50/50 challenge with Luke Armstrong. The real culprit (in our view) was Orient's captain, Jobi McAnuff, now in the twilight of his career after spells with Watford, Reading and several other clubs. At the other end of the field, he had been tackled as he prepared to cross the ball, raised his arms in an appeal to the referee that he had been fouled, and failed to chase back to tackle the defender who had legitimately dispossessed him, leaving him free to surge upfield and initiative the move that led to the goal.

Worse was to follow for the visitors. Shortly before Gateshead's goal, they had brought on a striker, James Alabi, for a midfielder, James Dayton, in an attempt to bring about that elusive winning goal. Shortly after, Alabi was deservedly sent off for a reckless tackle on Robert Tinkler, in full view of the home team bench, the fourth official and the most vociferous group of Gateshead supporters in the Main Stand. Was there any way back for Orient? As it happened, there was. A minute before the end of normal time, a corner from the left was not cleared and the ball fell to Marvin Ekpiteta, who smashed the ball home from an acute angle.

Orient held on without much trouble to secure the draw, which was the least their overall performance deserved. As a neutral, I was delighted that justice had been done, just as I had been when Ebbsfleet had managed a late equaliser at Brisbane Road a couple of weeks earlier.

We made our way back to Newcastle Central station by a different route, through an area of urban no-man's land. John drew my attention to a windowless building, which looked like a small storage depot and had the unlikely title 'Last Night of Freedom'. Was this a place where illegal immigrants were brought, before being deported? It wasn't, of course. It was a venue for stag weekends and hen nights – why go to Blackpool when you can come to a nondescript industrial estate on the edge of Gateshead? But business was good, or so its website claimed: 'We have been planning world-class stag-and-hen dos since 1999, and we now have 25,000 successful weekends under our belts.' So, in addition to a world-class concert hall (the Sage) and a world-class statue (the Angel of the North), Gateshead can also boast of a world-class stag and hen parties venue!

FYLDE

There'll be dancing in the streets of Kirkham and Wesham

In the Leach family album, there's a photograph of my mother, Margaret Mary, then only four or five months old, cradled in the arms of her mother, Isabella Newland, who is seated. It is early 1911. Next to Isabella stands her husband, William. In front of him stand Margaret Mary's sisters, Winifred (aged nine) and Phyllis (aged five). Everyone is looking stern, not to say uncomfortable, apart from Phyllis, in whose eyes there is a distinct twinkle. She is a beautiful little girl.

It is a typical example of the posed family photographs of that era, a time before the requirement to smile (or at least look cheerful) came in. There were no further additions to the family, no doubt to the disappointment of my grandfather William, who would most likely have been hoping for a son and heir.

With one exception, the only relatives we saw during my childhood were those on my mother's side. Dad had broken away from the Catholic Church in his early twenties, and this caused a major rift in the Leach family. I never met my paternal grandparents, nor Dad's sister, Mary, until she and Dad were eventually reconciled in the 1970s. There was an occasional childhood visit to Dad's half-sister, Margaret, in her gloomy house on Wilbraham Road in Chorlton-cum-Hardy, Manchester, but these visits soon petered out. It was over sixty-five years later that I met my long-lost cousin Ursula, by then eighty-eight, and discovered that we were soulmates, sharing a love of classical music (which I'd inherited from Dad) and literature.

The lovely Phyllis found herself pregnant at the age of seventeen, and, in line with the middle-class mores of the time, was expected to marry the father, Ambrose Taylor, a lower-rank civil servant, which she dutifully did. Uncle Ambi (as we knew him) was of Italian descent; his grandfather had walked all the way from Italy to Manchester to find work in the mid-nineteenth century, ending up in Ancoats, one of the less salubrious inner Manchester areas, where he prospered in the ice-cream business.

Their marriage survived until Phyllis died, although by all accounts it had its rocky moments, and their life together was beset with tragedy. Their daughter Shirley, whose birth followed shortly after their marriage, died at home at the age of four, when her nightdress caught fire in their living room. A second child was stillborn. Their other children, Pam and Max, did survive to adulthood, but Max was killed in a car crash in his mid-twenties. I well remember overhearing the tearful phone-call when Phyllis told Mum the bad news.

But this series of tragedies, which would have left many bitter and resentful, did not have this effect on Phyllis. Her positive, life-affirming spirit carried her through. She was my favourite auntie and was always affectionate with me, listening with apparent interest to whatever I had to say (which I suspect in many cases wasn't particularly interesting).

When I was a young child, Auntie Phyllis and Uncle Ambi lived not far away in Whalley Range, but, by the time I started at Manchester Grammar School, they had moved to Lytham, on the Fylde coast, to be near their daughter, Pam. Auntie Pam (as we called her, although technically she was a cousin) had married Jack Pemberton towards the end of World War Two. Uncle Jack was a well-off director of a Manchester-based publishing company called World Distributors Ltd, a title which I suspect gave a somewhat unrealistic impression of the scope of their business. I know they published Roy Rogers annuals (featuring his trusty steed, Trigger), because I often received one as a Christmas present. Dad intimated that some of their other publishing ventures were of a less wholesome nature; the equivalent of *Spick* and *Span* perhaps, which were furtively circulated behind the Scout huts at school from time to time.

Auntie Phyl was a heavy smoker (as was my mother) and contracted lung cancer in her fifties (my mother miraculously never did and survived to the ripe old age of eighty-eight). We saw her at our home in West Didsbury on her visits from Lytham to nearby Christie Hospital, which specialised in cancer treatment (and still does); in her case it could only delay the inevitable. 'She's going to Christie's' was a term of dread then, and no doubt still is.

Auntie Pam and Uncle Jack had set up house after their marriage in Fairhaven, which is midway between Lytham and St Annes-on-Sea and our family made periodic visits there. When Auntie Phyl and Uncle Ambi moved to Lytham, our visits increased in frequency. As its residents are only too ready to stress, these places are not Blackpool, which is six miles to the north and very different. This is the Fylde coast we are talking about, home to those who make their money in Blackpool (or in a few cases, including Uncle Jack, Manchester), but don't choose to live there. So, in a sense, my connection is not with Blackpool itself, but with the small towns to the south of it. But on our visits, there was often a trip from Lytham or St Annes to their gaudier, brasher neighbour to the north.

Auntie Pam inherited her mother's vivacity, but her life was beset with tragedy, too. Three of her five children died before their time. Uncle Jack developed circulatory problems (possibly as a result of his lavish lifestyle with frequent entertaining of business clients at Manchester's prestigious Midland hotel) and had both legs amputated before his system totally collapsed. But Pam retained her warmth and life spirit until she passed away in her late seventies. The year before Pam died, we visited her in St Annes-on-Sea, when Callum was ten and Fergus three. We had lunch at the beach café and rode on the little train with open carriages that operated nearby. She was lovely with the boys; it's a memory I treasure.

My memories of childhood are full of images of Lytham and St Annes: the windmill on Lytham Green, overlooking the sea; the white marble church at Ansdell, near where Pam and Jack lived; being dispatched to Auntie Phyl's to convalesce from one of the many diseases I contracted in childhood (whooping cough, as I recall); walking with my parents and my best friend John along a slippery jetty at Lytham, from which John fell into the sea and disappeared completely, before my dad managed to locate him and dragged him to the surface and safety; and staying with John at Auntie Pam's the night we went to see Manchester City play a cup-tie replay against Blackpool at Bloomfield Road in the 1960s (City lost 1-0).

I returned recently to explore the area. St Annes-on-Sea had a distinct air of prosperity about it. Judging from the number of wheelchairs, mobility scooters and stick-aided walkers, it has a predominantly elderly population, but that is true of many erstwhile seaside resorts. I made my way to the attractive pier, built in late Victorian times when the town was planned and developed as a seaside resort by a local businessman, Elijah Hargreaves. The 'pier experience' is marred by a large and noisy amusement arcade, which confronts you on entrance, but as soon as you get past that, there is much to admire: plenty of ornate wrought iron decorations and a view out to sea at the pier's end. At the time of my visit, the sea was a long way out, beyond a vast expanse of golden sand.

Lytham, two or three miles to the south, which describes itself as 'leafy Lytham' is an older settlement, with a degree of civic gravitas lacking in St Annes-on-Sea. The town also benefitted from the attention of a local Victorian landowner, John Talbot Clifton, who saw potential in transforming it from a small fishing village into an up-market seaside resort. Following his success in doing so, the opulent (in its day) Clifton Arms Hotel was built, together with the imposing Assembly Rooms and several other monuments to the town's growing status. The town lacks the golden sands of its close neighbour, but there is some compensation in the spacious green area that separates the sea front from the row of west-facing mansions adjacent to the town centre, on the edge of which is the recently restored Lytham Windmill. The town's impressive railway station has been preserved as a pub/restaurant; its grandeur contrasts with the neglected adjoining single-track line, on which you catch a train to Blackpool South or Preston, if you're lucky. After waiting twenty minutes for a train to Preston, I was called to the station frontage to board a bus, replacing a cancelled train, neither of which had been pre-announced.

The indeterminate status of Lytham St Annes – economically closely linked to and dependent on Blackpool, but physically separate from it and socially, a very different kind of place – presented me with a dilemma. Given that my personal affiliation is with Lytham St Annes, should my associated football visit be to Bloomfield Road, where Blackpool FC play? Or should it be to AFC Fylde's new stadium in Kirkham, which is within the boundaries of Fylde District Council, but ten miles to the east of Lytham?

Whereas most football clubs are rooted in an historic local community, AFC Fylde is an anomaly. It sprung from nowhere – a few seasons ago it was playing against the likes of Kendal Town before 150 spectators (on a good day) in a makeshift stadium surrounded by fields near the village of Warton, in the fourth tier of the non-league pyramid. In the 2016–17 season, I located this venue (with some difficulty) to watch them play Stockport County in what turned out to be an uninspiring goalless draw. By this time Fylde had moved up to level two of the pyramid, on the back of the generous financial resources injected by local businessman David

Haythornthwaite. The following season they made it to the National League, where they reached the play-offs, whilst Stockport, with no rich businessman to bankroll them, continued to languish in the National League North. Is there no justice?

Fylde as an area (Blackpool excluded) contains a dispersed pattern of small towns and villages with lots of open country-side separating them. The club did have some connection with Kirkham (and Wesham), where its owner chose to build the new stadium in 2015: indeed, that was what the club was called when David Haythornthwaite purchased it in 1998. He retitled it AFC Fylde as late as 2008. Although around a thousand spectators now turn up for the home games, in no sense can the club be rooted in the hearts and minds of Fylde's residents.

My hope was that at some point during the first few months of the 2018–19 season, Blackpool FC would escape from the clutches of the Oyston family. If this happy event occurred, I would travel with my friend Phil Hartley to be present at the first game following the takeover. It wouldn't matter who was involved in the change, the Blackpool Supporters' Trust (of which Phil is a member) would be out in force – all 2,000 of them – together with many others, to celebrate the disappearance from the scene of the hated Oyston. At that point in time, three thousand Blackpool supporters, at most, would turn up for home games, a deri-sory turn-out for a town of that size and football tradition (the Supporters' Trust has been boycotting home games since 2015). I could see little point in going along in those circumstances, where it was not unusual for opposition supporters to outnumber home fans. So, if there were no change of ownership as 2018 drew to a close, I would have to settle for AFC Fylde, which at least pro-vides a closer connection with where Auntie Phyllis, Uncle Ambi, Cousin Pam, *et al*, lived.

My recent friendship with Phil Hartley came about as a result of one of those amazing coincidences that life sometimes throws at you. When I returned to Birmingham University in 1977 to do an MA in public policy, I was in an unhappy state of mind and found it very difficult to settle. I didn't feel any affinity with the other members of my course, with one exception, a fellow exile from the Northwest (Whaley Bridge in Derbyshire). He helped to keep me sane during the first few weeks, but then decided that it wasn't the right course for him and departed for an alternative elsewhere. After his departure, my depression and feelings of insecurity increased, and I very nearly gave up on it. But I gritted my teeth, persevered and obtained the degree that was the passport to my subsequent academic career.

Fast forward thirty-eight years to 2015. My elder son, Callum, had a summer job as a car-park attendant at the Lake District National Park Centre at Brockholes, near Ambleside. I arrived there to give him a lift home and he asked if I could take back one of his fellow-workers, Tom, who also lived in Kendal. 'Of course,' was my reply. During the ensuing conversation, it emerged that I was writing a book about Blackpool FC. 'That's interesting,' said Tom, 'my dad's supported Blackpool since he was a lad. He's got a season ticket, but he doesn't use it any more, in protest at the Oystons. Perhaps he'd lend it to you.' We agreed that, even if he wouldn't, it would be useful for me to talk to him about the club. A meeting was duly arranged.

Phil proved most helpful in sharing his history of support for Blackpool, and his views on their current plight (and he did loan me his season ticket). Our third meeting was in a Kendal pub, where we began to chat about our own personal histories. I talked about my time at Birmingham University. He mentioned that, in his late teens, his family had gone to live in Whaley Bridge and that he'd studied at Birmingham. Suddenly, light-bulbs began to flash: it was an emotional moment for both of us, and a most unlikely reunion. What were the chances of us ever meeting again? But I'm delighted we did.

AFC FYLDE v GATESHEAD
National League, Tuesday October 30th, 2018

As we got towards the end of 2018, the Oystons were still in control at Blackpool. So, AFC Fylde it had to be. I made my way to Wesham, on a cold autumn evening, to watch them take on Gateshead. Both clubs were enjoying good runs and were respectively sixth and seventh in the National League table. Gateshead had won four games in succession, without conceding a goal. Fylde were unbeaten in the League for six matches, having conceded one. No expectations of a goal feast at Mill Farm stadium tonight, then! (Although Fylde had scored six at Maidenhead the previous Saturday.)

You can see the lights of the stadium from the M65, as you approach the turn-off to Kirkham. David Haythornthwaite, the club's millionaire owner, pays for the stadium always to be lit up at night, with the aim of heightening the club's profile and visibility. It is an impressive venue, dominated by an attractive and substantial main stand with a convex roof. Opposite is a smaller standing terrace, also with a convex roof, and at one end a similar structure reserved for away supporters. The other end is totally un-elevated, acting solely as a transit to the adjacent standing terrace, a phenomenon that evokes comparisons with Aldershot's Recreation Ground and Oxford United's Kassam Stadium. This is not conducive to a good atmosphere – it's hard to ignore the fact that there's a spectator vacuum behind one of the goals.

As the two teams warmed up on the pitch ten minutes prior to kick-off, the referee and the two linespersons (one female, I was pleased to see) did likewise, with some synchronised stretching exercises and gentle collective runs to and fro across the pitch.

I'd seen exactly the same ritual at other National League matches this season. It struck me as strange; were all officials issued with a proforma at the start of the season? You have to do a warm-up, and this is the specified sequence. Ignore it at your peril! It all seemed a tad farcical to me. Previously, the officials used to be first seen when the teams emerged from the tunnel, five minutes before kick-off, and rarely had any problems keeping up with the ebb and flow of the play. But maybe I need to shake off my traditionalist preconceptions.

There was plenty of ebb and flow when the game got underway. You could see why both sides had conceded so few goals recently: two strong, well-organised defences, with tall centre-backs who coped with anything that came near them in the air. It was one of those games where there was very little space in midfield; anyone receiving a pass was immediately hassled by one or more opponents. Despite this, both sides managed to create chances, typically from well-worked passing movements rather than high balls into the area. The overall quality of play was impressive.

One of Fylde's strikers was local legend Danny Rowe, whose goalscoring record since joining Fylde four seasons previously had been phenomenal, averaging around thirty goals a season, with ten already in 2018–19. He can appear ponderous, and he doesn't win much in the air, but he possesses a thunderous shot. So, it was a worry for the home supporters when, shortly before halftime, he collapsed on the pitch clutching his right thigh. Fortunately, the magic sponge (aided by a few sprays from an aerosol can) achieved the usual positive outcome.

Halftime came with no goals, but plenty to admire. Both sides were operating as coherent, well-drilled units, striving to play creative attacking football, rather than the long ball game not uncommon at this level. Fylde's supporters, wherever they had travelled from, were strangely quiet, but maybe that's inevitable for a club with so little in the way of a history or tradition. The two winners of the halftime draw both came from Lytham, which (with St Annes-on-Sea) is where the bulk of Fylde's population is located. I learned later that the club puts on free buses from Lytham for every game. Maybe the link with the home territory of my relatives was stronger than I'd thought.

The second half proved similar to the first; evenly matched, not many chances created (the two resolute defences saw to that), but plenty of good approach play. Amongst the players who caught the eye were Nick Haughton and Zaine Francis-Angol of Fylde, and Scott Barrow, Gateshead's captain. Both sides had opportunities to break the deadlock; it had long been clear that a single goal would win this match. But as the three minutes of injury time commenced, neither had done so, and a 0-0 draw, albeit one of the better ones, seemed a certainty. On this assumption, I left the ground with one minute of added time remaining. A big mistake! As I reached the nearby car park, there was a roar from the crowd that strongly suggested a goal; nothing too ecstatic (this is Fylde we're talking about) but one that years of experience of interpreting different crowd noises had 'goal' written all over it. And this proved to be the case. In the dying seconds, Francis-Angol had once again sped down the left flank and crossed into a crowded goal mouth, where Danny Rowe (who else?) had poked the ball home from close range. The moral? Don't leave before the end of a match when the scores are level, or if there's only one goal in it. But at least I hadn't missed one of Danny's trademark thunderbolts.

I felt sorry for Gateshead, who I felt had done enough to earn a draw. It would be a long journey back for the forty or so supporters who had crossed the Pennines on a cold October evening and provided support at a decibel level that belied their limited numbers. Meanwhile, AFC Fylde would be preparing for next Saturday's visit of league leaders Leyton Orient with enhanced confidence.

NORTHAMPTON

Sixty miles by road or rail to Northampton

I didn't really get to know Northampton until Callum gained a university place there in 2011. I wasn't even aware there was a university in Northampton, but what place of any size doesn't have one nowadays? And at least people will know where it is, unlike De Montfort University, where I ended my academic career.

Like many young people, Callum wasn't clear what he wanted to study at university. It would have been better (with the benefit of hindsight) if he'd taken a gap year. But 2011–12 was the last year when university fees were pitched at £3,000, before rising to a maximum of £9,000 the following year. We felt under a lot of pressure to get Callum established at university – somewhere, anywhere – before this tripling of the fees. So, he started on a computer studies course, switched after a year to media studies, before deciding that wasn't for him either. I was sympathetic and supportive; after all, I had also switched from chemistry to social science at Birmingham University. Nor could his mother really complain: after finishing school, she had not persevered with courses in teacher training and fine arts.

Even though there was no tangible outcome in terms of a qualification, Callum's two years in Northampton were by no means wasted time: he shared student houses, made several good friends, and matured as a person, a process invariably facilitated by living away from home.

I'd previously visited Northampton on a couple of occasions to do work for the local council. There is an impressive town hall, in the middle of a rather less impressive town centre: one long main street, full of all the usual suspects, with a slightly more interesting market square at one end. My impression was that the centre had failed to keep pace with the rapid growth of the town itself, which resulted from Northampton's designation as a new town in the 1960s and involved a substantial intake of overspill from London. The population more than doubled over a fifty-year period, transforming it from a medium-sized market town into a city-sized settlement.

Northampton Borough Council has also made several bids to extricate itself from the county council and become a 'unitary authority', which means taking over responsibility for education (or what little responsibility for it remains at local level) and social services, including the fast-expanding and grossly underfunded need for social care for the elderly. You wonder why they would want to take on these services, given the fact that austerity is highly likely to continue for the foreseeable future. However, this aim too is now unachievable. Northamptonshire County Council was the first local authority to go bust, towards the end of 2017. There are likely to be several more. The government's bizarre 'solution' has been to abolish the county council and the seven district councils within the county, including Northampton itself. At the time of writing, the town is due to become part of a new West Northamptonshire unitary authority, unwillingly conjoined with Daventry, Towcester, Brackley and vast swathes of the rural East Midlands. How this change is supposed to remedy the financial position the county is in is by no means clear; but the outcome is that there will be yet another real place – the town of Northampton – without a council to represent it. It is important that towns and cities which have strong local identities (as most of them do – as illustrated by the support for the local football team) are run by councils rooted in the town or city concerned. That interrelationship is good for local democracy: local people are more likely to become involved in civic issues if the council covers 'their town' (or city). So, given what's happened in Northamptonshire … Liverpool, Newcastle and Birmingham Councils had better watch out. If there is a financial crisis, it could be your turn to be abolished next!

Even more bizarre was the attempt made in 1980 by the Northampton New Town Development Corporation to encourage firms to relocate to the town by commissioning and issuing a pop record entitled *Energy in Northampton*. Singer Linda Jardim tells the story of a group of aliens, circling above middle England, who descend on the town and settle there because it had 'the energy and technology for which we have been searching'. It was a town where they 'knew they could be free'. The B-side, *Sixty miles by road or rail to Northampton*, contains the memorable (if unbelievable) line 'I just can't wait to be in Northampton'. I tried to envisage a Toyota executive playing the record, and thinking, 'Yes, that's the place for us', but it proved beyond the scope of my imagination. This historical curiosity can be accessed on YouTube.

Northampton is one of the candidates in the hotly contested 'where is the centre of England?' debate. This question is not capable of a logical resolution due to the waywardness of the English coastline. The preferred candidate of the Ordnance Survey, who are probably the most credible authority on the subject, is Lindley Hall Farm, near Atherstone in Warwickshire. In John Higgs's informative and entertaining travel book, *Watling Street*, he visits Northampton and meets Alan Moore, a local author, who points out that Hitler (amongst others) thought that Northampton was the centre of England. His invasion plan, Operation Sealion, came up from the south and ended in the town, because 'he reckoned that once he held the heart of England, the rest of the country would surrender'. There's also the old story of a medieval monk, told by an angel to carry a stone cross to the centre of England, who was intercepted by another angel, when he'd reached

Northampton, to be told that he'd reached his destination. This makes Northampton's case even stronger (and it's a much more interesting justification than the OS's argument for Atherstone).

Alan Moore also has an interesting view of Northampton as a 'black hole':

There's a lot of people in Northampton who came here for a weekend and are still wandering around, not entirely sure how they ended up here. They never get out. You can't get up the escape velocity to get beyond the town, and if you try, you'll inevitably be sucked back in. It's a place where people end up, rather than where people go to.

Maybe Callum escaped just in time!

And what of Northampton Town? I saw them in the late 1980s, when they still played at the County Ground, which they shared with Northants County Cricket club. It was disconcerting to see a sizeable gap between one side of the pitch and the stands on the east side of the ground. Our friends Hamish and Catherine Ross who spent over twenty years as medical practitioners in Northampton and were regular visitors to the County ground told me that this gap was often exploited by the home side late in the game, when hanging on desperately to a one-goal lead. There was a predisposition to hoof the ball in the direction of the cricket pavilion at every opportunity, and trust that the ball-boys would take their time retrieving it (this was before the days of 'added time' – the final whistle would be blown precisely forty-five minutes after the commencement of the second half).

Shared grounds with County Cricket clubs have been few and far between. Bramhall Lane, home of Sheffield United, was one such example (now reconstructed following Yorkshire's departure). Bradford Park Avenue was another, although both County

Cricket and football club have long since moved away. I've sometimes wondered how the cricket clubs on shared grounds coped with the early games of their season, when the football clubs were still using their pitches. With great difficulty, I should imagine, given the extent to which the surface becomes uneven and disfigured towards the end of the football season. Plenty of 'rough' for a wily spin-bowler to exploit, I would have thought.

In the game I saw, Northampton Town, then in the Fourth Division, had a big centre-forward by the name of George Reilly, who looked like he was destined for greater things. He scored an impressive hat-trick in a 4-2 win over opponents whose identity I can't remember. He was, indeed, on an upward trajectory. After starting his career with Corby Town (well, they've all got to start somewhere), where he worked as a bricklayer, he moved to Northampton Town, and then on to Watford, scoring the winning goal in the 1988 FA Cup semi-final against Plymouth Argyle (apparently, he is still the object of hatred amongst Plymouth fans of that era). He later joined Newcastle United and West Bromwich Albion, before returning to Corby and resuming his former bricklaying career. In 2006, he was invited by Watford to see his former club contest an FA Cup semi-final against Crystal Palace. He turned it down, preferring to watch the game from the comfort of his local pub, the Talisman, in the tough Danesholme estate in Corby where he grew up. It was seen (by the *Daily Mail*) as a 'typical gesture from the battle-hardened and bruised No 9, with most of his football money long since gone'. Personally, I think there's a lot to commend in his career trajectory: a high-profile footballer who chose, when his career was over, to return to his roots and resume his former manual occupation. They don't make them like that anymore! It's certainly hard to imagine any of the overpaid Premiership players following his example. But it's also hard to imagine any of them previously working as bricklayers.

The 1960s was the decade when it all happened for Northampton Town. After a relatively undistinguished forty-year stint in the Third Division South (1921–58), where they typically finished mid-table, Northampton Town burst into the lime-light when, after successive promotions, they reached the lofty heights of the First Division in 1965. Sadly, the euphoria lasted for one season only. One year later they were back in the Second Division and by 1969 back in the Fourth, which one feels is where they really belong. But what an achievement for an unfashion-able club to break through into that world! It can still happen, as Bournemouth has recently shown. But it becomes more and more difficult, as big money increasingly dominates the Premier League.

Since the heady days of the 1960s, Northampton have moved between the third and fourth tiers of the Football League, usually the latter, without ever looking likely to replicate their achieve-ments of that decade. In 1994, they moved from the increasingly decrepit County Ground to a new purpose-built stadium at Sixfields in the suburbs.

NORTHAMPTON TOWN v GRIMSBY TOWN
League Two, Saturday November 24th, 2018

On a bleak, cold late-November day, I travelled from my home in Cumbria to Northampton by train to watch the Cobblers take on the Mariners. The journey takes over four hours; you alight at Milton Keynes Central and then travel in the reverse direction to Northampton on a branch line. It would have been much more convenient if the burghers of the town had had the good sense in the 1850s to support the proposal to route the mainline to the Northwest and Scotland through the town. But they objected vehemently, and the railway company concerned lost patience and re-routed the line through Bletchley and Wolverton, to the benefit of Milton Keynes new town when it was established in the 1960s, and to the long-term detriment of Northampton, which ended up on a branch line with numerous stopping points between the town and London, and similarly onwards towards Birmingham and Crewe.

The town centre was bustling, as might be expected with only five weeks to go before Christmas. Northampton is steeped in history; it was one of the most sizeable and important towns in England in medieval times. Sadly, most of that historical infrastructure was destroyed in the Great Fire of Northampton in 1675, ten years after its much better-known counterpart in the metropolis. There were a few notable buildings that survived, including the Welsh House on Market Street, the impressive Norman church of St Peter's, close to the railway station and its near neighbour, Hazelrigg House. As I wandered around the town centre, I began to feel that my lack of enthusiasm on my previous visits was perhaps unjustified. The local limestone is of an attractive warm golden-brown colour, and it has been used in many of the post-1675 buildings. And the Market Square is distinctive and attractive, if you can mentally block out the funfair in its centre, and the new shopping centre that intrudes on one of its sides. I can think of many worse town centres (Wolverhampton, Rochdale and Grimsby, to name but three).

The town centre's environmental reputation has been enhanced by the demolition of the notorious Greyfriars bus station in 2016. Opened in 1976, and lauded (or derided) as a striking example of brutalist architecture, it came to be known locally as the 'Mouth of Hell' and was adjudged the third most-hated building in Britain, in a survey carried out in 2015 as part of the BBC series *Demolition*.

Like so many of the new (post-1990) stadia, Sixfields is inconveniently situated, close to a retail park, nearly two miles from the town centre. I decided to walk there, through a typical area of urban wasteland: council depots, waste-transfer stations, builders supply yards and the odd unkempt field or patch of scrubby vegetation. On arrival, you realise that the ground is situated in a low-lying area, with the retail park looking down on it. As I walked a circuit of the stadium, I reached a point at one of its corners where there was a good view of over half of the pitch, including the goal at the far end. It would be just about worthwhile for any supporters unable to afford the cost of a ticket to position themselves there.

Sixfields was another new ground for me, something that always generates a frisson of excitement as I approach and then enter it. Before doing so, I purchased a fanzine: *HotelEnders*, subtitled 'Talk of the Teyn, still only a peynd' (is that really the way they talk in Northampton?). Fanzines, as noted earlier, are an admirable institution, a welcome antidote to the (often anodyne) content of the official programme, and much to be preferred to the ranting and raving that typically dominate social media posts. *HotelEnders* did not disappoint. There were a couple of features assessing, in positive terms, the impact of Keith Curle's recent appointment as manager (replacing Dean Austin), and a witty take-off of a newspaper 'problems page' ('Dear Claire Rayner ... back with more problems on football and sex'). Prior to Curle's arrival, Town had managed a mere seven points from ten games. Since then, they had lost only once, amassed fifteen points from eight games, and moved to a position of mid-table respectability. His track record at Carlisle, his previous managerial position, was less then inspiring, but maybe a fresh challenge was bringing out the best in him.

Grimsby, too, had recovered well from a dismal start to the season, which included a sequence of six defeats in September, including an unlikely 2-0 reverse at home to my local club, Morecambe. Unlike

Northampton, they had stuck with their manager, Michael Jolley, but given that he'd been appointed six months previous in March 2019, it would have been premature, not to say callous, not to give him more time to turn things round (not that that has stopped other clubs from dismissing managers in similar circumstances). So, what on the face of it, might have seemed a routine mid-season fixture between two teams in the lower-middle reaches of League Two could more positively be viewed as one between two fast-improving clubs moving up the table.

The away end, with seats for around one thousand fans, was well filled with a lively set of Grimsby supporters – 'lively' in that they spent a good deal of the ten minutes before kick-off jumping up and down in unison and lustily chanting and singing refrains, much of the content of which was hard to decipher. I was impressed that so many had made the journey to a venue nearly a hundred miles from their hometown; but most League Two venues are even further away from Grimsby (Lincoln excepted). The Northampton fans, too, were making a lot of noise, and throughout the game demonstrated a passion for their team that I hadn't expected, given the town's laid-back reputation.

The Grimsby contingent was temporarily silenced after four minutes, when a right-wing corner found its way through to Andy Williams, who volleyed it home emphatically from close range, right before their eyes. Northampton continued to dominate the play, with Sam Hoskins regularly finding space down the right flank, and they created several opportunities to increase their lead, the home side twice being thwarted by good saves from Grimsby's keeper, James McKeown. But towards the end of the first half, Grimsby, in one of their few serious attacks, equalised, when Wes Thomas and Ben Pringle combined well on the left and the latter's cross was neatly controlled by Charles Vernan, before slotting the ball past David Cornell.

The game was proving a good advert for League Two football, with players of both sides demonstrating an ability to hold the ball and use it creatively. The second half developed a similar pattern to the first, except this time, it was Grimsby who dominated, creating (but not taking) a succession of chances. Northampton were hardly in the game but contrived to take the lead twenty minutes from the end, when Kevin van Veen scored with an immaculate free-kick from the edge of the area – its quality comparable with anything you might see in the Premier League. Undeterred, Grimsby resumed their domination, and deservedly equalised when substitute Harry Cardwell scored from close range in a crowded goalmouth. He and his teammates rushed to the wall adjacent to the goal and exchanged many a mutual embrace with the ecstatic Grimsby fans behind it. I much prefer this kind of celebration to the more prevalent 'silly dance' routines (individual or collective). It epitomises the strength of the inter-dependency between the team and the fans. Shortly before the end, van Veen was fouled by Grimsby's Harry Clifton when he had a clear run on goal. Clifton was deservedly red-carded, but van Veen couldn't manage a repeat dose of magic with the ensuing free kick.

I walked back to Northampton station with a feeling of quiet satisfaction. The match hadn't been a classic (games in League Two rarely are), but it was dramatic and had held my attention throughout. Both sides intermittently succeeded in playing attractive football, building up moves from the back. An invigorating atmosphere in the stadium with two passionate sets of fans, both of which came away with something. And a fair result, which is always a welcome outcome for the non-partisan outsider. What better way to spend a drab, cold Saturday afternoon in late November?

In the *Football League Paper* the following day the headline in the match report was *Curle calls on his side to kill off opponents*. Perhaps a rather drastic and high-risk response to a dropped point!

STOKE-ON-TRENT

The survival of the Football Special bus

The city known as Stoke-on-Trent consists of six separate townships, one of which is, confusingly, also called Stoke-on-Trent. The other five settlements comprise Hanley, Burslem, Tunstall, Fenton and Longton. The collection of townships is also traditionally known as the Potteries, reflecting the area's basic industry, although very little pottery is now manufactured in Stoke. In its industrial heyday, the area was a spectacular sight at night, illuminated by the flares from numerous pottery kilns.

This blend of diversity and communality in the different settlements is recognised in Arnold Bennett's early twentieth-century novel, *Anna of the Five Towns*, although one of the six listed above apparently failed to make the cut-off point. The recognised city centre is Hanley, two miles north-east of the railway station, whereas the township of Stoke-on-Trent, close to the station, is in a state of decline. But this is the area I know best, first because it is close to the Victoria Ground, which is where Stoke City used to play, and second because it is even closer to the council offices, where I've carried out various pieces of consultancy work over the years.

One of the assignments I carried out for Stoke City Council was a review in 2005 of their scrutiny arrangements. This involved the doubtful pleasure of interviewing a member of the British National Party, who were then well represented on the council, holding as many as a dozen seats. I expected a tirade of unmitigated racial prejudice, but it never materialised. The BNP were proving subtler in their approach than I'd anticipated; their argument was that they were there to advocate on behalf of their local communities, which may have been the main reason for their recent success in the local elections. The local Labour Party was notorious at the time for its out-of-touch elite of elderly male members, so accustomed to holding power on the council that they felt little need to bother themselves with the concerns of the communities they represented. They – the council – knew best, or thought they did.

Stoke has an unusual recent political history. In 2000, the *Stoke Sentinel* ran a campaign in favour of Stoke having an elected mayor, which was one of the options provided (and encouraged) in the 1997–2001 Labour government's vision for local government. There was a referendum, and the people of Stoke (or at least the 25% who could be bothered to turn out) voted to give it a try. Given the dominance of Labour on the council at the time, there was a widespread expectation that the Labour candidate would win. But no, the victor turned out to be an Independent – a young, gay community worker by the name of Mike Wolfe. It cannot have been a comfortable term of office for him, faced with a hostile Labour-dominated council who couldn't quite believe (nor accept) the outcome of the election. After four years of attrition, normality was restored when a Labour candidate won the mayoral election.

By 2014, the people of Stoke decided that having an elected mayor wasn't such a great idea after all and voted in a second referendum to return to the more traditional option of a council leader. When I returned in 2015 to do a further review of scrutiny, the BNP had lost all the seats they'd won in 2005, but there was a substantial opposition of Independents (again a reflection of the Labour Party's inability to develop a community-friendly approach) who were confident they could win the forthcoming council election. They didn't quite manage to gain a majority but did become the largest party and, with the support of a handful of

Conservatives, were in a position to run the council. The decline of Labour as a pro-active force became apparent in 2017, when the local Labour MP, Tristram Hunt, resigned from Parliament, and a by-election was held. There was an expectation that this might prove a breakthrough for UKIP, who put forward their leader, Paul Nuttall, as their candidate. In the event, he narrowly failed to win the seat.

Stoke City are probably best known as the club at which Sir Stanley Matthews began and ended his playing career. They have rarely won anything of note but, since World War Two, have enjoyed regular periods in the top tier. In 1998, they moved from the Victoria Ground to the Britannia Stadium (now renamed the bet365 Stadium, a change that well illustrates the growing role of betting in football), which is a windswept arena situated on the top of a hill, a mile and a half to the south. I remember the Victoria Ground well; it was a traditional stadium built as early as 1878. You had to walk from the station through Stoke-on-Trent township centre and then through an area of terraced housing to reach the ground, a familiar sequence in the 1960s and '70s, before grounds began to be relocated in fringe locations, typically close to or within a modern business park or retail development.

My earlier visits to the Victoria Ground included one in 1965–66, the season Manchester City were promoted to the First Division, having been relegated in 1961. The visitors were on a roll at the time and won 2-0. I remember little about the game itself, but more about the disgruntled looks I was subjected to from my then girlfriend – as a result of late departure from Stoke of the Football Special bus, I turned up half an hour late for the start of *The Sound of Music*, which I'd arranged to see that evening at a Manchester cinema. That was the last time I endeavoured to combine trips to away fixtures with evening cinema visits.

More memorable was the visit in 1997 of Stockport County,

then in the third tier, who were drawn away to Stoke in the third round of the FA Cup. This was the season County reached the semi-finals of the League Cup and achieved promotion. It was a misty night and I saw little of Kieron Durkan's first-half goal at the far end of the ground. But I was in a perfect position to see the talented Alun Armstrong slide in the second, a few minutes from the end. Armstrong was released by Newcastle United at the age of eighteen, and their loss was County's gain. He went on to play for Middlesbrough and later Ipswich Town in the Premier League. County were defeated at Birmingham City in the fourth round, but it was a season to remember, and a bitter reminder of how far they have fallen, forty years on. On the way back to Leicester, where I was working at the time, I was caught by a speed trap – a small price to pay for a memorable evening.

STOKE CITY v DERBY COUNTY
The Championship, Wednesday November 28th, 2018

It was a wet afternoon, when I booked in at the North British Hotel, conveniently close to Stoke-on-Trent railway station. In the invaluable *Football Grounds: A Fans' Guide*, Duncan Adams quotes one correspondent who claims that you can walk from the station to Stoke City's ground in less than thirty minutes, by following the towpath of the Trent and Mersey Canal. I might have considered that option on a fine Saturday afternoon in autumn, but certainly not on a wet evening in November. The memories of nearly falling into the Leeds and Liverpool Canal, where it passes through Wigan, after witnessing a game at the DW stadium on just such an evening in 2016 were too recent. But Adams's book also indicated that you could catch a Football Special from Stoke's town centre, five minutes' walk away. I went to investigate and discovered that indeed you could. So, I did, using a form of match-day transport that was common in the 1950s and '60s. The all-male clientele and the excited hubbub of pre-match speculation were just as I remembered it as a young adult. The main difference was the absence of the clouds of cigarette smoke which swirled around the bus interior in that era.

Stoke City had been relegated at the end of the 2017–18 season after ten years of survival in the Premier League. They never finished higher than ninth, and more typically in the bottom half of the table, but their survival was a creditable achievement for a side that has never been a 'big club' in the Chelsea/Arsenal/ Man United mould and has never been owned by oil sheiks or Russian oligarchs with bulging wallets. They were typically viewed as one of the less attractive sides in the Premier League, playing under the 'no frills' management philosophy of Tony Pullis and Mark Hughes. A Stoke City/ West Bromwich Albion clash was rarely worth staying up for on *Match of the Day*. They are probably best remembered for their effective use of 'long throw' tactics, before they became commonplace, Rory Delap being the most famous (or notorious?) exponent. In recent years, they provided an opportunity for Peter Crouch to enjoy the twilight of his illustrious career. Towards the end of his tenure he was no longer a regular but continued playing as an intermittent second-half substitute, coming on to score the occasional crucial goal, typically a header, soaring above defenders.

Stoke had been widely tipped to bounce straight back to the Premier League, aided by the (arguably unjust) system of parachute payments. They had held on to several of their key players, notably Ryan Shawcross, Joe Allen, Jack Butland and Saido Berahino, and had made some impressive close-season signings, including Tom Ince from Huddersfield Town and Ashley Williams from Everton. But they had found adjustment to life in the Championship difficult. Their struggles were highlighted by a 0-3 home defeat at the hands of Wigan Athletic in August (the visitors' only win on the road so far that season), following which the Potters were languishing in 22nd position. There had since been an improvement, and they were currently in 12th position, having lost only one of the previous nine League games.

The visitors, Derby County, had fared better, under their new manager, Frank Lampard (his first managerial appointment). They were currently in sixth position, which is where they finished the previous season. The last time Derby had tasted Premier League football is forever etched on the psyches of their supporters. The season was 2007–08. Newly promoted County ended up with the worst record ever of any club in the Premier League, or indeed in the forty-odd post-war years of First Division football that preceded it. They recorded a single victory, drew eight of the remaining games and lost twenty-nine, leaving them with a meagre total of eleven points (twenty goals scored, eighty-nine conceded). It was hardly surprising that they continued to struggle for the next few seasons after an experience like that, twice narrowly avoiding a further relegation. But their fortunes had since improved, and in three of the past six seasons they had reached the play-offs, but progressed no further.

The bet365 Stadium is a typical example of the growing number of out-of-town grounds, located in industrial wastelands. In his book *Going to the Match*, Duncan Hamilton describes how the stadium 'sits in a landscape so unlovely that the blandness of its own architecture is – temporarily, at least – forgotten when you take in the rest of the neighbourhood'. Fortunately for me, the ugliness of the adjacent environment is much less apparent when it's dark. The warehouses, industrial units and the waste-recycling factory had not gone away but had merged into a blur of indistinctness and darkness, a process accentuated by the powerful light emitted by the stadium. After a quick admiring look at the evocative Stanley Matthews statue behind the Boothen End, I made my way to the Q-railing (no idea what that title signifies) West Stand, the tallest in the stadium.

There is a Stoke City fanzine that is an impressive example of the genre. It is entitled *Duck*, for reasons that are not immediately apparent. I was hoping to locate a *Duck* seller before the game, but either the fanzine wasn't on sale that day, or if it was, not near a part of the ground that I passed; a pity, because I'd enjoyed the previous issues I'd seen. Like Wigan's *Mudhutter*, it covers topics other than football; there was a moving piece in Issue 42 by a supporter who had mental health problems and wanted his fellow fans to understand what it was like. Issue 43 was a retrospective celebration of the 1992–93 season, when Stoke were promoted from the third tier to the second.

In that issue a good deal of attention was paid to the rivalry between Stoke City and Stockport County. I'd forgotten what an important part County had played in the history of Stoke City around this time. The previous season (1991–92), both clubs had reached the play-offs and met in a semi-final, Stockport securing a 2-1 win on aggregate. But Stoke got their revenge at Wembley a week later when they beat County in the final of the Autoglass Trophy (now the Leasing.com Trophy, at the time of writing), which was a bigger deal then than it is now. There was a lot of bad feeling between the two clubs at this time: allegations of racial abuse directed at Mark Stein by Jim Gannon, and hostility between the two sets of fans. It all seems a long time ago, particularly (as *Duck* is happy to remind us) given that County are now several tiers below Stoke. Twenty-five years ago, the two clubs were both at level three. Such are the changing fortunes of clubs in the Football League.

My seat was ideally located in a central position, at the front of the upper tier and well away from the rain, which was periodically pelting down. To my right, adjacent to the corner from which the teams were to emerge, was the Southern (Marstons Pedigree) stand, half of which was reserved for visiting supporters. It was packed today. Derby County versus Stoke is something of a local derby; the two cities are less than forty miles apart. There was a particular edge to the rivalry tonight. The previous season, Derby had been managed by Gary Rowett, who had taken them to a play-off place. Defeat by Fulham followed, and a month or so later, Rowett left Derby for Stoke City. The away fans had brought with them a plethora of snakes (of the green plastic variety, I should add) to signify their collective view of the questionable morality of Rowett's switch of clubs.

Duncan Hamilton considers that the bet365 Stadium lacks character, having been built 'without grandeur ... There is no designer chic, no signature creative flourish and no elegant land-mark feature about it. The bet365 looks as though it arrived in kit form, the pieces bolted together afterwards'. I am sure he is right, when viewing the empty stadium (as he did on his visit). But as it quickly filled up before kick-off, I found it an exhilarating place to be. Both sets of supporters were in good voice and an air of excitement was building up nicely. When the teams emerged, Gary Rowett, did, as expected, receive a hostile reception from the Derby fans, whose repertoire of insults included, 'Gary Rowett, your football is shit!' But not so shitty as to prevent Derby from making it to the play-offs last season!

In the early stages, the build-up of Derby's attacks was more fluent and incisive than those of Stoke. But the home side were the first to create goal chances and began to dominate the game. Their reward came in the 24th minute, when the lively Joe Allen crafted a lovely through pass to send Sam Clucas with a clear run on goal. Clucas managed to steer the ball past the advancing Scott Carson, for his first goal after a long absence through injury.

Ten minutes later came a game-changing incident. Stoke's Peter Etebo raced in to tackle Derby's Richard Keogh on the far side of the pitch from where I was sitting. As Keogh fell to the ground, players from both sides converged on the scene for a free-for-all, in which blows were exchanged, necks held in a clinch and it looked like Derby's Bradley Johnson bit the neck of Joe Allen. When calm had been restored, the referee, after a long consultation with the linesman, who had been well placed to observe the initial incident, sent off Etebo, and booked Johnson for 'ungentlemanly conduct'. A halftime viewing of the video evidence confirmed that the sending-off had been justified; the offending tackle had been over the ball and straight onto Keogh's shin.

'Well, that's ruined the game,' said the bloke sitting next to me, and I feared that he was right. Derby were an in-form side and would be highly likely to take advantage of the extra man, with two-thirds of the match remaining. Nevertheless, Stoke survived until halftime, through some well-disciplined defending, although they rarely progressed outside their own half.

When the teams came out for the second half, it was announced that Bradley Johnson had been substituted, 'presumably for dental work', as the *Stoke Sentinel* put it the next day, but more likely as a 'precautionary measure', pending a possible second booking. It did not take Derby long to take advantage of their superior numbers. The visitors won a free kick on the edge of Derby's penalty area, and the impressive Harry Wilson, on loan from Liverpool, stepped up and curved his kick over the wall and just inside the far-post. Cue for delirious celebration from the Derby fans behind the goal, who proceeded to jump up and down in unison – an impressive sight when over two thousand individuals are involved.

There was an air of resignation amongst the Stoke fans around me. The expectation was that this goal would be the first of several, which would surely result from the waves of Derby attacks in the forty minutes of the match remaining. That expectation was strengthened as the visitors continued to press forward relentlessly. But, gradually, a subtle change in the balance of play became apparent. Stoke began to mount attacks of their own, with players surging out of defence when the opportunity arose. They began to put the Derby defence under pressure from corners and free kicks. The crowd quickly responded to the evidence of City's increasing ability to overcome their one-man disadvantage and provided an intensity of vocal support that can sometimes change the outcome of a game. And sure enough, with twenty-five minutes remaining, the tenacious Saido Berahino won the ball in midfield, found Sam Clucas in space on the left, and from his low cross, Tom Ince swept the ball home.

In the main stand, we were all on our feet cheering ecstatically, including me, a neutral outsider with no commitment to Stoke City. But how could I not respond to one of those magical moments that football matches can provide? The question then became, could Stoke hold on to this one-goal lead in the time that remained? Fifteen minutes elapsed, and they were holding on, aided by some brave goalkeeping by Jack Butland, and some resolute defending, in which Ashley Williams was outstanding, not least in the quality of his interceptions. The ability to 'read the game' had a particular resonance in his case. It is only fair to add that Derby showed precious little imagination in their attempts to break down Stoke's defence. The 'extra man' bonus only makes a difference if it can be effectively exploited, and the visitors were proving incapable of doing so.

More time passed: five minutes of added time were signalled and still Stoke held on. At the final whistle, a collective throaty roar echoed round the ground, followed by a blast of 'When the Reds go marching in', which the *Stoke Sentinel* suggested 'might have bought a tear to your eye'. We stood to applaud the Stoke players from the field. It had been a game that illustrated so much of the best of football: a courageous display by a side reduced to ten men who had plucked an unlikely victory from the prospect of a seemingly inevitable defeat. Tom Ince received the Man of the Match award; personally, I would have given it to Ashley Williams, whose early career with Stockport County I had witnessed in the mid-1990s. He was outstanding even then.

The Derby County fans, who I suspect couldn't believe they had ended the match pointless, had a further setback to face. There was a loudspeaker announcement that there had been a major incident on the A50, the main road linking Stoke and Derby, and that long delays were expected. Insult added to injury! Meanwhile, we happy Stoke supporters (in my case, on a temporary basis) made our way back on the waiting Football Special. It was a joyful journey back to the town centre, with crucial elements of the game recalled and celebrated. It is evenings like this that help one understand football's universal appeal.

BIRMINGHAM

Cardboard pasties and volleys of expletives

I've spent over twenty years living and studying or working in Birmingham. But I've never really warmed to the city. I first went there in 1961, and returned in 1976, having vowed I never would, to do a one-year masters course in public policy at the Institute of Local Government Studies (INLOGOV). But at the end of the course, I was persuaded to stay on as a research fellow at INLOGOV, where I remained until the end of 1995, when I moved on to De Montfort University in Leicester.

In 1961, I opted for Birmingham rather than Bristol (where I had also been offered a place) because John Smith, my best friend at Manchester Grammar School, had been accepted there to study biochemistry, and there was no one I knew who was going to Bristol. That friendship helped me adjust to the strange and unsettling experience of living away from home for the first time. Our interests gradually diverged; he became an enthusiastic rock-climber, and was away most weekends doing just that, whereas I wasn't and didn't. That turned out not to be a problem; my social life was kick-started by my good fortune in finding myself sharing digs with five other students in the lodging-house in Gillott Road owned and managed by the formidable Mrs Smith (see the Kidderminster chapter). There were other lodgers there, too: a middle-aged Polish refugee; a deaf, half-paralysed old man; a blind Irishman; and a grossly overweight, middle-aged lady (a Miss Burbage). They, with Mrs Smith, would have made an ideal cast for a Harold Pinter play

Gillott Road was a long curving road of Victorian houses that would once have been owned by middle-class families, with space for a servant or two. Not in 1961. The house across the road was a brothel; we students watched the comings and goings with considerable interest. Many of the other houses were multi-occupied, either by students like us, or a variety of loners, drifters and illicit couples. But for a reserved middle-class lad like me, 479 Gillott Road with its five ready-made student drinking companions, proved an ideal base for enjoying university life.

Although Wolves were the most successful of the West Midlands teams during my three years at Birmingham University, the club I most enjoyed watching was Birmingham City. They were then a lower table side in the top tier, whose attacking abilities were counter-balanced by their defensive frailties. Many of their most prominent players – forwards Mike Hellawell, Ken Leek and Jimmy Bloomfield, and midfielders Mathew Beard and Terry Hennessey – have become club legends, particularly given the absence of credible competition since the team's decline from the 1980s onwards. But my favourite player was the mercurial Scottish left-winger Bertie Auld, inspiring on his day for his formidable dribbling skills, but on his off-days, likely to spend most of his time running into cul-de-sacs. Life was never boring at St Andrews. I warmed to the passion of their long-suffering supporters, and much preferred my visits there to those to the Hawthorns (at the time, notable for its high proportion of hard-to-please moaners) and Villa Park, which somehow lacked the intensity of atmosphere of St Andrews.

I turned out regularly for the Faculty football team in the fixtures against other departments. There was also the occasional visit to other universities, to play the Social Science departments there. On a visit to Manchester University, two goals from me had kept us in the game. We were 3-2 down with a couple of minutes to go when we were awarded a penalty. I was deputed to take it. With the personal glory of a hat-trick and the chance to earn

Birmingham an honourable draw beckoning, I ballooned it over the bar. When numerous England players in World or European Cup matches did the same in penalty shoot-outs, I knew exactly how they felt.

When I returned to Birmingham in 1976, on route to eventually becoming a local authority chief executive (or that was the plan), I had no intention of extending my stay beyond the nine months of the course. Indeed, I was so miserable during the first term, I very nearly packed it in and took a welfare rights advice job in Manchester. Instead, I gritted my teeth, persevered with the course and, in the spring term, began to enjoy life in Birmingham. I joined Birmingham Friends of the Earth, where I co-authored an 'alternative plan for the city centre', which included as one of its recommendations the creation of dedicated cycleways. This was an idea ahead of its time. In 1977, it was ridiculed in the pages of the *Birmingham Mail*, but forty years later, most cities and towns have introduced them. When, shortly before graduation, I was offered a one-year post of research assistant at the university, I put my previous career aspirations on hold and decided to take it.

This decision had a lot to do with the fact that I had met someone who would later become my (first) wife. She had separated from her husband the previous year and moved to Birmingham with her two daughters, Eleanor and Anna (aged seven and five respectively, when I first met them). Although we had both been at Birmingham University between 1961 and 1964 in the same Faculty (Commerce and Social Science), I had absolutely no recollection of her (nor she of me). Despite having then made such a profound non-impression on each other, we started going out together, and shortly after taking up my research assistant post in November 1977, I moved into her terraced house in Gaddesby Road, Kings Heath, and became a de facto stepfather. The following year we moved to a larger Victorian house in nearby

Cambridge Road, which we shared with another single mother and her two daughters.

Next door to us in Cambridge Road was a house which appeared to be shared by a fluctuating population of people in their twenties. The members of the band UB40, including Robin and Ali Campbell used the house as a rehearsal venue and could often be seen in its garden. Indeed, the whole area was a diverse and cosmopolitan one. David Edgar, the playwright, lived just down the road. Around the corner lived Stuart Hall, the influential West Indian social and political thinker, with his wife Katherine, and their two children, Becky and JJ, who were part of Eleanor and Anna's circle of school-friends. Various other high-powered academics based at Birmingham University also lived in the area, several of whom were friends or acquaintances of my new partner. It was an unfamiliar social milieu for me, and I found it uncomfortable and challenging; Liverpool Polytechnic's Town Planning department may have just about qualified as academia, but it was in a different league to Birmingham University, where I was now seeking to establish myself.

I went on to spend a total of nineteen demanding but rewarding years at INLOGOV. My partner and I were married just before moving to Silverdale, north Lancashire, in 1982. The marriage did not last; we separated in 1989 and were divorced three years later. But happily, the relationship with my stepdaughters did survive. I had been there for them throughout their childhood and adolescence, and thirty years on, our relationship remains as close as would be the case if they were my natural children.

What with the demands of my new job and family life, I didn't have a lot of spare time to indulge my passion for watching football. When I did, it was to my old favourites Birmingham City that I returned. In 1976, when I came back to Birmingham, they were continuing in their familiar (from the early 1960s) vein of under-performing First Division strugglers. I saw the hugely impressive seventeen-year-old Trevor Francis on a couple of occasions before he departed for Notts Forest. In 1979, they were relegated, but bounced straight back, securing promotion in the final game of the season at St Andrews. I was there to witness a typical maverick City performance. Their opponents were Notts County, safe in a lower-middle table position with little to play for (or so you would have thought). But a lack of motivation on the part of such opponents can never be relied upon. Three times Birmingham went ahead; three times Notts County equalised. Had the visitors scored a late winner, Birmingham would have been overtaken by Chelsea. But a draw was just enough to secure promotion.

At this time, under the benign management of Jim Smith, Birmingham had the nucleus of a good side, a mixture of younger players, including the skilful midfielder Kevin Dillon, and the formidable (if temperamental) defender Mark Dennis, and their more experienced teammates, including Alan Curbishley, Colin Todd, Archie Gemmill and Frank Worthington. They managed a mid-table finish the following season (a rare achievement for them), and survived a further two seasons in the First Division, before returning to the Second Division in 1984, by which time I was living in the Northwest (although still working in Birmingham).

I also made the occasional visit to the Hawthorns, mainly because I enjoyed watching Willie Johnston, a talented, mercurial but inconsistent (and notoriously short-tempered) left-winger from Scotland, in the mould of Bertie Auld. Johnston was sent home in disgrace from the 1978 World Cup in Mexico for failing a drugs test, although he always vehemently denied any wrongdoing. He was a delight to watch in his West Bromwich days. How rare it is nowadays to see a player who stays on the wing and sees it as his job to dribble past defenders before crossing from the bye-line. There is very little scope for such specialism in the modern game. They don't make them like Bertie Auld and Willie Johnston anymore – or, if they do, their natural instincts soon become submerged in a rigid game plan.

When my stepdaughter Anna decided she was a Liverpool supporter, we went to the Hawthorns to watch them play there; a 1-1 draw, with Cyrille Regis, then in his prime, scoring the equaliser for the Albion. The most successful local team of the time was Aston Villa, twice League champions and twice European Cup winners. They were in decline when I got around to watching them entertain Manchester City in 1982. City proceeded to out-play Villa and ran out 5-1 winners (of which David White scored four), much to my delight.

It is always fascinating to research the history of football clubs, to observe the fluctuations involved, and to remind ourselves of various unlikely phenomena: for example, that lowly Bury won the FA Cup twice in the early twentieth century and were First Division regulars until 1930; that Premier League Watford never once emerged from the lowest tier of League football until 1970; that Northampton Town, Leyton Orient, Carlisle United and Oxford United have all played in the First Division (pre-Premier League) over the past sixty years; that Glossop North End once played against Liverpool, Everton and Manchester City in the First Division (and yes, they still exist); and that, for a brief period in the 1890s, two Burton-based clubs – United and Wanderers – played out local derbies in the Second Division.

But another insight from studying the history of football clubs is the recognition that we sometimes have an inaccurate picture of their achievements (or lack of them) over time. Take Birmingham City. I'd always assumed that the four 'big clubs' in the West Midlands had broadly similar records of success over the years, with City perhaps lagging slightly behind the others. I was wrong. Painstaking research has revealed that whereas Aston Villa, West Brom and Wolves have won between them twenty-six League and FA Cup titles, City have managed precisely none. There have been two League Cup wins (1963, against local rivals Villa – I bet they enjoyed that) and as recently as 2011, when they defeated Arsenal. But if you add in the League Cup wins of the other three, the outcome is that City's tally is a mere two of the thirty-six trophies won. They are, without doubt, the poor relations (discounting Walsall) of the West Midlands football world.

City have spent nearly as much time outside the top division as in it, including a couple of brief spells at the third level, and with recent narrow escapes from repeating this fall from grace. Probably their most outstanding achievement has been to reach the final of a long-forgotten competition called the Inter-Cities Fairs Cup, which was a forerunner to the UEFA Cup, but with somewhat obscure criteria for entry (representing a big city seemed to be adequate). Birmingham reached their finals in 1960 and 1961, losing to Barcelona and AS Roma, 4-1 and 4-2, respectively). No mean feat for a club that had never previously won anything (apart from a handful of Second Division titles).

The experience of the West Midlands 'big four' since 1983 lends credence to Anthony Clavane's hypothesis that there is a link between economic decline and the fortunes of local football teams. As in Yorkshire, the fortunes of Birmingham and the Black Country was devastated by the Thatcher government's economic policies of the 1980s. What have Aston Villa, Birmingham City, West Brom and Wolves achieved over the past thirty-five years?

There was no question that it would be Birmingham City that I would go to watch on my nostalgic return trip to the city, rather than the Villa, or West Brom. The last time I'd seen them at St Andrews was in 1997, playing Stockport County during the latter's brief spell of glory in the second tier. The game was marred by a leg fracture suffered by County's midfielder Tom Bennett, the sound of which echoed round the ground. It took ten minutes to strap him up and get him off the pitch, after which the result seemed irrelevant. Then, towards the end of the 2017–18 season, I had seen City achieve a deserved 1-0 win at Bolton, spurred on by over five thousand passionate visiting Brummies, a key landmark in their great escape that year.

BIRMINGHAM CITY v BRISTOL CITY
The Championship, Saturday December 8th, 2018

With Christmas looming, all the trains going south were packed. The route was a familiar one; I'd travelled it on a regular basis between 1982 and 1995, when I was living in Silverdale and working in Birmingham. In his epic *English Journey*, written in the 1930s Depression, J.B Priestley described the section between Wolverhampton and Birmingham New Street as 'possibly the ugliest stretch of railway line in the whole country'. But it has greatly changed since then: most of the heavy industry that flourished in the Black Country has gone. The Bilston steelworks has disappeared from the face of the earth, as have many of the smaller-scale premises that manufactured nuts, bolts, rivets, nails, screws and many other small artifacts of metal construction. There is now a surprising amount of open space, albeit much of it scruffy and unkempt in appearance. Canals still appear at regular intervals; the Black Country is an urban canal enthusiast's paradise.

In West Bromwich, we passed the site of the old factory operated by the Kenrick family (manufacturers of large metal products). The Kenricks were one of the big names of Birmingham entrepreneurship in Victorian times, not quite in the same league as the Chamberlains and Cadburys, but not far behind.

In the early 1990s, I lodged in Harborne with the widow of one of this renowned dynasty. Her son was then running the business, which had downsized markedly since its heyday, partly as a result of a predecessor Kenrick, who in the 1930s became chairman of the city's education authority and had apparently found the job infinitely more interesting than running a large industrial concern. His consequent neglect of the 'day job' weakened the competitive edge of the company, which it never quite recovered.

Then came the familiar sight of Winson Green Prison to the left and Smethwick High Street to the right, before the train arrived in the subterranean and totally confusing New Street station. If ever you need to change trains there, be sure to leave yourself at least ten minutes to find your way around.

I had planned my trip to enable me to spend an hour or so in Kings Heath, the Victorian suburb where I spent five years with Eleanor and Anna and their mother, before we moved up north in 1982. Cambridge Road was much as I remembered it, the spacious terraced residences still occupied by middle-class families (judging from the accents I overheard) or, in other cases, shared by students. Gaddesby Road also hadn't changed significantly; here the terraced houses are smaller and the population, then as now, more diverse in terms of income and ethnicity. Moving on to the shopping area, marred by the traffic on the busy main road running through it, I noticed that this diversity is reflected in the mix of shops – trendy café-bars, halal butchers, and 'alternative' health centres offering treatments such as acupuncture, together with the familiar array of Poundlands, charity shops, Greggs, Starbucks and the like. The site of the old cinema, which became a bingo hall when we lived there, was now an Asda supermarket. The previous switch from cinema to bingo was not to the liking of Eleanor, who organised demonstrations with groups of her school-friends on Saturday mornings, marching round the cinema chanting, 'Bingo is boring!'

It was just as well that I had arrived at St Andrews with plenty of time to spare. It took all of thirty minutes for me to join a queue for a ticket, undergo the five minutes of questions felt to be necessary before being sold one, be misdirected to a turnstile different from the one through which my ticket entitled me to enter, be redirected through a number of side streets to the Gil Merrick Stand and then be searched, before finally being allowed into the ground. There must be a simpler way of dealing with one-off visits from neutral outsiders. It was never like this at Morecambe!

Once in the ground, in one of those unfriendly cavernous areas under the stand that appear to be built into the design of all new stadia, I surveyed the food options available. There were the usual suspects: burgers, hot dogs and pies. I opted for a cheese and onion pasty. A mistake, as it turned out – it had been so long overheated that the base was like congealed cardboard, and the contents so scaldingly hot that it was a further ten minutes before I could contemplate a mouthful. So far, my nostalgic return to St Andrews had not gone well. I made my way to my seat, which was high up in the stand in the corner of the stadium, adjacent to the main stand, the only element of the old ground I used to frequent that had survived.

Birmingham were on a good run. After a slow start, dominated by drawn games, they had moved steadily up the table, and currently lay ninth, one point and one place behind arch-rivals Aston Villa. If this outcome appears unremarkable, it should be remembered that in three of the previous five seasons, they had secured survival in the Championship only on the final day. Garry Monk, their manager since February 2018, had a run of good seasons with Swansea City in the Premier League, before they were relegated in 2017. He has made an impressive start at St Andrews. Bristol City, their opponents today, were currently a few places below their hosts, but well clear of the relegation slots.

The game started slowly, with both sides intent on weighing each other up and not trying anything too adventurous. It could surely only improve. But it showed little sign of doing so. Shots on (or off) target were rare. The visitors dominated possession, but struggled to translate it into goal opportunities, apart from of one good attempt from Andreas Weimann, which Birmingham striker Lukas Jutkiewicz did well to clear off the line. The best the home side could offer in return was a penetrating run from pony-tailed Jacques Maghoma, which took him into the penalty area, where his progress was halted – unfairly, he and most of the home crowd thought – but not in the view of the referee (nor me). There was a frustrating succession of moves that started with one or other of the keepers and ended up, after five or six passes, back where they'd started, without crossing the halfway line. Come on, Birmingham and Bristol, you can do better than this! Sadly, by halftime there had been little to suggest that this was the case.

At the interval, I made my way back to the grim refreshment area to check on the halftime scores elsewhere. Usually, you can guarantee Sky Sports being on view in such venues. But not at St Andrews. It was a Blues TV channel, featuring a boring interview with some club official about the boring first half we had seen.

Was there to be any improvement in the standard of play in the second half? There was not. Birmingham's two strikers, Ché Adams and Lukas Jutkiewicz, had an impressive joint tally of nineteen League goals to their credit this season, but neither looked remotely like adding to it today. Bristol continued to look marginally more motivated than their lack-lustre opponents. Then in the sixty-third minute came an unexpected goal. A right-wing corner found Bristol's Senegalese striker, Famara Diédhiou, in space, and his glancing header wrong-footed the Birmingham keeper. Diédhiou was delighted, as well he might be. It was at St

Andrews the previous season that he had been sent off and then banned for six matches for allegedly spitting on an opponent, an offence he vehemently denied.

The home side then came more into the game, and Jutkiewicz was unlucky when his powerful header rebounded back from the angle of post and crossbar. There were a couple of penalty appeals, neither of them conclusive, neither awarded. During this period of Birmingham dominance, the crowd around me became increasingly angry with the referee and used a range of expletives to express their anger, which was, I thought, grossly insensitive in an area of the stand where there were a lot of young kids. In the final minute of injury time, a free kick was scrambled off the line by a Bristol defender, and that was it – Birmingham's first home defeat of the season. Did the visitors deserve it? Probably, just about, on balance. But a 0-0 draw would have been the most fitting outcome to an arid game. There had been so little in the way of silky skills, imagination or indeed anything that was at all memorable. If this was the Championship, give me League Two, or the National League, any day.

With my gripes about ticket purchasing arrangements, cardboard pasty casings, tedious halftime entertainment and insensitive crowd behaviour unregistered, I made my way out of the ground and down the hill towards the city centre. The route passes along Fazeley Street, through a dimly lit, neglected inner area of the city, which used to be dominated by small business enterprises dating from Victorian times. Many of the buildings remain, some converted to other uses, others derelict. As a relic of the Industrial Revolution, the area had a certain charm. I was particularly struck by an impressive old building that housed (or so it claimed) 'Fellows, Morton and Clayton – Canal Carriers'. Could it really still be operational? Is there any demand for 'canal carrying' nowadays?

The report in the *Football League Paper* the next day awarded the game three stars, despite the managers describing it (rightly) as 'a dogfight', 'a lacklustre performance' and 'frustrating'. Had reporter Olly Barker been at the same game as I had? I then noticed that the vast majority of the thirty-six games covered by the *Paper* were given three stars. So, either the correspondents can't be bothered to take the rating system seriously (which would be understandable), or they didn't want to offend anyone.

LINCOLN

The remarkable programme notes of Colin Murphy

The significance of Lincoln in my life is not so much the town itself (impressive though it is), but rather a large field on a farm (Tupholme Manor) about ten miles to the east of the city, near to a village called Bardney. The year was 1971, and the occasion was one of the great music festivals of the early 1970s. I came over with a group of friends who frequented the Crossfoxes folk club in Chester, where I lived and worked at the time. It was one of those days that I recall as being idyllic. It was July: the sun shone down (but not too fiercely), we sat on the grass with a clear view of the stage, shared our picnic food, and listened to an historic line-up of bands and individuals.

It was billed as a folk festival, but that was to use the term 'folk' in a very broad sense. I don't think the headliners, The Byrds, who were into their *Eight Miles High* phase, would have seen themselves (or been thought of) as a folk group. But who cared, all the music was fantastic. There was an earnest young singer-songwriter with long dark hair, James Taylor, who sang movingly of the suicide of a close friend (*Fire and Rain*); and another, Tim Hardin, whose own life was to come to an untimely end within a couple of years, whose set included his most renowned song, *If I Were a Carpenter*, which had been made famous by Bobby Darin. Sandy Denny, who had recently left Fairport Convention to pursue a solo career, did a set that later appeared as 'The North Star Grassman and the Ravens' album, ably supported by a band including her former Fairport sparring partner, Richard Thompson. Steeleye Span (or Steel Ice-Pan, as one of the Chester contingent thought they were called) were at a relatively early stage in their career and had recently acquired the services of Maddy Prior, who sang and pranced energetically around the stage. Buffy Sainte-Marie sang passionately about the plight of the Native Americans. Also appearing were Dave Swarbrick and Martin Carthy, Dion (without the Belmonts), the Incredible String Band, Pentangle, Ralph McTell, Steve Terry and Brownie McGhee and possibly Tom Paxton. One report claims he didn't show up, but I have a reasonably clear memory of seeing him there. Has there ever been a folk festival with such an impressive line-up?

There was no evidence of the drunkenness, drug abuse or aggression that became commonplace a few years later. I can recall a visit to a festival in Milton Keynes with my stepdaughter Anna in the early 1980s, where half-empty plastic bottles of beer (or in some cases, I suspect, piss) were hurled with monotonous regularity at whoever was on the stage. Nothing like that at Bardney, possibly because folk music was a genre that appealed largely to nice middle-class families, like mine. We listened attentively, applauded appreciatively, but generally behaved ourselves. Tickets cost £2, and the audience was estimated at sixty thousand.

What made the Bardney Festival so special for me was that it brought together three strands in the development of popular music which really excited me at the time: folk music, protest songs and the increasing poetic and literary quality of some lyrics. It took place soon after the end of the 1960s, a decade which had seen popular music transformed out of all recognition. The first half of the 1950s seemed to me, then in my early teens, a relatively barren phase in the history of the genre, although I later came to recognise the craftsmanship of some of the leading songwriters of the time. The music scene was highly commercialised, ruled by the paunchy ageing barons of Tin Pan Alley. Ballads, mostly American in origin, were the order of the day, sung by 'showbiz' celebrities such as Frankie Laine, Alma Cogan, Eve Boswell and the Beverley Sisters. The most outrageous act, as far as I was concerned, was Johnnie *Cry* Ray, who revelled in lyrics laced with fake, over-the-top emotion, and had a penchant for bursting into tears at crucial moments in his awful songs.

There were signs of improvement in 1955, with the first appearance of what came to be known as rock and roll, in the rotund form of Bill Haley and the Comets, who starred in the film *Rock Around the Clock*, which had teenagers screaming and jiving in cinemas across the country, and, in some venues, ripping the seats apart. Then came Elvis Presley, whose R & B-inspired singles (and his dynamic appearance and stage act) added further impetus to rock and roll's increasing popularity. Unfortunately, his manager, Colonel Parker, contrived a change of direction into the middle of the road, where Elvis's popularity and sales increased, but his vitality and authenticity diminished.

The year 1957 saw the appearance of skiffle on the scene, which inspired the formation of numerous local bands, using home-made or cut-price instruments such as washboards, harmonicas, acoustic guitars, kazoos and basses built into tea chests. This development really did feel like a revolution. The best-known exponent was Lonnie Donegan, who sadly also went the way of Elvis. His first hit single was a version of an old Leadbelly song, *Rock Island Line*. Three years later, it was *Does Your Chewing Gum Lose Its Flavour (On the Bedpost Overnight)?*, at which point I lost interest. Another original talent transformed into an all-round entertainer.

By the end of the decade, the skiffle boom had burned itself out. But it proved hugely influential in the musical development of The Beatles and many of the other groups who made their names in the early 1960s, which was when the real transformation took place. The first strand of this sea change was the blossoming of folk music and folk clubs, where you could hear authentic traditional songs, mainly from the British Isles or the USA, sung by the likes of Martin Carthy, Shirley Collins, Ewan MacColl and Peggy Seeger and the Watersons – songs about real people and places performed by singers totally dissociated from the world of commercial pop. There were parallels with the growth of skiffle, but the revival of folk music lasted longer; indeed, it still thrives today. And we all could (and did) join in the choruses.

The second was the spread of the protest song, epitomised by the early recordings of Bob Dylan, which was music to the ears of politically aware young people like me. At last there was someone singing songs about issues that really concerned us: the threat of nuclear war (*A Hard Rain's A-Gonna Fall*), the defence industry (*Masters of War*) and the battle for civil rights (*Only a Pawn In Their Game*). It's difficult to overstate the impact of this development on our hearts and minds.

Third, by the mid-1969s, the quality of the lyrics in popular music came of age. No longer were we exposed to moons and Junes, and the like. Well, we were, but there was now an alternative to such familiar platitudes. Again, Bob Dylan was a leading figure in this change. From his fifth album ('Bringing It All Back Home') onwards, his lyrics developed a quality that can only be described as poetic, and would have been unthinkable in the world of popular music, two or three years previously.

I later returned to Lincoln in a professional capacity. It was 2007, and there was yet another local government reorganisation looming. Lincolnshire County Council and the six district councils engaged me and a De Montfort University colleague to provide some expert advice. David Miliband was the government minister involved at the time, and I very nearly met him, which, as an academic involved in politics, would have been a big deal. Unfortunately, I was committed to working for another council on the day of his visit to Lincoln, so my university colleague had to fill in for me.

And then there was the trip to Lincoln on a freezing cold day early in 2013, to watch a Conference match between Lincoln City and Barrow – my first ever visit to Sincil Bank. Lincoln City were struggling at the time, having just sacked their manager, and escaped with an undeserved 0-0 draw. But, unlike Barrow, they managed to avoid relegation. They continued to struggle for the next three seasons, but came good in 2016–17, under the joint managership of the Cowley brothers, Jason and Nicky. A spectacular FA Cup run endeared them to football fans across the country – they defeated Burnley and Ipswich Town, and reached the quarter-finals, before going down to Millwall. They also finished up as National League champions, returning to the Football League after a six-year absence.

Lincoln City have never been a major force in the Football League, but then you wouldn't expect that from a town of modest size (it's technically a city, but only because there's a cathedral there). But they've had their moments. In 1976, a certain Graham Taylor was their manager, and they stormed away with the Fourth Division title, winning thirty-two of their League fixtures. At Sincil Bank they proved invincible, winning twenty-one of their games and drawing the other two. Lincoln amassed seventy-two points in total, which would have been 104 if three points had been awarded for a win, as is now the case. Not even Manchester City, in the 2017–18 season when they ran away with the Premier League title, could match that home record.

Lincoln were first relegated to the Conference in 1987 but bounced back the following season under the idiosyncratic manager Colin Murphy. Colin gained cult status for his notes in the match day programmes, which have since become collectors' items. Here is one example:

Of the keys on the ring at the moment, we should be selecting more correctly to unlock opposing mechanisms. However, there is not a lock that cannot be unlocked, so we shall endeavour to unlock the lock, but in doing so, we must not get locked out.

Erm ... could you run that past us again, Colin?

LINCOLN CITY v NEWPORT COUNTY
League Two, Saturday December 22nd, 2018

The day after the winter solstice. Three days before Christmas Day. I had planned to come over the previous Saturday to watch Lincoln take on Morecambe (the Imps versus the Shrimps!), but the onset of Storm Dennis, and the repeated 'don't travel unless absolutely necessary' warnings dissuaded me. Probably just as well: Morecambe were 3-0 down after thirty-five minutes, which I wouldn't have enjoyed, before they pulled a goal back in the second half. So, I settled for today's visit of Newport County. I travelled to Lincoln by car, given that the alternative was a convoluted train journey from Kendal (four and a half hours, with three changes). Approaching from the north, the city's spectacular cathedral can be seen directly ahead, beckoning one forward. To avoid the congestion of the city centre, I parked the car near the cathedral, and descended the steep path to the main shopping area. It was heaving with frenetic, bag-laden Christmas shoppers. The route to Sincil Bank passes alongside the Sincil Drain, a conduit, serving as an overflow from the River Witham, which runs through the city centre.

Sincil Bank has changed greatly since 1987, when Simon Inglis described it, in his book *Football Grounds of Britain*, as 'having retained much of its picturesque quality'. 'Picturesque' is not a word one would now use. There is a utilitarian main stand (the Selenity Stand), completed in 1989, two similar low-rise all-seater terraces at each end of the pitch, one (the Bridge McFarland Stand) with a row of executive boxes built into its roof, above an area reserved, wholly or partly, for away supporters. Today, the Newport travelling contingent looked to be less than two hundred, but then it was the week before Christmas. The jewel in the crown was the imposing Co-operative Community Stand, completed in 2010. Taken as a whole, Sincil Bank now looks totally unlike the stadium depicted in Inglis's book.

I took my seat in the Stacey West Stand, named after the two Lincoln City supporters who perished in the fire at Bradford's Valley Parade on the last day of the 1984–85 season, when Lincoln were the visitors. The change in Lincoln's fortunes since I was last here in 2013 was apparent. As the team emerged from the dressing room as League Two leaders, both the big stands were packed. There was a lively atmosphere, sustained by much singing from the home fans, which persisted throughout the game.

Lincoln had done well in 2017–18, their first season back in the Football League, making it to the play-offs. This season they had started with five wins in their first six League matches, and continued in similar vein, with only three defeats so far in twenty-one games. Their opponents, Newport County, were also flourishing (apart from an inexplicable 6-0 home defeat at the hands of lowly Yeovil Town) and were currently lying in sixth position. Although none of Lincoln's team were familiar to me, I did know Newport's leading scorer, Pádraig Amond, who had previously spent two moderately successful seasons with Morecambe. The Newport line-up also included a couple of survivors from the team I saw gain promotion from the Conference in 2013: defender David Pipe and midfielder Robbie Wilmott. It felt like I was renewing acquaintance with old friends.

Both David Pipe and Robbie Wilmott had spent spells away from Newport since 2013; Pipe returned in 2017 and Robbie Wilmott more recently, after stints at Ebbsfleet, Eastleigh and Chelmsford City. He even had a spell working in a supermarket, when he was 'between football jobs'. Prior to joining Newport in 2012, he had played for Cambridge United and Luton Town. His career pattern is typical of so many of those players who rarely make it as far as the Championship: a series of short-term contracts and loan spells at clubs ranging from League One to the National League South or North. You can imagine the pressures that this level of job insecurity places on partners and young families. 'We're moving where? We've only been in Dover two years and now it's Barrow!' This is the reason why one encounters so many 'old friends'. If they're approaching thirty (as Wilmott was), they're probably at their sixth or seventh club, and it's quite likely that you will have come across them previously, somewhere or other.

For the first half-hour, Lincoln showed why they were heading the table. They moved the ball around purposefully, rarely misplacing a pass, and created many scoring opportunities, two of which they converted. As early as the third minute they went ahead when leading scorer John Akinde's deflected shot left Newport's keeper, Joe Day, wrong-footed. Their second goal, four minutes later, was in a different class. Winger Harry Anderson cut in from the right and found the net with a fierce cross-shot. But although the home side continued to dominate possession, the visitors always looked dangerous in their breakaway attacks, with Jamille Matt controlling the ball and distributing it impressively. And in the last minute of the first half, they pulled a goal back, with Pádraig Amond netting from close range after Luton defenders had failed to deal with a corner. That was good news, as far as I was concerned; it kept the game alive as a contest.

At halftime, I asked a friendly steward what the three large green tanks, situated between the Stacey West and the Selenity Stands, contained. The answer was water, which apparently is needed to top up the normal supply, to prevent the toilets in the ground from getting clogged up on match days. This problem is caused by the difficulties of maintaining the water pressure at a ground as low-lying as Sincil Bank. The presence of the tanks is, I would guess, a unique feature at Football League stadia.

Having pulled themselves back into the game just before half-time, Newport proceeded to dominate it in the second half, with some forceful attacking football, which restricted Lincoln to the occasional breakaway. Particularly impressive was Newport's defender Dan Butler, who made regular forays down the left and proved adept at curling a series of dangerous crosses into the box, well placed to find the heads of the in-rushing Pádraig Amond or Jamille Matt. It felt like an equalising goal must come soon. It was not long before a goal did come, but it was at the other end. A headed knockdown from John Akinde sent Tom Pett clear on the left and his accurate cross-shot was too good for the Newport keeper. But back came Newport, a few minutes later, when a miskick from Lincoln's keeper, Grant Smith, found Matt, whose well-judged pass set up Amond, who slotted the ball home beyond the stranded keeper to make it 3-2. Shortly afterwards, Lincoln brought on Matt Rhead as substitute. He had scored some crucial goals in his previous three seasons with the club and had become something of a local icon. Overweight and ponderous, he achieved little in the time that remained, and it may have been that he was nearing the end of his illustrious (at this level) career. But the crowd clearly had a great affection for him, greeting his appearance with chants of 'Rhead, Rhead' (repeated at intervals thereafter) and proving tolerant of his limited contribution to the game.

As an objective neutral, I was willing Newport to manage an equaliser, for that is what their second half display merited. But it was not to be. Lincoln remained top of the table and Newport slid down a couple of places. It had been an exhilarating game, well worth the long journey east. What a contrast with the barren Birmingham/Bristol City match that I'd endured a couple of weeks earlier! Danny Cowley, the Lincoln manager, acknowledged that his team had faded badly after the first thirty minutes, 'which was probably the best we've played during my tenure'. He was 'frustrated and disappointed in equal measure' (but, perhaps, even more relieved?). Newport's manager, Mike Flynn, claimed that his side was the better team by a mile after the first twenty-five minutes, and rather than being encouraged at the way his side had pushed the League leaders all the way, felt Newport should have won. I could see his point. Both teams would, I was confident, be vying for promotion come April. As I walked back into the town centre, the floodlit cathedral, on top of Lincoln Edge was in full view, reminding us of the city's historical significance.

Two weeks later, both clubs were faced with Premier League opponents in the third round of the FA Cup. Lincoln certainly didn't disgrace themselves in a narrow 1-2 defeat at Everton. But it was Newport who made the headlines with the biggest upset of the round: a 2-1 win over Leicester City at Rodney Parade. I watched the game on TV and relished the ability of a League Two club to take on and defeat a club seventy-two places above them in the League. Jamille Matt gave them the lead in the first half with a well-placed header from a penetrating cross by Robbie Wilmott. And then, six minutes from the end, Pádraig Amond coolly converted the penalty that won them the match.

WALSALL

Whatever happened to Bill 'Chopper' Guttridge?

Walsall is one of the larger of the many Black Country towns. You pass close to it on the M6 as you approach the M5 junction, travelling south; indeed, the Bescot Stadium, Walsall FC's home since 1990, is very close to the motorway, an easy target for travelling football ground-spotters. I first watched the club during my undergraduate days at Birmingham University (1961–64), when I fancied a change from my staple diet of Aston Villa, Birmingham City, West Bromwich Albion and Wolves (then all in the First Division). It wasn't a bad time for Walsall FC. Between 1961 and 1963, they were in the Second Division – for the first time in their history – although they were relegated in 1963. Their ground was then Fellows Park, famous for its 'laundry end', which constituted a brick wall, directly behind one of the goals. There was a paltry five or six steps of terracing, and then the wall, with plenty of scope for goal efforts to ricochet back from it, or sometimes disappear over its top. I much preferred the homely atmosphere of Fellows Park to the utilitarian Bescot Stadium, to which I made one visit in the early 1990s.

But it was not until much later that I discovered Walsall as a town. I retired from my post at De Montfort University in 2009 but continued to carry out occasional pieces of work for councils who remembered me, or to whom I had been recommended. In 2012, I received a call from Walsall Council, asking if I would chair their members' allowances panel (an independent body, which all local authorities are required to appoint in order to make recommendations about how much councillors should get paid), which I was happy to do. A couple of years later they asked me to carry out a review of their scrutiny committees.

I developed an affection for Walsall. It is not pretty; none of the Black Country towns are. But it has a lively town centre, with market stalls running down the centre of the pedestrianised high street, and the people are friendly, speaking in their lugubrious Black Country accent, which is subtly different from the Brummie accent, a fact they will hasten to point out to anyone who isn't aware of the distinction. I usually stayed at a pub/hotel called Lyndon House, just north of the town centre, which has a previous history as a leather factory and (more recently) a Salvation Army hostel. In the bleak environment around Walsall's town centre, it is a pleasant surprise, a hidden gem. To quote the *Birmingham Mail*: 'The red brick building, with its Mediterranean-style terrace, stands like a monument to a bygone age, stubbornly remaining on its hillside perch.'

Walsall Council, like others in the Black Country, incorporates several smaller towns, such as Willenhall, Darlaston and Bloxwich, each with its strong community identity and distinctive industrial history. For example, Darlaston's speciality was the manufacture of nuts, bolts and gun locks, whereas in Willenhall, it was locks and keys. But what characterised all these communities (and indeed the whole of the Black Country) was the large majority in favour of breaking the ties with the EU in the 2016 referendum. The residents of Walsall voted decisively for Brexit: 68% in the borough as a whole, and well over 70% in Blakenall Heath, a large impoverished council estate to the west. It was argued in a recent *Guardian* article that this high figure could be explained by the inappropriateness of the case being made for remaining by the then Tory leadership: 'Think what you've got to lose if we leave the EU' was what the residents of Blakenall Heath were asked to reflect upon. Unsurprisingly, most of them considered that they had very little to lose. The advantages of being in the EU had by-passed the Blakenall Heaths of this world, and there was a sense that at a time of proliferating food banks, low-paid and insecure employment and reduced welfare benefits, things could hardly get worse if Britain opted out.

The newly expanded Walsall Borough Council, which was created in 1974, has had an interesting, not to say turbulent history since its inception. Its Labour administration soon recognised what other authorities in the Black Country failed to do, namely that the new Walsall was in fact a conglomeration of towns with distinctive identities. So, under the leadership of the visionary Dave Church, a system of devolution of decision-making to neighbourhood councils was introduced, based on real places like Willenhall. It was widely seen at the time as a welcome counterbalance to the large authorities introduced in 1974, although few followed Walsall's example.

Dave Church had other qualities untypical of council leaders. He did not trust the council's senior officials and went out of his way to emphasise the right of his Labour administration to ignore the advice they provided, or to take decisions contrary to such advice. This attitude might sound idiosyncratic and counterproductive, but, if not carried to excess (which it sometimes was), it can be seen positively, in democratic terms. The 1970s was a decade when professional officers knew best – or thought they did. There were too many local authorities where senior officers were dominant, with leading councillors much less prepared than Dave Church to challenge their advice.

In the late 1990s, when Dave and his radical neighbourhood strategy had faded from the scene, Walsall was judged by the Audit Commission to be a 'failing authority' and a panel of expert outsiders was brought in to sort out its flawed decision-making and management arrangements. Just as well it didn't happen in 2018, otherwise the likelihood is that, like Northamptonshire, Walsall Council would have been abolished. Ever since 1974, local government in Walsall has usually been eventful, if unstable, and rarely dull. In recent years, control has fluctuated between Labour and the Conservatives, who have strongholds in the more affluent settlements of Aldridge and Streetly, to the east of the town, though not in the town of Walsall itself. Since 2011, it has been a continuous challenge to seek to protect council services from the impact of successive governments' commitment to austerity.

Walsall FC does not have a particularly distinguished history, but then very few 'small town' clubs do. They are known as the Saddlers, reflecting the town's once-dominant leather-manufacturing industry. There aren't any saddles made in Walsall nowadays, but there aren't any hats made in Stockport or Luton (both known as the Hatters), nor fish caught in Fleetwood (the Fishermen, or Cod Army). Nicknames of football clubs often provide important clues to their towns' economic past.

Walsall Swifts were one of the founding members of the Second Division in 1892, where they survived for three seasons, lost their place in 1895, regained it the following year (renamed as Walsall FC), lost it again in 1901, and then disappeared from sight (or at least from the Football League) for the next twenty years. In 1921, they became a member of the Third Division North. They were switched from time to time to Third Division South (and back) over the next thirty-eight years, but never achieved promotion. In fact, between 1951 and 1954, they finished bottom of the Third Division South for three successive seasons (a rare achievement). By far their most notable success during these otherwise unremarkable years was the 2-0 defeat of Arsenal at Fellows Park in 1933, justifiably regarded as one of the giant-killing feats of all time (Arsenal went on to win the League title that season).

With the 1958–59 League realignment, Walsall emerged in the Fourth Division. Then came two successive promotions, up to the Third Division in 1960, and the then Second Division in 1961.

One of their key players at this time was Bill 'Chopper' Guttridge, who I must have seen in my occasional visits to Fellows Park, but sadly I have no recollection of this formidable-sounding defender. After relegation in 1963, and a further one in 1979, Walsall spent most of the rest of the twentieth century in the third and fourth tiers of the League. Any promotions were short-lived – how quickly triumph turned to disaster for the Walsall faithful. But the club bounced back, and they actually managed three seasons in the second tier, between 2001 and 2004, before sinking back to their accustomed third-tier location.

WALSALL v LUTON TOWN
League One, December 29th, 2018

This trip to Walsall was the final game in a sequence that started in Barrow on December 30th, 2017. Luton Town were the visitors; it was the Saddlers versus the Hatters. West Bromwich Albion, five miles down the road, were also at home, but why watch West Brom when you can watch Walsall? I took the train from Kendal to Wolverhampton and then caught the 529 bus, which takes just over half an hour to cover the six miles to Walsall.

The easiest way to get from Walsall town centre to the Bescot Stadium is by rail; it's a five-minute journey to a station that is close to the ground. But I'd arrived in Walsall with plenty of time to spare, with the intention of walking the mile and a half to the stadium through a sector of Walsall that was unknown to me. As I emerged from the station, I passed an establishment with a sign which boasted '100 million ears pierced!' Surely not all in Walsall? Then I made a detour to facilitate a nostalgic return visit to the afore-mentioned Lyndon House Hotel for a pint of Batham's bitter, which you don't find anywhere outside the Black Country, before setting out in the general direction of the ground, along Bradford Street.

Bradford Street is one of those areas adjacent to a town centre that has seen better days; an air of dilapidation is apparent in the houses and in the shops, which are intermingled with them. It was something of a surprise to come across an establishment which called itself the Touch of Elegance Boutique, and which proclaimed that its clothes were designed for 'Weddings, Church, Races, Proms and many more...'. Could this really be Walsall? But good luck to the place; maybe it had established a reputation when Bradford Street was more up-market, and had retained its former clientele, despite the growing dereliction around it.

Moving on to a lively local shopping centre, where the mix of shops and their clientele indicated that this was a predominantly Asian area (one of several such in the town), there was one of those unexpected architectural gems that you come across from time to time: a Carolean manor house called the White Hart, dating from the seventeenth century. Its drab surroundings were not able to provide the most appropriate setting for it, but in a sense that added to its attraction; it had survived (with a bit of help from the council) in unlikely circumstances – a bit like the Touch of Elegance Boutique.

Bescot Stadium was one of the first of the new grounds to be built in the 1980s and '90s. Scunthorpe United led the way with Glanford Park in 1988, but Walsall was the next pioneer in 1990. Duncan Adams describes it as 'a fairly simple affair', which is the way I remember it from my only previous visit in the early 1990s. It had more than a touch of an identikit self-assembly quality about it, with four identical stands, each with around fifteen rows of seats. But this uniformity was mercifully dispelled in 2003, when the stand at one end was transformed into a much larger two-tier affair, free of the large number of supporting pillars found on the other three sides. This is where Adams advises neutrals to sit, and I followed his advice, which turned out to be sound. Halfway up the stand, and to one side, I had an excellent view of the pitch, and was close (but not too close) to a vociferous group of home supporters positioned behind the goal. The Pukka steak pie I purchased was in a different league to the cardboard-encased pasty I'd mistakenly bought at St Andrews – tasty and not so hot as to scald the inside of your mouth. My last book-related day out was so far going well.

Luton Town were on a roll, unbeaten in their previous eleven League games, and currently second in the table, a single point behind leaders Portsmouth. They are a well-supported club, and their travelling fans filled the stand opposite the one I was in, plus an overspill into a third of the adjacent stand. Walsall had started the season well – in early October they were fifth – but had proved inconsistent since, with commendable victories (2-1 against Coventry City three weeks previously) alternating with disappointing defeats against lowly-placed opponents (1-2 at home to Bristol Rovers on Boxing Day). They were currently in mid-table, ten points behind the last of the play-off contenders and ten points ahead of the highest-placed team in the relegation positions. Another month or so of average results and their season could effectively be over.

As noted in the previous chapter, one of the delights of travelling around the country to watch matches is the chance of encountering 'old friends' on the pitch; that is, players one had previously come across in one's travels. In today's line-ups, there were two such examples. Walsall's Andy Cook had been a prolific goalscorer for Barrow a couple of seasons previously, before moving to Tranmere Rovers, where he continued to demonstrate his goalscoring ability in their promotion season from the National League. But the move to Walsall raised him two levels above what he had been used to. Had he been able to deliver at this level or was he now out of his depth? Five goals in twenty-four League appearances (five as substitute) implied an open verdict at this stage.

The other was Luton's Elliot Lee, who came through West Ham's academy, although his subsequent first-team appearances there were rare. I saw him a couple of times when on loan to Blackpool in the 2015–16 season, when they were relegated from League One to League Two. He made very little impression, and became an object of ridicule at Bloomfield Road, when he revealed that he was homesick and wanted to return to London, which he quickly did. He moved to Luton halfway through the 2017– 18 season and his career had flourished since then: twelve goals in nineteen starts in the previous season, and ten goals already in the 2018–19 season. The Blackpool nightmare must be fading fast.

In the early stages of the game, Luton exuded confidence, as might be expected from a team with a long unbeaten run. Their approach play was crisp and incisive, with passes invariably finding their targets. In contrast, there was little coherence in Walsall's build-up, with too great a reliance on long aimless balls booted out of defence towards well-marked strikers. The visitors seemed to have more time on the ball to consider what to do with it, unlike the home side, whose decisions were more rushed and correspondingly less effective. Unsurprisingly, it was Luton who were creating the chances, including a shot from the exotically named Pelly-Ruddock Mpanzu, which rebounded back from the angle of post and crossbar. But they were unable to turn their superiority into goals and fell behind in the 26th minute, against the run of play, when Walsall's skipper, George Dobson, was needlessly fouled in the area by Jack Stacey, and Morgan Ferrier confidently put away the resulting penalty. That changed the balance of the game. Walsall grew in confidence, whilst Luton lost their early momentum, showing little in the way of penetration. The home side were certainly showing commitment. 'There's more fight about them today,' my neighbour observed, comparing the game with the defeat against Bristol Rovers four days earlier.

At halftime, I wandered up to the spacious and well-appointed bar at the back of the stand, checked on the halftime scores, and witnessed an impressive sunset through the large windows overlooking the pitch. The proximity of the M6 motorway to the stadium is apparent from this vantage point; the cars and lorries were flowing endlessly above the opposite stand, where the Luton supporters were located.

Halfway through the second half, Walsall scored again. The increasingly impressive Morgan Ferrier found space on the left, slipped and fell but recovered his balance and retained possession of the ball, before dispatching a dangerous cross, which a Luton defender misjudged, leaving Andy Cook in the clear to volley the ball home from close range. Luton's unbeaten run was beginning to look extremely vulnerable, but not for long. Five minutes later, Luton's James Collins swivelled neatly in the box, to create the space to reduce the arrears. Two minutes later, it looked like they had equalised, with Jack Hylton nodding home Mpanzu's ambitious long-range volley. But the goal was controversially disallowed for offside. Could Walsall hold out for the remaining eighteen minutes (plus stoppage time)? They gave every appearance of being able to do so, with some resolute defending. Indeed, they came close to adding a third in occasional breakaways. But then, in the final minute of added time, following a disputed free kick awarded to the visitors, substitute Kazenga LuaLua equalised with a neat flick from the side of his boot. Delirium and rapture ensued at the Luton end, resignation amongst the Walsall fans.

The game had been a thoroughly absorbing one, with the result in doubt up to the very last minute. As a neutral, I felt that justice had been done. Luton had played the more imaginative football, and it would have been unfair if they had come away with nothing. But, equally, Walsall had shown great spirit and resilience, and they too deserved something. A satisfying outcome to my final game of the year. I made my way to Bescot station, having checked the timetable and discovered a rare phenomenon – a Birmingham-bound train that doesn't normally stop at Bescot, but does on Saturday afternoon matchdays. Would that all railway companies displayed this degree of customer-friendliness.

My view about the justice of the outcome was not shared by the two managers. Luton's Nathan Jones was adamant that Luton should have had all three points, arguing (with some justification, on the basis of the video evidence) that Hylton's 'goal' should not have been disallowed, and had it stood, Luton would have probably gone on to win. Unsurprisingly, Walsall's Dean Keates did not agree. He described the free kick decision that led to Luton's equaliser as 'shambolic' and added that 'we fully deserved to be 2-0 up against what is probably the best team in the division'. But then what else would you expect from opposing football managers in a closely contested game? 'We were lucky to come away with anything'? I don't think so!

WHAT HAPPENED NEXT ...

In this chapter, I look at the subsequent fortunes of the eighteen clubs visited, up to the end of the 2018–19 season. Were hopes fulfilled or worst fears realised, as the season progressed? Who ended up celebrating promotion, who relegation, and for whom was mid-table mediocrity the outcome?

Clubs visited in 2017–18

With only two exceptions, the futures of the ten teams from the towns I visited in the second half of the 2017–18 season remained uncertain until its last two or three weeks. In three cases their fate was decided on the final day of their programme.

The two exceptions were Carlisle United and Chester. By the end of January, Carlisle were mid-table and still had an outside chance of making the League Two play-offs. I thought this was still a possibility after witnessing the admittedly uninspiring 1-0 win against lowly Forest Green Rovers. But the inconsistency that had plagued the team all season continued. Commendable away victories were followed by points dropped at home to mid-table sides. By the start of April, it would have taken a run of four or five straight victories to reach the play-offs, and that wasn't going to happen. United were unfortunate in the sustained absence through injury of Nicky Adams, without doubt their most creative and dynamic attacking player. At the end of the season, manager Keith Curle decided he'd achieved as much as he could at Carlisle and voluntarily stepped down (perhaps with an inkling that his contract might not be renewed anyway). His successor, John Sheridan, was appointed in July.

Carlisle's pattern of inconsistency was repeated in the 2018–19 season. At times, it looked like they might sneak into a play-off position, but whenever this happened, they would suffer a couple of defeats and slide back into mid-table oblivion. John Sheridan left Carlisle in December 2018 for struggling National League side Chesterfield (a move difficult to comprehend) and was replaced by Steve Presley, who proved unable to alter the inconsistent pattern of their results.

By the time I saw Chester play Tranmere in early April 2018, their position in the bottom four of the National League looked hopeless, and their 2-0 defeat that afternoon sealed their relegation fate. With the pressure off, they brought in several untried youngsters and experienced a minor revival: two wins in the last four games. But it was the National League North for them the following season. Despite signing the managerial duo who had steered Salford City from the middle reaches of the non-league pyramid into the National League, at the same time as Chester were being relegated from it, they failed to take the National League North by storm and finished short of a play-off position.

When I visited Stockport County and Kidderminster Harriers in mid-April 2018, their places in the National League North play-offs looked virtually certain. And that is what transpired: they finished fifth and fourth respectively, earning home ties against Chorley and Bradford Park Avenue. But they both proceeded to blow it, failing to capitalise on home advantage and losing out to their respective lower-placed opponents; the Harriers 0-2 to Bradford, who had emerged from mid-table obscurity in the final few weeks of the season, and County 0-1 to a resolute, defence-minded Chorley side. This was Kidderminster's second successive failure at the play-off stage, but at least it represented progress of a kind for County – the first time they'd reached this stage since being relegated in 2013.

Kidderminster were up with the leaders for the first half of the 2018–19 season, but then fell away, not helped by changes of manager (the owner taking over at one stage – never a good idea) and the departure of key players, and finished in a disappointing mid-table position. Stockport's achievements in 2018–19 are covered at the end of this chapter.

Wigan Athletic, Accrington Stanley and Macclesfield Town all ended up as champions of their respective divisions. Wigan suffered one or two blips after I saw them scrape a 1-0 win against Rochdale, but they managed to avoid the familiar sequence of poor results when a lower league team finally goes out of the FA Cup after an unexpected run of success (Wigan were defeated by Southampton in the quarter- finals, after victories over Premier League Bournemouth, West Ham United and, unbelievably, Manchester City). Promotion to the Championship was assured with three games to play, and they clinched the title with a 1-0 win at Doncaster on the final day of the season, courtesy of a second-half goal from – who else? – Will Grigg. They deserved to win the League; the quality of their football was superior to that of the more prosaic Blackburn Rovers, who came a close second. The abiding memory of the Wigan season for me was the form of Nick Powell, a true artist in a division dominated by hard-working journeymen. He was always a delight to watch.

Wigan's sequence of relegation from the Championship (2015 and 2017), followed by promotion back to it (2016 and 2018), looked from Christmas 2018 onwards increasingly likely to be continued. Although their home form was reasonable throughout the season, their away record was abysmal. An early encouraging win at Stoke City was followed by a long series of defeats, punctuated by the occasional draw. Then, in a crucial game late in the season away to second-placed Leeds United, a minor miracle occurred. Twenty minutes into the game, a Wigan defender was harshly adjudged to have handled the ball on the goal-line and was sent off. The resulting penalty was saved, but Leeds took the lead five minutes later. The result appeared to be a foregone conclusion. But thanks to some heroic goalkeeping from Chris Walton and two well-taken counter-attack goals from Gavin Massey, Wigan took the lead and managed to hold on to it, to record a famous victory. That turned the tide, and Wigan ended up comfortably clear of relegation. Which was just as well for popular manager Paul Cook, whose future would have been in jeopardy had Wigan been relegated.

Accrington Stanley went from strength to strength in League Two after their stirring comeback against Port Vale, which I witnessed, lifted them into an automatic promotion slot in January. They suffered only two defeats in the remainder of the season, a sequence that included a 2-1 win at the much-fancied (and financially much better-off) Luton Town, and secured promotion with five games to play. They were crowned as champions with two weeks of the season remaining. Promotion to League One is their greatest achievement so far, since rising from the dead in 1968 and returning to the Football League in 2004. Huge credit was due to manager John Coleman and his deputy John Bell, who put together a side of unproven youngsters and seasoned professionals (with relatively undistinguished previous careers) and welded them into a cohesive unit that was a treat to watch. They fully deserved to win the title.

In the early stages of the 2018–19 season, Accrington surprised everyone by being up with the League One leaders. Their form subsequently declined, but their survival at this level was confirmed on the penultimate Saturday of the season with an emphatic 5-1 win at home to Plymouth Argyle in driving winds and heavy rain, a game I witnessed in the company of a very disgruntled Argyle supporter. Realistically, survival was the most that could be expected from a club with a home support base of less than two thousand and a meagre budget, compared with the likes of Sunderland and Portsmouth. It was good to see so many of the 2017–18 squad, such as Sean McConville, Billy Kee, Lee Clark and Martin Hughes, still turning out for the club. This was a big part of John Coleman's success – keeping a settled squad together over successive seasons.

Macclesfield Town proved to be a similar success story. Despite having to manage without the talented Elliot Durrell, whose season was curtailed by injury soon after I saw him play a major part in their 3-1 win against Barrow, their consistency ensured that their nearest National League challengers, Sutton United and Tranmere Rovers, were unable to keep up with them. Mike Marsh, who wasn't playing when I saw them, came into the side and scored some crucial goals, including one in the 2-0 win at Eastleigh on the penultimate Saturday of the season that secured the title. They had continued to play attractive football and demonstrate exemplary teamwork, losing only once since the Barrow game early in March. They are not a well-off club and had been tipped for relegation rather than promotion at the start of the season. An inspirational manager, John Askew, and a group of highly motivated players were the key factors.

John Askew departed in the close season and was replaced by Mark Yates from Solihull Moors. By the end of October 2018, an immediate return to the National League looked virtually certain. Town had not won a match and were firmly entrenched at the foot of League Two. Then they became national news. Having sacked Mark Yates, they appointed Sol Campbell in his place. After a distinguished career with Spurs, Arsenal and England, Campbell had long been trying and failing to land a managerial role with a League club. Macclesfield decided to give him that opportunity – very much a case of 'starting at the bottom' for him. And it worked;

slowly but surely the team's form improved and escape from the two relegation slots became a distinct possibility. However, it was not until the last day of the season that a draw at home to Cambridge United, coupled with fellow strugglers Notts County's defeat at Swindon, ensured survival. Campbell left in the close season, but they will certainly remember him in Macclesfield.

On the final day of the 2017–18 season, three of the teams I'd seen that year faced a survival battle. Barrow were still in with a chance of avoiding relegation from the National League because of their away record. At home, they had recorded a paltry four wins; only already-relegated Guiseley had a worse record. But their fate was in their own hands. Either they or Woking would be relegated. Barrow started the day one point ahead with a better goal difference. To stay up, they had to match Woking's result (or, if Woking drew, that would be enough to keep Barrow up). On paper, they looked well placed to do so, with a game at home to already-relegated Chester, whilst Woking hosted Dover, who were in the frame (depending on other results) for a play-off place.

My friend John Pearce invited me to attend Barrow's match but I was not able to – as things turned out, I was fortunate to have missed it. Barrow went behind midway through the first half, as did Dover. But Woking equalised just before halftime. The tension on the Holker Street terraces, John told me later, was palpable. Then, early in the second half, Barrow equalised. The tension reduced. But soon afterwards, Chester regained the lead. This meant that if Woking scored again and the results stayed that way, Barrow would be relegated. Barrow rarely looked like equalising but were rescued by a late Dover winner at Woking. The celebrations were understandably muted, after what John described as an abysmal performance from the home side. But at least Barrow were still in the National League.

The following season was relatively uneventful, by Barrow's standards. Having replaced Ady Pinnock with Ian Evatt and with an almost wholly new squad, they never looked like achieving a play-off place in 2018–19, but nor did they ever seem in danger of relegation. Their workmanlike but uninspiring side occasionally enthused their regular 1,200 home crowd, but more often bored or disappointed them.

Morecambe faced a similar situation to that of Barrow. They had continued to struggle since I had seen them in January: numerous draws (the most in League Two) but only the occasional win (a rare highlight was a 4-2 victory at promotion candidates Wycombe). On the final day of the season, either they or Barnet would be relegated. Morecambe began with a two-point advantage and a seven-point better goal difference than their fellow strugglers. But Barnet had what was, on the face of it, an easy home fixture against already-relegated Chesterfield, whilst Morecambe had to travel to Coventry City, an in-form side who needed one point to be certain of making the play-offs. If Barnet won and Morecambe lost, that was it. The Shrimps' eleven-year stay in the Football League would be at an end.

Before an unfamiliarly large crowd of nearly 16,000, Morecambe were on the defensive right from the start. Two brilliant saves from veteran keeper Barry Roche (aged thirty-six) kept them in the game. Barnet were 1-0 up shortly before the interval, and it looked like Morecambe would need a draw to survive. This they achieved, thanks to further goalkeeping heroics, and a slackening of the pace of Coventry's attacks in the last twenty minutes, when it became clear that their play-off place was assured. Barnet ran out 3-0 winners, but to no avail. Great was the relief amongst the Morecambe players and travelling supporters when the final whistle was blown. They had had a turbulent couple of years, with changing ownership, and one felt that if they were relegated, they would not find it easy to return to the League. The formidable Jim Bentley had once again inspired survival.

Morecambe started the 2018–19 season once again every pundit's tip for relegation and, for a while, looked likely to justify that prediction, starting the campaign with a 6-0 drubbing at Crewe and winning only one of their first ten League games. But once again, Jim Bentley proved equal to the challenge. Having assembled a team more or less from scratch in the close season, he moulded them into a cohesive unit and inspired a steady improvement, his team finishing on fifty-four points, comfortably clear of the two relegation places.

Which leaves us with Bolton Wanderers. Since I watched them go down 1-0 to fellow strugglers Birmingham City, they managed only a single point in the subsequent five Championship games. On the final day of the 2017–18 season, they had to beat mid-table Notts Forest at the Macron Stadium to stand any chance of survival. The other two relegation candidates, Barnsley and Burton Albion, had difficult away fixtures at Derby and Preston respectively. But such had been the dire quality of Bolton's recent performances, it was to imagine them beating anyone.

It was 0-0 at halftime, but early in the second half, Adam le Fondre gave Bolton a precious lead. But with ten minutes to go, Notts Forest scored twice to take the lead, and all seemed lost for the Wanderers. But in an unexpected final twist, they equalised through David Wheater and, in injury time, substitute Aaron Wilbraham met a right-wing cross with a glancing header to secure a win. Barnsley and Burton had both obligingly lost and Bolton, against all the odds, were still in the Championship.

I was pleased that Wilbraham, aged thirty-eight, had scored the crucial goal. His first club was Stockport County, for whom he scored in his debut against Manchester City towards the end of the 1996–97 season, and he had gone on to register plenty of goals for Norwich City and Bristol City, amongst others. He had signed for Bolton the previous December and had appeared mainly as a late substitute. But he, and 20,000 Bolton fans, will long remember his contribution on May 6th, 2018. Le Fondre, who scored the first goal, also had a long spell with Stockport in the early 2000s. So, it was a case of two former County players saving Bolton's bacon!

Bolton started the 2018–19 season impressively and, for a while, a more comfortable Championship campaign seemed a possibility. But it wasn't to last and their form deteriorated from late September onwards. The club then found itself in serious financial difficulties; the owner Ken Anderson was unable to provide the financial support needed to keep it solvent. Players were paid late or, in the last month of the season, not at all, resulting in the squad refusing to turn out for the penultimate game of the season at home to Brentford. With no acceptable new owner appearing on the scene, Bolton went into administration at the end of the season and started 2019–20 in League One on minus 12 points.

Clubs visited in 2018–19

Leyton Orient finished the 2018–19 season as National League champions, fending off powerful challenges from Salford City and Solihull Moors in the last few weeks of the season. I welcomed their success; their relegation in 2017 had been the consequence of the disastrous regime of owner Francesco Becchetti. With their strong and passionate fan base (averaging over five thousand in 2018–19) and proud tradition as a small-time east London club, they were back in the League, where they belonged. The euphoria following promotion was, however, abruptly punctured in June 2019 by the sudden death from a heart attack of popular manager Justin Edinburgh.

Gateshead looked like they might make the National League play-offs, despite a small and relatively docile support base, but faded in the last couple of months and finished in ninth position, four points behind seventh-placed Eastleigh. In May 2019, misfortune struck. Gateshead's owner, who'd only been there for twelve months, opted out; the club hit financial difficulties and subsequently had nine points deducted from the 2018–19 total. They were relegated to the National League North (Aldershot were the lucky beneficiaries).

AFC Fylde continued to punch above their weight, given their small-town location and limited support base. What weight they do possess comes from the financial largesse provided by wealthy Brexit-enthusiast owner David Haythornthwaite. Finishing fifth in the National League, Fylde defeated Harrogate Town and Solihull Moors to earn themselves a Wembley play-off final date with Salford City. Sadly, they were outplayed on the day and went down 3-0 before a meagre crowd of eight thousand. They did, however, end the season in style, defeating Leyton Orient 1-0 in the final of the FA Trophy, again at Wembley (the scorer was Danny Rowe – of course!), possibly inspiring dancing in the streets of Kirkham and Wesham.

The positive response in November in the Northampton Town fanzine *HotelEnders* to the appointment of Keith Curle as manager may well have become hedged with reservations by the end of the season. True, he had lifted them out of the League Two relegation zone by the time I saw them in late November, but he wasn't able to sustain the momentum and Town finished the season in a safe but disappointing mid-table position. The problem was a profusion of drawn games: nineteen, the highest total in the division. Town did finish the season well, however, winning 5-2 at Oldham.

Stoke City suffered an even worse case of drawn games: twenty-one of their Championship fixtures resulted in this outcome.

One of the few highlights in a hugely disappointing season was the heroic victory over Derby County, when playing two-thirds of the game with ten men, which I witnessed in November. Manager Gary Rowett did not see the season out; he was dismissed in January, no doubt to the delight of the betrayed Derby County supporters, and replaced by Nathan Jones from high-flying Luton Town, who failed to move Stoke from their position of mid-table mediocrity. For a team expected to bounce straight back into the Premier League, the 2018–19 season will be quickly forgotten.

Birmingham City, who were in contention for a Championship play-off place when I saw them lose to Bristol City in December, then lost momentum. Like Northampton Town and Stoke City, their record included too many drawn games (twenty) to remain as serious contenders, but even if they had been able to improve their win/draw ratio, it would have been to no avail. The nine-point penalty imposed on them in March 2019, as a result of breaching League financial rules, put paid to any promotion prospects. However, there were enough points in the bank to allay any fears of relegation, and Garry Monk deserves credit for transforming the disorganised and under-performing squad he inherited in 2018 into a more coherent and consistent unit. His 'reward' was to lose his job at the end of the season, following a dispute with the club's owners.

Lincoln City went on to win the League Two title, losing only five games all season. Newport County, their impressive opponents in the game I saw at Sincil Bank in December, scraped into the play-offs with a 1-1 draw at Morecambe, courtesy of an 87th-minute equaliser from Jamille Matt. Celebrations were delayed until the result of the Exeter City/ Forest Green Rovers result came through, but then erupted when the team and the eight hundred travelling fans learned of the outcome. I was pleased for them; their FA Cup run earlier in the season had endeared them to supporters of underdogs throughout the country. They progressed to the play-off final, where they lost to Tranmere Rovers in the final minute of extra time. How cruel can it get!

Walsall, who came close to inflicting a rare defeat on eventual League One champions Luton Town in the game I saw in December, continued their slide down the table in the following months. Manager Dean Keates was sacked in January, but his successor was unable to turn things round, and Walsall's relegation was confirmed on the final day of the season.

But the highlight of the 2018–19 season for me was the achievement of Stockport County in winning the National League North title. This doesn't sound like a big deal, but if you've supported a club since 1957, as I have Stockport, it certainly is, particularly when it is recalled that as recently as 2001–02, they were gracing the second tier of the League with their presence. Stockport fans had endured five years of purgatory since relegation from the Conference in 2013. But in 2018–19, it all came good and we were back in the big time (relatively speaking) after a season of high drama. In mid-November, County were languishing in mid-table, with even the play-offs seeming a remote possibility. Then came a run of fifteen successive League victories, which put them within a point of long-term League leaders, Chorley.

I was at Edgeley Park in March 2019 for the clash with third-placed Spennymoor Town, which County won 1-0 in front of a crowd of 6,300, the biggest ever by far for a National League North fixture. I was also at Chorley in April, when both clubs had three games remaining. Whoever won would be guaranteed the title, if they won their remaining two games. On an unseasonably hot spring afternoon, Chorley prevailed with a 2-0 win, and that appeared to be that. Except that it wasn't. On the penultimate Saturday of the season, County managed a routine 2-0 home win against mid-table Curzon Ashton. Chorley were playing at

Spennymoor, then fourth in the table. Three times the home side, who dominated the game, hit the woodwork. Then, with fifteen minutes to go, Chorley were awarded a penalty, which was brilliantly saved by the Spennymoor keeper. In the 90th minute, following a corner, Spennymoor's John Taylor found the net with a powerful header. I was following the game on Flashscores and leapt to my feet and punched the air with delight when the news came through. The following Saturday, all Stockport had to do was win at bottom-of-the-table Nuneaton Town (four wins all season), which they duly did 3-0, in front of three thousand travelling supporters. The ability of football to stir the emotions, even at National League North level, was once again demonstrated.

REFLECTIONS

My final visit to a 'football town' (Walsall) was on December 29th, 2018, exactly 365 days after the first (Barrow) on December 30th, 2017, a satisfyingly neat outcome: job completed within a year, leaving me with a host of memories. In *Saturday, 3pm*, many of Daniel Gray's 'fifty eternal delights of modern football' struck a chord with me, as my journeys through my past took me around the country. But other delights that I experienced did not feature in his book. Set out below is a mixture of our shared enthusiasms and some of my own.

Football as drama

Football matches can be likened to plays (in two acts, with an interval) filled with some combination of heroism, villainy, pathos, farce, tragedy, comedy, and unexpected twists to the plot in the final few minutes. My visits provided plenty of confirmation of the appropriateness of this metaphor. Two dramas with unexpected outcomes stand out.

At a crucial stage in Accrington Stanley's push for promotion from League Two in January 2018, they found themselves at half-time two goals down to visitors Port Vale. Drawing on reserves of commitment and self-belief, they turned the game round in the second half, to end up as 3-2 winners. I was behind the goal that Accrington were attacking, close to their most vociferous supporters, and was totally caught up in the atmosphere.

The second was Stoke City's heroic achievement in overcoming the dismissal of a player, with two thirds of the game remaining, to beat Derby County in a Midlands derby in November 2018. When Derby equalised five minutes into the second half, no one would have put money on Stoke getting anything out of the game. But with a combination of resolute defending and well-judged counter-attacks, they not only prevented the visitors from scoring again, but engineered a match-winning goal later in the game. The collective euphoria on the Football Special back to the town centre was a delight to experience.

Celebrations of the travelling fans

Elsewhere, there were winning goals, deep into added time (Fylde, which I missed, having wrongly and unwisely decided it wasn't going to happen), and late equalisers (Luton at Walsall; Leyton Orient at Gateshead) that I did see. Whenever an away side scored a decisive goal towards the end of a game, at the end of the ground where their supporters were located, the team (goalkeeper apart) typically raced over to celebrate with them, with many wall-straddling embraces and sometimes a player or two leaping over the wall into the crowd. Having endured other, less palatable forms of post-goal celebrations in recent years, I approve of this practice. It provides an acknowledgement, on the part of the visitors, that the club's existence (and their own pay cheques) are dependent on the fans who turn out every week to watch them, of whom the group who have made the trip to a distant destination are likely to be the most committed. And there is an element of spontaneity about it, unlike the rehearsed routines, such as the synchronised dives across the grass, which were prevalent in the 2015–16 season, when I was following the fortunes of Wigan Athletic and Blackpool. The most annoying examples were (and still are) the 'silly dances', sometimes performed by the goalscorer himself, sometimes as an ensemble piece, which dominate Premier League celebrations – the silly dances now performed by players with an increasing abundance of silly haircuts!

The celebrations with the visiting fans have a special poignancy when there aren't very many of them present. In the National League, it is not unusual for their number to be in double figures, sometimes as low as the twenties or thirties, if you're talking about a visit to, say, Hartlepool on a wet Tuesday evening in February. In the first match of my sequence, Barrow against Solihull Moors at the end of December 2017, the travelling fans numbered twenty-seven. When Solihull scored a late penalty to seal a deserved win, fans and team came together at the wall in front of the adjacent visitors' enclosure for mutual celebrations. Unlike my disgruntled Barrow-supporting companion, I felt pleased for them. Their long journey on a perishing cold December day had proved worthwhile.

Meeting 'old friends'

If you've watched a lot of football at different locations over the years, as I have, it is always enjoyable, when scanning the programme, to recognise players you have seen before, playing for other teams at other grounds. In the lower divisions and the National League in particular, short-term contracts often predominate, and it is not unusual for a player in his thirties to have been with eight or nine different clubs (more if you count loan spells), which enhances the chances of having seen them before somewhere. There were numerous such examples encountered in my visits, many of whom I had first come across in the 2012–13 season, when I visited all the twenty-four clubs then in the Conference.

It was good to see the formidable Steve McNulty turn out for Tranmere Rovers in their game at Chester. Now, as then, he looked like he could usefully lose a couple of stone in weight, but his bulk proved no impediment to accomplished defensive performances.

Striker Matt Rhead, also of considerable bulk, came on as a late substitute in Lincoln's game against Newport in December 2018.

I'd seen him make a similarly late appearance for Mansfield Town in their game at home to Nuneaton Town. 'He's our secret weapon,' the bloke in the stand next to me said. 'He's not fit enough to last ninety minutes, but he's scored some crucial late goals.' In neither of the games I saw did he manage one, and at Lincoln he looked ponderous and not desperately interested, but he'd delivered for them over the previous three seasons and was clearly held in great affection there.

Carlisle United's Jamie Devitt, last seen with Grimsby Town in 2013, turned in an impressive performance (and scored the winning goal) in Carlisle United's 1-0 defeat of Forest Green Rovers. And Danny Rowe, who endured an unrewarding season with relegated Barrow in 2012–13, was scoring prolifically for AFC Fylde for the fourth successive season and poked home the winner in the game I saw against Gateshead.

Visiting a ground for the first time; and standing on the terraces

There's always a frisson of excitement as you approach a previously unvisited venue, enhanced by the proximity of scarf- and T-shirt-bedecked home supporters, likewise converging on the stadium. Six of my eighteen visits were to grounds I'd not been to before, one of which was 'traditional' and the other five post-1990 constructions. On most occasions, I travelled by train, and then completed the journey on foot, or, occasionally, by bus. To do so allows you to savour a gradual build-up of anticipation prior to entering the new ground, which is why I try to avoid parking my car, in the rare circumstances that I use it, close to the ground.

My preference is for traditional stadia, rather than the new grounds built from the 1980s onwards. Scunthorpe United's Glanford Park was the pioneer, opened in 1988; there have since been a further thirty or so examples. In addition to the pervasive sense of nostalgia, and the historical associations (often over a hundred years of hosting fixtures), it is much more likely, at a traditional ground, that there will be a standing terrace from which you can watch the game. Macclesfield Town's Moss Rose Ground and Accrington Stanley's Wham Stadium both provide this opportunity. But so, to be fair, did AFC Fylde's Mill Farm Stadium, and Morecambe's Globe Arena, both relatively recent constructions. At Carlisle United's Brunton Park, there is a paddock of around fifteen steps, running in front of the old Main Stand for its full length, an ideal vantage point from which to watch a match.

Traditional stadia also typically consist of a seemingly random mixture of stands and terraces in different architectural styles, some of them there from time immemorial, others more recent additions or modifications. That unplanned feel to such grounds is part of their charm. There are some particularly picturesque examples at National League level. At Woking's Kingfield Stadium, there are a couple of small adjacent stands that are reminiscent of cricket pavilions. At Hereford's dilapidated Edgar Road ground, there are two of the narrowest cantilever stands I've ever come across.

But the new stadia have diversified since their early days, when there was a sense of the identikit about them. Bolton's Reebok Stadium (now renamed the University of Bolton Stadium) and AFC Fylde's ground both have stands with convex curving roof lines, which are much more aesthetically pleasing than the uniform vertical and horizontal features of Stoke City's Britannia Stadium and Chester's Deva Stadium.

Post-match reviews

It's always interesting to compare one's own impressions of a match with those of others. I enjoy checking what the *Football League Paper* or the *Non-League Paper* made of a game I have seen the previous afternoon. Sometimes I wonder if their reporters and

I have been at the same match! The rating system – five stars for a classic, one star for a load of rubbish – sometimes generates an outburst of disbelief: 'Did the reporter really think that that pedestrian affair was worth four stars?' I have similarly sceptical reactions to the ratings (within a range of one to ten) awarded to individual players, but it must be hard for one reporter to keep tabs on the performances of twenty-two of them (plus substitutes). I suspect a lot of it gets made up. I just hope players don't harbour a burning sense of injustice if they are scored a five but feel that they were Man of the Match candidates!

Daniel Gray enthuses about the Sunday score pages. 'The double page results spread is a work of art and a triumph of the factual,' he writes. 'Nothing in the whole paper looks as good or is as accurate.' No doubt, like me, it is the first thing he turns to when he opens the Sunday paper. Team composition, sequence, timing and scorers of goals, attendances, league tables: there in all its fascinating detail, although for such information about the National League, you need to buy the *Non-League Paper*.

For me, attendance figures are of special interest: how were Borehamwood going to survive in the Football League, if they won the National League play-off final in 2018, when their average home gate was around six hundred? (They didn't, so we'll never know). The published figures can't always be relied on, however. It's normal to include in the figure the totality of season ticket holders. Normally, that is not a threat to accuracy, but it was in the 2015–16 season, when around two thousand Blackpool season ticket holders boycotted all the home games, in protest against the way the Oyston family ran the club. There were several instances where the number of away supporters outnumbered the home fans, which is most unusual. I remember a large contingent from Coventry City chanting as a large flock of seagulls hovered above Bloomfield Road: 'You've got more seagulls than fans.'

For someone like myself, who has been to eighteen different grounds in a single year, the Sunday score pages have a much broader scope of interest than if you are primarily concerned with the fortunes of a particular team, one you have supported since childhood. There were several clubs for whom I developed an affection, which led to me closely scrutinise their subsequent results. Having witnessed Accrington Stanley's impressive comeback from 2-0 down against Port Vale, to win 3-2, I was willing them to win promotion, which in due course they did, as League Two champions. Macclesfield Town's classy display in their 3-1 win over Barrow generated a strong hope that they too would be promoted, which they duly were, as National League champions. Leyton Orient's revival, following the departure of their much-reviled owner Francesco Becchetti, coupled with the fact that one of my best friends supported them, resulted in them joining the increasing list of my priorities, as they battled in the 2018–19 season for promotion back into the Football League. The quality of Newport County's football in their unjust 2-3 defeat at Lincoln elicited a similar enthusiasm, and a sense of delight when they defeated Leicester City in the FA Cup, three weeks later. And this close attention is in addition to that of the details of the matches played by the three local clubs I watch regularly: Morecambe, Barrow and Carlisle United.

* * *

'When most football fans think of a place, they think of the team.' That's the claim of Daniel Gray, and I'm sure he's right. When, as a lad, my visits to football grounds were confined to Maine Road, Old Trafford and Edgeley Park, I listened every Saturday to the football results, and began to wonder what these many other football-related places were like. I located most of them readily enough in my dad's motoring atlas, but in some cases, had to carry out a bit of detective work to discover where they were. Scotland was a particular challenge in this respect. Where on earth did Albion Rovers play, not to mention St Mirren, St Johnstone, Queen of the South and, until they went out of business, Third Lanark? I nearly got myself into trouble in the penultimate year of my primary school education. During a geography lesson, our teacher, the formidable Mrs Wood, referred to a place called Hartlepool, which I well knew from *Sports Report*. But she mis-pronounced it 'Hart-el-pool'. I was just about to stick up my hand and say, 'Miss, Miss, it's not Hart-el-pool, it's Hart-le-pool.' Fortunately, some internal braking mechanism stopped me from doing so. Just as well – Mrs Wood was notorious for her fiery temper and wouldn't have been best pleased at being corrected by some youthful smart arse.

In the sixties, when John Davies and I began to venture further afield, I discovered the reality behind some of these magic names, familiar from years of listening to *Sports Report*. So, this was what the towns of Rochdale, Bradford, Burnley, Crewe and Rotherham were really like! By 1970, I had visited nearly sixty of the Football League grounds (and associated towns), a wonderful, participative way of becoming familiar with the geography of Great Britain. As Gray perceptively points out, football towns 'are often post-industrial towns where the football club has become a beacon and something to cling on to. As people can no longer anchor themselves to a factory or shipyard, they cling to their football club. Identities become joined and the team and town are one.' How well this quote illustrates the strength of the links between place, personal histories and the football team. In the post-industrial wilderness of places like Barnsley, Burnley, Walsall and Hartlepool, the football club does provide for many an important element of continuity in a changing world.

There were other football-associated delights in my youth that have sadly long-since fallen by the wayside: the stirring music played by the Beswick Prize Band (vocalist, Sylvia Farmer) before the home games of Manchester City and United, and the way the bandmaster would hurl a long pole into the air as the band marched around the pitch... and always catch it; the thump of the string-tied bundles of the *Football Pink* (*Manchester Evening Chronicle*) and *Football Green* (*Manchester Evening News*) as they hit the pavement outside the local newsagents, having been hurled from a company van, with a sizeable clientele always in waiting, eager for the news of the performance of their favoured team; the thrill of boarding a steam train-hauled Football Special bound for some FA Cup replay at Shrewsbury or Stoke-on-Trent, although given the Football Special's later reputation for violence and damage, it's probably just as well that they are a thing of the past; and occasionally, as a child, being granted free admission at Maine Road or Old Trafford, when the bloke manning the turnstile allowed my dad to lift me over it. All these delights are now part of history – but, fortunately, many others remain.

The trashing and subsequent withdrawal of the Football Specials remind us that there is a dark side to football, as there is to most elements of our cultural heritage. The hooliganism, gang warfare (fortunately on the decline), and the racist and sexist behaviour and chanting (now better regulated by the clubs, but sadly, still persistent) should serve to prevent us from becoming too starry-eyed and rose-tinted-spectacled about the beautiful game. But once you move away from the international scene and the Premier League (and Millwall!), it is rare, at least in my recent experience, for the dark side to intrude. I came across very few instances in my travels: the baiting of the Tranmere Rovers fans by a couple of aggressive home supporters at Chester (where the Tranmere response was a model of low-key humour); the inappropriately coarse language at Birmingham City, in a part of the ground where a lot of family groups were located; and the over-the-top abuse directed at the match officials which you often hear at Barrow. But that was about the sum of it. Otherwise, my visits to eighteen different towns and matches provided unmitigated enjoyment.

Such enjoyment came from several different sources, in a way which illustrates that there is much more about 'going to the match' than the match itself. There is the anticipation – reading up about the teams and watching footage of their recent games (many thanks to Sky Sports for this facility). There is the journey to familiar and unfamiliar places (in my case, usually by train) and then the walk to the ground, joining a tide of colourfully dressed groups of home supporters, and enjoying the infectious enthusiasm of the many youngsters present. There is the ritual of the pre-match pint, particularly enjoyable if you have a companion, but fine even if you don't. There is the excitement of visiting a new ground or returning to one you have not been to for ages and taking in the changes.

But the quality of 'going to the match' that struck me most forcibly was its illustration of the strength of the link between the local community and the football club; indeed, the way that football clubs act as an expression of the community identity of the place. It really felt like that when Carlisle United were cheered on to the pitch by a crowd double the average gate, in the first match back at Brunton Park in the aftermath of Storm Desmond, after which the Carlisle players had put in numerous hours of voluntary work, helping local residents clear up the devastation to their homes caused by the storm. Or when, in 2016, I joined with over two thousand Blackpool supporters on a protest march about the damage the Oyston family was doing to their beloved club, with visiting fans from Wigan, seated outside pubs, cheering us as we passed them (there is a real bond between club supporters in such situations). Or watching the young ball-girl at the Chester/Tranmere match, utterly absorbed in the game and her role in it.

I also relished the distinctive characteristics of the towns I visited in my personal odyssey: down-to-earth Wigan, with its unexpectedly impressive high street; Accrington, with its lovely curving railway viaduct and its streets of terraced houses climbing the Pennine moors; Barrow, with the shipyard buildings dominating the view from the football ground; and Stockport's lively historic quarter, with its iconic market hall at its centre. Many of the towns I visited had suffered from the decline in their basic industry, be it cotton-spinning, tourism, shoe-making or pottery, but all had retained their unique identities, and in each case, I sensed the importance of the football club as an important continuing source of local pride and community identity.

* * *

The pleasure of supporting your local team, particularly when it seems the most positive aspect of community life in a town in long-term economic decline, has been seen by some as a form of escapism that is harmful. This is certainly the view of the writer Terry Eagleton. For him, football is the new 'opium of the people', or, to update the metaphor, he likens its influence to that of crack cocaine. For him, football is a distraction from the need to challenge the inequalities and injustices found in society. He argued in a *Guardian* column that 'if every rightwing thinktank came up with a scheme to distract the populace from political injustice and compensate them for lives of hard labour, the solution in each case would be the same: football'. He adds that 'nobody serious about political change can shirk the fact that the game has to be abolished'. Fat chance of that happening, I'd say, Terry!

Eagleton's thinking owes much to the writings of Karl Marx. It has long been unrealistic for Marxists to argue that, in Britain at least, such distractions are preventing the growth of a collective consciousness within the working class, which (if they were absent) would ultimately lead to revolution and the overthrow of capitalism. That outcome just isn't going to happen, not least because of the virtual disappearance of the traditional strongholds of working-class activism, such as mining, shipbuilding and the iron and steel industry. But there remains a plausible argument that football and other forms of 'escapism' are preventing or limiting the growth of political awareness and activity of the kind that might provide a serious challenge to the inequalities which are so dominant in our society – and perhaps lead to, if not revolution, then at least radical social change.

Stuart Jeffries (himself a football enthusiast), also writing in the *Guardian*, took up this argument in the wake of the 2018 World Cup euphoria that swept the country, when England unexpectedly made it to the semi-final. He reminds us of the Marxist view that capitalism has become increasingly sophisticated, deploying the leisure industry to control our 'free' time and co-opting us to facilitate the smooth running of a system that oppresses us. He quotes Leon Trotsky: 'The revolution will inevitably awaken in the British working class the deepest passions which have been diverted along artificial channels with the aid of football.' 'You'll notice,' comments Jeffries wryly, 'that this hasn't happened. We're too busy gawping from the terraces and sofas to seize control of our own destinies.' He concludes (possibly tongue in cheek), 'Sport, then, is the nightmare from which we dare not awake. For if we did, we would see it as the emblem of an intolerable world and burn our season tickets.'

Jeffries' views rang alarm bells: I, for one, wouldn't want to feel that I was helping to perpetuate an unjust economic system by the choice of my leisure interests. However, there are two important rejoinders to the 'crack cocaine of the people' argument. First, as we have seen, there is evidence that support for your local football team can actually lead to a growth of political awareness and activity, rather than stifling it, as illustrated by what has happened at Blackpool, Charlton Athletic, Wimbledon, Leyton Orient and Bury.

Second, the nature of the distraction involved in watching a football match differs markedly from drug or alcohol abuse, gambling or incessant computer gaming, all of which would typically be seen as destructive (and certainly not life-enhancing) activities. Not even the most committed Marxist would be likely to deny the positive contribution that certain cultural activities (art, music, drama) make to our personal development and the enrichment of our collective social life.

In my view, there is a case for including football amongst these kinds of enriching cultural activity. The parallels between football and drama (each game as a play in two acts with a mystery ending) were drawn out earlier in this chapter. Nor is it too fanciful to draw parallels between football and ballet. A Wigan Athletic supporter, describing to me the first game he had seen, highlighted a defence-splitting pass as a 'thing of beauty'. So too (I would argue) are: the goal scored from an overhead scissors-kick; the dummy that leaves the defender trailing in the wake of its perpetrator; a flying finger-tip save by a goalkeeper; the ball brought down immaculately from chest to foot with an astute shrug of the shoulder; and the well-timed interception by a defender astute at 'reading the game'. Make your own selection.

There were several responses to Terry Eagleton's views that rightly emphasise the artistic qualities of football. In fact, even Eagleton makes the point himself in the same article, when he argues that football allows ordinary people to witness 'displays of sublime artistry by men for whom the word genius is sometimes no mere hype'.

On *The Blizzard* website, sports journalist Alex Keble argues:

Watching live football is, I believe, fundamentally a unifying experience with infinite scope for social change and artistic beauty. Being given the opportunity to witness this first hand is a privilege that should not be taken lightly ... For ninety minutes, people from contrasting backgrounds become a collective force sharing in the universal language of football. Twenty-two people kicking a ball on a patch of grass becomes the primary focus and concern of thousands of people united in a shared moment of solidarity. It is a brief glimpse of utopia.

Writing in the *Socialist Worker*, Dave Zirin regards Eagleton's arguments as 'elitist hogwash':

We don't love sports because we are like babies suckling at the teat of constant distraction. We love them because they're exciting, interesting and, at their best, rise to the level of art ... By rejecting football, Eagleton also rejects what is both human and remarkable ... We can stir our soul with gospel music even while we understand that its existence owes itself to pain as much as hope. Similarly, amid the politics and pain that engulf and sometimes threaten to smother professional sport, there is also an art that can take your breath away.

And we haven't yet mentioned the happiness generated by seeing a goal being scored (preferably by the team you support). Alex Keble considers it one of life's rare high points, producing 'feelings of ecstatic joy and euphoric completeness'.

The content of all these responses makes sense to me. The only other comparable source of collective euphoria, in my experience, is the impact of a rock concert: Bob Dylan singing *Masters of War* at Manchester's Free Trade Hall in 1965; Neil Young singing *Heart of Gold* at the Liverpool Echo Arena in 2017, and four thousand Merseysiders singing along with every word.

After a year of visits to a series of fascinating places and absorbing football matches, I would add my own response to Terry Eagleton's view that football should be regarded as the 'crack cocaine of the people'. To me, football is an important expression of a place-related collective identity, which operates as an important antidote to our increasingly atomised society. It can stimulate, rather than constrain, the development of social awareness and political action. And, at its best, it can become a thing of beauty, an art form, rather than a distraction fuelled by drugs or fantasy. Let's continue to celebrate it.

ACKNOWLEDGEMENTS

There are many people who have made valuable inputs to this project. My step-daughter Eleanor, an accomplished proof-reader, read through drafts of all the chapters, and provided invaluable advice, not just about repetition and my misuse of brackets, exclamation marks, colons and semi-colons, but also about the content – misguided attempts at humour, unbalanced negative portrayals of certain towns and references (particularly to local government issues) that would be likely to confuse or bore the reader.

I also circulated to friends those chapters that included material about them, which led to a good deal of helpful feedback. In this context, thanks are due to John Davies (Manchester, Stockport and Gateshead), Tony Simey (Wigan), Phil Hartley (Fylde), Roger Perrin (Kidderminster), John Pearce (Barrow), Tony Hogg (Leyton) and Harry Pearson (Carlisle). My wife, Karen Lloyd, read and commented on chapters that discuss our family life (Gateshead, Barrow and Northampton). Dennis Reed provided a helpful critique of my introductory chapter. Martin Tarbuck, editor of the excellent Wigan Athletic fanzine *Mudhutter*, provided much valuable input in relation to Wigan, other fanzines, and his own experience supporting his local team over a period of thirty years. My editor, Craig Hillsley, did an impeccable job and made many helpful suggestions for improvements to the text. Thanks to all these people, and to anyone else I've inadvertently omitted.

Thanks are also due to the various writers and experts quoted in this book.

Finally, I owe a great debt to Sara Hunt, of Saraband, who saw enough merit in the proposal and draft chapters I sent her to agree to publish the book. Without her positive response and subsequent encouragement and support, I doubt whether *Twenty Football Towns* would have ever seen the light of day.

INDEX

268